Commercial Facilities Sector-Specific Plan

An Annex to the National Infrastructure Protection Plan

2010

Homeland Security

Preface

The Commercial Facilities (CF) Sector is widely diverse in both scope and function. A dominant influence on the Nation's economy, this sector includes retail centers, hotels, casinos, theme parks, motion picture production studios, office and apartment buildings, convention centers, sports stadiums, and other sites where large numbers of people congregate to pursue business activities, conduct personal commercial transactions, and enjoy recreational pastimes and accommodations. The sector is composed primarily of privately owned facilities that operate on the principle of open public access, meaning the public may move freely throughout these facilities without the deterrent of highly visible security barriers. Each owner and operator has distinct assets, operational processes, business environments, and risk management approaches that vary across all business lines because of the considerable diversity in their objectives. These characteristics require an integrated and comprehensive approach to protecting critical infrastructure and key resources (CIKR) in the sector.

The CF *Sector-Specific Plan* (SSP) complements the *National Infrastructure Protection Plan* (NIPP) by developing efforts to improve the protection of the CF Sector in an all-hazards environment. This SSP describes the processes used to identify, assess, and protect CIKR; and the plans to implement these processes and measure effectiveness. The SSP also helps define the partnership between the Commercial Facilities Sector-Specific Agency (CF SSA), other SSAs, and those additional partners protecting the sector through implementation of risk mitigation activities.

This 2010 release of the CF SSP reflects the maturation of the CF Sector partnership and the progress of the sector programs first outlined in the 2007 SSP. Examples of CF Sector accomplishments since the publication of the 2007 SSP include the following:

- Worked in partnership with the Emergency Services Sector and the Retail Subsector to develop training and awareness materials entitled, *"Active Shooter: How to Respond."*

- Developed the *Risk Self-Assessment Tool for Stadiums and Arenas* and the *Evacuation Planning Guide for Stadiums*.

- Expanded cybersecurity outreach efforts by partnering with the National Cybersecurity Division (NCSD) to distribute its tools and services to sector partners.

- Partnered with the CF Sector Coordinating Council (SCC), IICD, and HITRAC in developing the criteria to be used for the Level 2 and Sector lists.

- Improved information sharing through the sponsorship of security clearances for more private sector partners.

- Worked with U.S. sports leagues to improve their security processes. For example, the National Football League implemented emergency drills/tabletop exercises at all 31 of its stadiums.

The CF SSA will continue to work with its partners to ensure that the sector remains strong and resilient by continuing to develop and execute a broad set of risk mitigation activities, like those summarized above. For example, the CF SSA will continue to produce Protective Measures Guides that address the needs of specific subsectors, as well as ones that address cross-sector concerns. Additionally, the CF SSA has engaged in a series of subsector outreach and information-sharing initiatives at the direction of DHS Secretary Napolitano. These have demonstrated that the CF SSA can work with its sector partners in a sustained way on an initiative that strengthens information sharing and leads to the creation of new products. For example, the Retail and Lodging Outreach Initiative had a number of important components, including a Table-Top Exercise, Protective Security Advisor (PSA) visits to mall owners and operators, and the development of new products including two threat recognition training tools and one video designed for retail and shopping center staff. The CF SSA will be engaging in similar initiatives targeted at additional subsectors. These and other risk mitigation activities highlight how the sector is strengthened through active engagement and partnership.

Each year, the CF Sector CIKR Protection Annual Report will provide updates on the sector's efforts to identify, prioritize, and coordinate the protection of its critical infrastructure. The Sector Annual Report provides the current priorities of the sector as well as the progress made during the past year in following the plans and strategies set out in the CF SSP.

The CF SSP establishes a relationship between the government and the private sector to foster the cooperation necessary to improve the protection and resilience of the sector from a natural or man-made disaster. The CF SSP reflects the collaborative efforts between government and private sector stakeholders who are dedicated to the protection of CIKR within the CF Sector.

The CF Sector Government Coordinating Council is pleased to support this CF SSP and looks forward to a continued partnership to sustain and enhance the protection and resilience of CIKR in the CF Sector.

Todd M. Keil

Assistant Secretary for
Infrastructure Protection
U.S. Department of Homeland Security

W. Craig Conklin

Director
SSA Executive Management Office
U.S. Department of Homeland Security
Chair, Commercial Facilities GCC

Turner D. Madden

Co-Chair
Commercial Facilities
Sector Coordinating Council

Joseph B. Donovan

Co-Chair
Commercial Facilities
Sector Coordinating Council

Table of Contents

Preface i

Executive Summary 1

    1. Sector Profile and Goals 1

    2. Identify Assets, Systems, Networks, and Functions 2

    3. Assess Risks 2

    4. Prioritize Infrastructure 3

    5. Develop and Implement Protective Programs and Resilience Strategies 3

    6. Measure Effectiveness 3

    7. CIKR Protection Research and Development 3

    8. Manage and Coordinate Sector-Specific Agency Responsibilities 3

Introduction 5

1. Sector Profile and Goals 7

    1.1 Sector Profile 7

        1.1.1 Commercial Facilities Subsectors 8

        1.1.2 Interdependencies and Relationships with Other CIKR Sectors 9

    1.2 CIKR Partners 11

        1.2.1 DHS as the Sector-Specific Agency 11

        1.2.2 CIKR Owners and Operators, Including Private and Public Entities 12

        1.2.3 U.S. Department of Homeland Security 12

        1.2.4 Other Federal Departments and Agencies 13

        1.2.5 State, Local, Tribal, and Territorial Governments 13

        1.2.6 Regional Coalitions 14

        1.2.7 International Organizations and Foreign Countries 15

    1.3 Sector Goals and Objectives 15

        1.3.1 Commercial Facilities Sector Goals 16

    1.4 Value Proposition 16

2. Identify Assets, Systems, and Networks 19

    2.1 Defining Information Parameters 20

2.1.1 Infrastructure Data Warehouse (IDW)... 23

2.1.2 CF SSA Role in Inventory Development and Maintenance 25

2.1.3 Identifying Cyber Infrastructure.. 26

2.2 Collecting Infrastructure Information 27

2.2.1 Commercial Facilities Sector Partners Contribution.......................... 29

2.3 Verifying Infrastructure Information 30

2.4 Updating Infrastructure Information 31

3. Assess Risks... 33

3.1 Cyber Risk.. 34

3.2 Use of Risk Assessment in the Sector... 35

3.3 Screening Infrastructure... 36

3.4 Assessing Consequences 37

3.5 Assessing Vulnerabilities... 39

3.6 Assessing Threats.. 42

3.7 Calculating Risk 43

4. Prioritize Infrastructure.. 45

5. Develop and Implement Protective Programs and Resilience Strategies 47

5.1 Overview of Sector Protective Programs and Resilience Strategies............... 47

5.1.1 Implementation 48

5.1.2 SSA Programs 48

5.1.3 Cybersecurity 50

5.2 Determining the Need for Protective Programs and Resilience Strategies 51

5.3 Protective Program/Resilience Strategy Implementation.............................. 53

5.4 Monitoring Program Implementation 53

6. Measure Effectiveness 55

6.1 Risk Mitigation Activities... 55

6.2 Process for Measuring Effectiveness 56

6.2.1 Process for Measuring Sector Progress.. 56

6.2.2 Information Collection and Verification 57

6.2.3 Reporting 57

6.3 Using Metrics for Continuous Improvement 57

7. CIKR Protection Research and Development 59

7.1 Sector R&D Requirements... 59

7.2 Sector R&D Plan 61

7.3 R&D Management Processes 62

8. Managing and Coordinating SSA Responsibilities 63

   8.1 Program Management Approach 63

   8.2 Processes and Responsibilities 65

      8.2.1 SSP Maintenance and Update 65

      8.2.2 SSP Implementation Milestones 65

      8.2.3 Resources and Budgets 66

      8.2.4 Training and Education 66

   8.3 Implementing the Sector Partnership Model 67

   8.4 Information Sharing and Protection 68

      8.4.1 Information Sharing 68

      8.4.2 Protecting Information 70

Annex 1: Entertainment and Media Subsector 73

   1. Entertainment and Media Subsector Profile and Goals 73

      1.1 Entertainment and Media Profile 73

      1.2 Entertainment and Media Subsector Goals 75

      1.3 Authorities 75

   2. Identification of Assets and Facilities 76

   3 and 4. Risk Assessment and Prioritization 76

   5. Develop and Implement Protective Programs 76

   6. Measure Progress 77

   7. Research and Development 77

Annex 2: Gaming Facilities Subsector 79

   1. Gaming Facilities Subsector Profile and Goals 79

      1.1 Gaming Facilities Profile 79

      1.2 Gaming Facilities Subsector Goals 82

      1.3 Authority 82

   2. Identify Assets and Facilities 82

   3 and 4. Risk Assessment and Prioritization 83

   5. Protective Programs and Resilience Strategies 83

   6. Measure Progress 84

   7. Research and Development 85

Annex 3: Lodging Subsector 87

   1. Lodging Subsector Profile and Goals 87

      1.1 CIKR Partners 88

      1.2 Distinguishing Characteristics 88

1.3 International. 89

1.4 Cyber Systems 89

1.5 Lodging Subsector Key Issues 89

1.6 Lodging Goals and Objectives. 90

1.7 Authorities 90

2. Identify Assets and Facilities. 91

3. Assess Risks 91

4. Prioritize the Lodging Infrastructure. 91

5. Develop and Implement Protective Programs. 91

6. Measure Progress 92

7. Research and Development 92

Annex 4: Outdoor Events Subsector 93

1. Outdoor Events Subsector Profile and Goals. 93

1.1 Outdoor Events Profile. 93

1.2 Outdoor Events Subsector Goals 95

1.3 Authorities 95

2. Identify Assets 95

3 and 4. Risk Assessment and Prioritization 96

5. Develop and Implement Protective Programs. 96

6. Measure Progress 97

7. Research and Development 97

Annex 5: Public Assembly Subsector 99

1. Public Assembly Subsector Profile and Goals 99

1.1 Public Assembly Profile 99

1.2 Public Assembly Goals and Objectives 103

1.3 Authorities 103

2. Identify Assets, Systems, Networks, and Functions. 104

2.1 Defining Information Parameters 104

2.2 Collecting Infrastructure Information. 104

2.3 Verifying Infrastructure Information. 104

2.4 Updating Infrastructure Information 104

3. Assess Risks 105

3.1 Use of Risk Assessment in the Public Assembly Subsector. 105

3.2 Screening Infrastructure. 105

3.3 Assessing Consequences. 105

    3.4 Assessing Vulnerabilities 105

    3.5 Assessing Threats 106

  4. Prioritize the Public Assembly Infrastructure 106

  5. Develop and Implement Protective Programs 106

    5.1 Determining Protective Program Needs 107

    5.2 Protective Program Implementation 108

  6. Measure Progress 108

  7. Research and Development 108

Annex 6: Real Estate Subsector **111**

  1. Real Estate Subsector Profile and Goals 111

    1.1 Real Estate Subsector Profile 111

    1.2 Goals and Objectives 115

    1.3 Authorities 115

  2. Identify Assets and Facilities 115

  3. Assess Risk 116

    3.1 Vulnerability Assessment for the Real Estate Subsector 116

    3.2 Risk Assessment 116

  4. Prioritize the Subsector Infrastructure 117

  5. Develop and Implement Protective Programs and Resilience Strategies 117

    5.1 Security Personnel Training 118

    5.2 Measure Effectiveness 119

  6. Measure Progress 119

  7. Subsector Protection Research and Development 120

Annex 7: Retail Subsector **121**

  1. Retail Subsector Profile and Goals 121

    1.1 Retail Profile 121

    1.2 Goals and Objectives 125

    1.3 Authorities 125

  2. Identify Assets and Facilities 125

  3. Assess Risks 126

  4. Prioritize the Subsector Infrastructure 126

  5. Develop and Implement Protective Programs and Resilience Strategies 127

    5.1 Security Guard Training 127

  6. Measure Progress 128

  7. Research and Development 128

Annex 8: Sports Leagues Subsector 129

    1. Sports Leagues Subsector Profile and Goals.. 129

        1.1 Sports Leagues Profile 129

        1.2 Sports Leagues Goals and Objectives... 136

        1.3 Authorities 136

    2. Identify Assets and Facilities.. 136

    3. Assess Risks 136

    4. Prioritize the Sports Leagues Infrastructure 137

    5. Develop and Implement Protective Programs and Resilience Strategies 137

    6. Measure Progress 138

    7. Research and Development 138

Appendix 1: List of Acronyms and Abbreviations 139

Appendix 2: Glossary of Key Terms 145

Appendix 3: Review of Authorities 149

    1.1 Commercial Facilities Sector Federal Authorities 149

        1.1.1 U.S. Department of Homeland Security.. 149

        1.1.2 U.S. Department of Commerce, National Institute of Standards and Technology 150

        1.1.3 U.S. Environmental Protection Agency.. 150

        1.1.4 Federal Emergency Management Agency 151

        1.1.5 National Institute for Occupational Safety and Health............................. 152

        1.1.6 U.S. Centers for Disease Control and Prevention.................................. 152

        1.1.7 U.S. Department of Labor.. 152

        1.1.8 General Services Administration 152

        1.1.9 U.S. Department of Justice 153

        1.1.10 Federal Aviation Administration.. 153

    1.2 State and Local Governments.. 153

        1.2.1 State Police Fusion Programs 154

    1.3 Private Sector Authorities... 154

        1.3.1 American Society for Industrial Security International.............................. 154

        1.3.2 National Fire Protection Association 154

        1.3.3 International Code Council 155

        1.3.4 American Society for Testing and Materials 155

        1.3.5 National Research Council... 155

    1.4 Other Guides.. 156

    1.5 Commercial Facilities Subsector Authorities.. 157

1.5.1 Entertainment and Media Subsector Authorities 157

1.5.2 Gaming Facilities Subsector Authorities 157

1.5.3 Lodging Subsector Authorities 157

1.5.4 Outdoor Events Subsector Authorities 158

1.5.5 Public Assembly Subsector Authorities 158

1.5.6 Real Estate Subsector Authorities 159

1.5.7 Retail Subsector Authorities 160

1.5.8 Sports Leagues Subsector Authorities 160

List of Figures

Figure ES-1: NIPP Risk Management Framework 2

Figure 1-1: Set Goals and Objectives 15

Figure 2-1: Identify Assets, Systems, and Networks 19

Figure 3-1: Assess Risks 33

Figure 4-1: Prioritize Infrastructure 45

Figure 5-1: Develop and Implement Protective Programs and Resilience Strategies 47

Figure 6-1: Measuring Effectiveness 55

List of Tables

Table 1-1: Commercial Facilities Sector Dependencies and Interdependencies with Other CIKR Sectors 10

Table 2-1: Taxonomy for the Public Assembly and Sports Leagues Subsectors 21

Table 7-1: National Critical Infrastructure Protection R&D Plan 60

Executive Summary

The Commercial Facilities (CF) Sector-Specific Plan (SSP) was created to complement the National Infrastructure Protection Plan (NIPP) by developing efforts to improve the protection of the CF Sector in an all-hazards environment. The CF-SSP establishes a relationship between the government and the private sector to foster the cooperation necessary to improve the protection of the sector from natural or manmade disasters. The CF-SSP sets a path forward for the sector to collectively identify and prioritize assets, assess risk, implement protective programs, and measure the effectiveness of protective programs. The CF-SSP reflects the collaborative efforts between government and private sector stakeholders who are dedicated to the protection of key resources within the CF Sector. The CF-SSP is divided into eight chapters and is described as follows.

1. Sector Profile and Goals

Sector Profile. The CF Sector is represented by a wide range of asset categories, including, but not limited to, hotels, commercial office buildings, convention centers, stadiums, theme parks, residential buildings, shopping centers, and other sites where large numbers of people gather to pursue business activities, conduct personal commercial transactions, or enjoy recreational pastimes. The CF Sector is a dominant influence on the Nation's economy; for example, according to the National Retail Federation, the retail subsector alone conducted more than $4.6 trillion in annual sales in 2008.

The majority of the facilities in the CF Sector operate under the principle of "open public access," meaning that the public may move freely through these facilities without the deterrent of highly visible security barriers. Commercial facilities are generally owned and operated by the private sector and have operated with minimal interaction with the Federal Government or other regulatory entities.

CIKR Partners. A variety of different entities play a role in helping to secure each of the 18 critical infrastructure and key resources (CIKR) sectors, including stakeholders from all levels of government and the private sector. The majority of the facilities within the CF Sector are owned and operated by the private sector. Commercial facilities owners and operators are ultimately responsible for assessing the vulnerabilities of their facilities to all hazards. As a result, the private sector is an integral partner in the efforts to protect the CF Sector. Representatives from industry associations and individual companies serve on a CF Sector Coordinating Council (SCC). This council serves as the coordinating body for private sector participation in CIKR protection issues.

The CF Sector Federal Government stakeholders include the U.S. Department of Homeland Security (DHS), as well as other Federal agencies. Federal Government stakeholders can influence sector activities and provide tools and resources that can benefit private sector partners. Federal agencies are represented on the CF Government Coordinating Council (GCC), which is chaired by DHS.

Sector Goals. The vision statement and strategic goals for CF Sector security are set forth in the CF-SSP. These elements have been developed by members of the SCC, the eight subcouncils, and the GCC.

> ### Mission Statement for the Commercial Facilities Sector
>
> *The Commercial Facilities Sector envisions a secure, resilient, and profitable sector in which effective and non-obstructive risk management programs instill a positive sense of safety and security in the public and sustain favorable business environments that are conducive to attracting and retaining employees, tenants, and customers.*

2. Identify Assets, Systems, Networks, and Functions

The identification of assets and facilities is necessary to define the CF Sector and to develop an inventory of assets that can be further analyzed with regard to criticality, vulnerability, and the protective actions that are required to achieve the goals established by the sector.

Information on the sector's infrastructure is maintained by the DHS Infrastructure Information Collection Division (IICD) through the Infrastructure Data Warehouse (IDW). The CF Sector-Specific Agency (SSA) continues to work with the sector partners to populate the IDW with information regarding each facility's functionality within the sector and to refine the sector's taxonomy terminology to accurately categorize the various commercial facilities infrastructure elements that are maintained in the IDW.

A recent focus of the CF Sector has been the assessment of the sector's cyber systems and their associated security issues. Unlike with some sector assets, working cyber assets within the sector are virtual rather than physical. Relevant assessments used by owners and operators include potential vulnerabilities and likely avenues of attack.

3. Assess Risks

The risk management framework highlighted in the NIPP is the cornerstone of the CF-SSP (see Figure ES-1). The CF-SSP complements the NIPP and describes the processes and methodologies used by the sector to carry out an all-hazards risk management framework throughout the sector.

Figure ES-1: NIPP Risk Management Framework

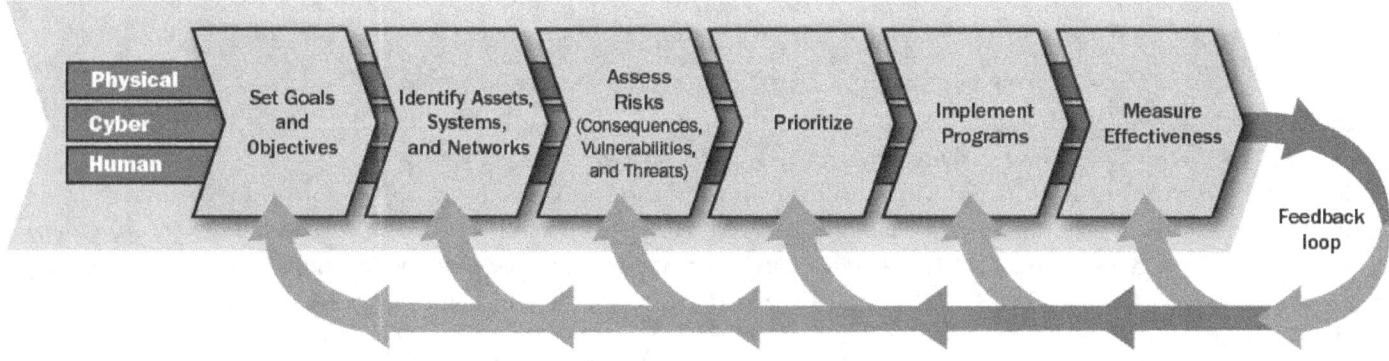

Continuous Improvement to enhance protection of CIKR

Because the risk environment is dependent on many variables, to mitigate risk throughout the CF Sector it is imperative to conduct a comprehensive risk assessment at many levels, including the facility, regional, and national levels. In an effort to collect risk information and create a CF Sector-wide risk profile, the CF SSA has been working with sector partners to develop risk assessment tools and assessment reports that identify the risks of concern to the sector. One example is partnering with the International Association of Assembly Managers (IAAM) to create a risk assessment model for use by stadium owners and operators. The Risk Self-Assessment Tool (RSAT) assists stadium and arena managers with the identification and management of vulnerabilities to reduce the risk to their facilities. It is the goal of the CF SSA to create risk assessment tools (e.g., RSAT modules or risk assessment methodologies) based on the Federal Emergency Management Agency (FEMA) Risk Management Series for facilities across all CF subsectors.

4. Prioritize Infrastructure

The CF-SCC and the CF SSA do not believe that it is appropriate to develop a single overarching prioritized list of assets for the CF Sector. Instead, assets are categorized using a consequence methodology that allows the CF SSA to drive sector-wide protection efforts.

5. Develop and Implement Protective Programs and Resilience Strategies

Protective programs involve measures designed to prevent, deter, detect, and defend against threat; reduce vulnerability to an attack or other disaster; mitigate consequences; and enable timely, efficient response and restoration in any post-event situation. Protective programs that benefit the CF Sector are in place at many facilities. Individual owners and operators apply effective implementation and evaluation of protective programs and resilience strategies.

6. Measure Effectiveness

An important function of the CF SSA is to respond to the changing risk environment and needs within the CF Sector. As the CF Sector is largely unregulated, the tasks of assessing, prioritizing, and implementing physical, cybersecurity, and preparedness measures are left up to owners and operators. The CF SSA works with the CF-SCC and CF-GCC to collectively identify gaps, implement protective programs, and measure the effectiveness of protective programs.

7. CIKR Protection Research and Development

Research and development (R&D) of new technology is valuable to the sector to improve knowledge pertaining to threats, vulnerabilities, consequences, and the subsequent risks associated with assets and facilities subject to manmade attacks or natural disasters. While individual commercial facility owners and operators employ new technologies, only a limited few actually have the resources available to engage in their own R&D. Therefore, the CF Sector is engaged in determining what new technical capabilities need to be developed to benefit the sector. A significant focus of the sector includes R&D initiatives related to preserving the open-access model for facilities while at the same time enhancing overall safety and security in response to all hazards.

8. Manage and Coordinate Sector-Specific Agency Responsibilities

The Secretary of Homeland Security has designated the DHS Office of Infrastructure Protection (IP) to carry out the SSA mission for 6 of the 18 CIKR sectors: the Chemical, Commercial Facilities, Critical Manufacturing, Dams, Emergency Services, and Nuclear Sectors. IP executes SSA functions for these six CIKR sectors through the SSA Executive Management Office (EMO). The SSA EMO has established five primary program areas through which to support implementation of the SSPs and the NIPP risk management framework: Planning and Project Integration, Education and Training, Partnership and Information Sharing, Exercises and Incident Management, and Assessment and Integration.

Introduction

Terrorist attacks and natural, manmade, or technological hazards against critical infrastructure and key resources (CIKR) could produce catastrophic losses in terms of human casualties, property destruction, and economic effects. Moreover, they have the ability to profoundly damage public morale and confidence. Accordingly, protecting the CIKR of the United States is essential to the Nation's security, public health and safety, economic vitality, and way of life.

The unifying framework established in Homeland Security Presidential Directive 7 (HSPD-7) provides the national approach for CIKR protection. This directive establishes the U.S. policy for "enhancing protection of the Nation's CIKR" and mandates a national plan to actuate that policy. In HSPD-7, the President designates the Secretary of Homeland Security as the "principal Federal official to lead CIKR protection efforts among Federal departments and agencies, State and local governments, and the private sector," and assigns responsibility for CIKR sectors to Federal Sector-Specific Agencies (SSAs).

In recognition of the unique characteristics associated with different infrastructure assets, systems, networks, and functions, HSPD-7 divides the Nation's infrastructure into 18 distinct CIKR sectors, and the coordination of CIKR protection responsibilities for each sector is assigned to a specified Federal agency, referred to as the SSA. The U.S. Department of Homeland Security (DHS) is the designated SSA for the Commercial Facilities (CF) Sector. Pursuant to the responsibilities for CIKR protection, DHS, in conjunction with partners from all levels of government and private sector partners from all sectors, developed the National Infrastructure Protection Plan (NIPP). The NIPP establishes the overarching concepts relevant to all CIKR sectors identified under the authority of HSPD-7, and addresses the physical, cyber, and human considerations required for effective implementation of protective programs and resilience strategies.

The NIPP, a comprehensive and well-coordinated protective strategy for all CIKR sectors, is an essential component of the homeland security mission to make America safer, more secure, and more resilient with regard to terrorist attacks and natural and manmade hazards. The NIPP provides the framework for the cooperation needed to develop, implement, and maintain a coordinated national effort that brings together government at all levels, the private sector, and international organizations and allies.

A fundamental objective of the NIPP is to identify actions to protect or improve the resilience of infrastructure that is identified as critical. In the NIPP context, protection efforts include actions to prevent, deter, neutralize, or mitigate the effects of deliberate efforts by terrorists to destroy, incapacitate, or exploit elements of our Nation's CIKR. Protection can include a wide range of activities, including hardening of facilities, building resilience and redundancy, incorporating hazard resistance into initial facility design, initiating active or passive countermeasures, installing security systems, and implementing cybersecurity measures.

Along with the NIPP's complementary Sector-Specific Plans (SSPs), the NIPP provides a consistent, unifying structure for integrating both existing and future CIKR protection efforts. Within each CIKR sector, the NIPP and the corresponding SSP provide the core processes and mechanisms to enable government and private sector CIKR partners to work together in implementing CIKR protection initiatives within each sector. The NIPP consists of a six-step risk management framework structured to continuously improve and enhance CIKR protection. The framework focuses sector activities on efforts to (1) set goals and objectives; (2) identify assets, systems, and networks; (3) assess risk based on consequences, vulnerabilities, and threats; (4) establish priorities based on risk assessments and, increasingly, on return-on-investment for mitigating risk; (5) implement protective programs and resilience strategies; and (6) measure effectiveness.

Given that the CF Sector is largely unregulated and extremely diverse, many facets of the NIPP risk management framework are applied at will by individual owners and operators. Corporate entities and industry associations, as well as owners and operators, carry out risk management decisions and the tasks of assessing, prioritizing, and implementing security and preparedness.

The CF Sector's six-step NIPP risk management framework provides for the following guidance:

1. **Set Goals and Objectives.** The CF SSA uses sector goals that define specific outcomes, conditions, end points, or performance targets as guiding principles to collectively constitute an effective risk management posture.

2. **Identify Assets, Systems, and Networks.** The identification of assets and facilities is necessary to develop an inventory of assets that can be analyzed further with regard to criticality and national significance. Because of the diverse nature of assets within the CF Sector, the CF SSA works with the DHS Infrastructure Information Collection Division (IICD) to identify and validate these assets. In addition to its collaboration with the IICD, the sector also identifies assets through interaction with trade associations and corporate owners and operators.

3. **Assess Risks.** The CF Sector approaches risk by evaluating consequence, vulnerability, and threat information with regard to a terrorist attack or other hazard to produce a comprehensive, systematic, and rational assessment.

4. **Prioritize.** The CF Sector Coordinating Council (SCC) and the CF SSA have found that it is not appropriate to develop a single, overarching prioritized list of assets for the CF Sector. Instead, assets are categorized by using a consequence methodology that allows the CF SSA to drive sector-wide protection efforts.

5. **Implement Programs.** Given the size and diversity of the CF Sector, there is no universal solution for implementing protective security measures. The owners and operators of CF Sector facilities implement the most effective protective programs based on their own assessments. Protective programs address the physical, cyber, and human dimensions.

6. **Measure Progress.** The CF SSA has developed relationships with both public and private sector partners, including trade associations, corporate entities, and industry subject matter experts. Information sharing through these partnerships is used to assist in measuring progress through the creation of sector metrics. By measuring the effectiveness of protective programs and their actions, the CF Sector can continually improve the infrastructure at the facility and subsector levels and improve security overall at the sector level.

As part of the implementing structure for the NIPP, each SSA coordinates the development of an SSP that follows and supports the NIPP's risk management framework. The CF SSP provides descriptions of the processes used to identify, assess, and protect CIKR; processes used to measure effectiveness; plans for implementing these processes, including lists of projects, initiatives, activities, time frames, milestones, and resource limitations; and the status of any ongoing activities designed to support these efforts, including best practices identified, challenges encountered, and products generated. The SSPs also help define the roles and responsibilities of the SSAs and others involved in securing the sector through implementation of the SSPs.

The SSA, in active coordination with its public and private sector CIKR partners, developed this document. The remainder of this SSP is structured around each of the steps outlined in the NIPP risk management framework.

1. Sector Profile and Goals

The CF Sector is primarily composed of privately owned facilities that operate on the principle of open public access, meaning that the public may move freely throughout these facilities without the deterrent of highly visible security barriers. Each owner and operator has distinct assets, operational processes, business environments, and risk management approaches that vary across all business lines because of the considerable diversity in their objectives. This chapter of the document characterizes the CF Sector's CIKR partners, their roles and responsibilities, and describes the CF Sector's goals for CIKR protection and desired outcomes.

1.1 Sector Profile

The CF Sector is widely diverse in both scope and function. A dominant influence on the Nation's economy, this sector includes retail centers, hotels, casinos, theme parks, motion picture production studios, office and apartment buildings, convention centers, sports stadiums, and other sites where large numbers of people congregate to pursue business activities, conduct personal commercial transactions, or enjoy recreational pastimes. Highlighting the vitality of the sector in the American economy, the retail industry conducted more than $4.6 trillion in annual sales in 2008. The retail industry has more than 1.6 million U.S. establishments and more than 24 million employees (about one in five American workers).[1] In addition, the hotel industry generated $139.4 billion due to tourist and business travel in 2007[2] and commercial casinos paid more than $5.7 billion in direct gaming taxes in 2008.[3] And more than one-third of all workers in commercial buildings (roughly 35 million out of 82 million) work in office buildings.[4]

Some facilities within the CF Sector also serve to establish a sense of civic pride among Americans, bringing communities together within sporting venues, entertainment districts, and local and special events. In 2008, three major sports leagues, the National Football League (NFL), Major League Baseball (MLB), and the National Basketball Association (NBA), had a combined attendance of more than 118 million fans.[5] In the same year, box office receipts for the motion picture industry totaled nearly $9.8 billion based on an attendance of 1.4 billion.[6] In 2007, entertainment and family-oriented venues, such as amusement and theme parks, were visited by 341 million people and generated $12 billion in revenue.[7] State and local parks, recreational

---

[1] National Retail Federation, **http://www.nrf.com.**

[2] American Hotel and Lodging Association, **www.ahla.com.**

[3] American Gaming Association, **www.americangaming.org.**

[4] Energy Information Administration, **www.eia.doe.gov.**

[5] ESPN, **www.sports.espn.go.com.**

[6] Motion Picture Association of America, **www.mpaa.org.**

[7] International Association of Amusement Parks and Attractions, **www.iaapa.org.**

facilities, and community events (e.g., holiday parades) are used regularly to conduct local business ventures and express community pride.

Private companies own the majority of the facilities in the CF Sector, and these private sector owners and operators have minimal interaction with the Federal Government and other regulatory entities. Because the majority of the assets within the sector are privately owned, commercial facility owners and operators are responsible for assessing the vulnerabilities of their specific facilities to terrorist attack and natural, manmade, or technological hazards, and practicing prudent risk management and mitigation measures. While there is no single solution or standard that would serve the sector as a whole, through threat assessments conducted at the sector and facility levels, the CF Sector's priority is to enhance the protection and resilience of facilities and the public from all hazards without compromising accessibility and profitability.

Commercial facilities have cyber systems related to their operations (e.g., access control; loss prevention systems; fire and intrusion alarms; communication/dispatch centers; heating, ventilation, and air conditioning systems (HVAC); lighting; closed-circuit television (CCTV); property management; reservations, ticketing, and human resources; and financial management). While the CF Sector utilizes cyber systems in day-to-day operations, a cyber event affecting the operations of one facility is not likely to affect cyber assets at other facilities within the sector. However, the CF Sector would certainly be affected by any mass communications failure. Decisions about implementation of cyber protective programs are made at the ownership level. Additionally, protection for back-end cyber infrastructure may not always be implemented according to best practices because of the need to adhere to building codes and architectural considerations.

The CF Sector is one of the few CIKR sectors that terrorists have attacked successfully. Commercial facilities are especially vulnerable due to the large inventory of buildings across the Nation that are open to the public and are populated by large numbers of people on a daily basis. Commercial facilities are designed to be welcoming and attractive to customers and can be contrary to design security principals. Typically, these facilities are built in accordance with building codes and lack substantial design considerations intended to prevent or minimize the impact of chemical, biological, radiological, or explosive attacks.

1.1.1 Commercial Facilities Subsectors

As explained above, a wide variety of assets, systems, and networks (e.g., stadiums, movie theaters, hotels, theme parks, fairs, arenas, and office buildings) make up the CF Sector. To help facilitate coordination among those commercial facilities with similar functions and operations, the CF Sector has divided itself into the following eight subsectors:

The **Entertainment and Media Subsector** represents the owners and operators of media production facilities (e.g., television and motion pictures), print media companies (e.g., newspapers, magazines, and books), and broadcast companies (e.g., television and radio stations). This subsector has close business ties with the Outdoor Events and Real Estate subsectors.

The **Gaming Facilities Subsector** (formerly called the Resorts Subsector) represents the owners and operators of casinos, as well as the hotels, conference centers, arenas, and shopping centers associated with those casinos. The subsector's assets are located primarily in Las Vegas, Reno, Detroit, Atlantic City, the Gulf Coast States, and on tribal lands. During the review process for preparation of this SSP, CF Sector partners decided that the name of the subsector would be changed to "Gaming Facilities" to more accurately reflect the industry represented within the subsector and to eliminate any possible confusion with other resort facilities. This subsector has close business ties with the Lodging, Public Assembly, Entertainment and Media Retail, and Real Estate subsectors.

The **Lodging Subsector** represents the owners and operators of non-gaming resorts, hotels and motels, hotel-based conference centers, and bed-and-breakfast establishments. This subsector has close business ties with the Public Assembly, Entertainment and Media, Real Estate, and Gaming Facilities subsectors.

The **Outdoor Events Subsector** represents the owners and operators of amusement parks, fairs, exhibitions, parks, and other outdoor venues. This subsector has close business ties with the Entertainment and Media, Public Assembly, Real Estate, and Sports Leagues subsectors.

The **Public Assembly Subsector** represents the owners and operators of convention centers, auditoriums, stadiums, arenas, movie theaters, cultural properties, and other assets where large numbers of people congregate. Cultural properties are a very large and very diverse segment of the Public Assembly Subsector. Cultural properties include, but are not limited to, museums, zoos, planetariums, aquariums, libraries, and performance venues. Formation of a separate, ninth subsector for cultural properties is under consideration by the SCC. This subsector has close business ties with the Lodging, Outdoor Events, Real Estate, Gaming Facilities, and Sports Leagues subsectors.

The **Real Estate Subsector** represents the owners and operators of office buildings and office parks, apartment buildings, multi-family towers and condominiums, self-storage facilities, and property management companies. The Real Estate Roundtable, a key subsector partner, hosts the Real Estate Information Sharing and Analysis Center (RE-ISAC), which is an information-sharing mechanism between the real estate industry and DHS. The Real Estate Subsector is the only subsector that hosts an ISAC; however, the Real Estate Roundtable has members from the Lodging and Retail subsectors in addition to the Real Estate Subsector. This subsector has close business ties with all subsectors except Sports Leagues.

The **Retail Subsector** represents the owners and operators of enclosed malls, shopping centers, strip malls, and freestanding retail establishments. As retail establishments are often collocated with other facility types, this subsector has close business ties with the Real Estate, Lodging, Gaming, and Public Assembly subsectors.

The **Sports Leagues Subsector** represents the major sports leagues and federations and a sports broadcasting network. This subsector has close business ties with the Public Assembly and Outdoor Events subsectors.

Additional information on the characteristics, goals and objectives, protective programs, and resilience strategies of each subsector can be found in the eight subsector annexes. The information contained in the annexes reflects the current protective status of each subsector based on input provided by subsector CIKR partners.

1.1.2 Interdependencies and Relationships with Other CIKR Sectors

Many assets, systems, and networks are dependent on elements of other assets, systems, and networks to maintain functionality. In some cases, a failure in one sector will have a significant impact on the ability of another sector to perform necessary functions. This reliance on another sector for the functionality of certain infrastructure is called a dependency. If two pieces of infrastructure are dependent on one another, they are interdependent. At the sector level, as well as at the asset, system, and network level, it is important to identify dependencies and interdependencies to understand the consequences of a terrorist attack and natural, manmade, or technological hazards on a piece of infrastructure and to identify the manner in which incidents at other infrastructure could impact an interdependent asset, system, or network.

The CF Sector is dependent on many other sectors to maintain full functionality. For instance, it relies on technology solutions from the Communications Sector to support operations and communications. The CF Sector is also highly dependent on the Transportation Systems Sector to provide rail, shipping, and trucking services for the secure transport of its retail products. Conversely, many sectors are reliant on the CF Sector. The National Monuments and Icons Sector is dependent on the Lodging Subsector of the CF Sector to provide overnight accommodations for people visiting national monuments and icons. The Defense Industrial Base Sector depends on retail products purchased by the Federal Government to operate military services. Government agencies, as well as banking and finance companies, often rely on the Real Estate Subsector for office space. More information on the CIKR sectors that depend on or are interdependent with the CF Sector can be found in table 1-1.

Table 1-1: Commercial Facilities Sector Dependencies and Interdependencies with Other CIKR Sectors

Sector (Sector-Specific Agency)	Dependency/Interdependency/Overlap with the Commercial Facilities Sector
Agriculture and Food (USDA and HHS)	The CF Sector depends on the Agriculture and Food Sector for the food and beverages served and sold in commercial facilities. Many commercial facilities rely on restaurants located in their facilities as the reason why the public visits their facilities (e.g., restaurants in malls and shopping districts). Many fairs and festivals feature special types of food and beverages.
Critical Manufacturing (DHS)	The CF Sector relies on the Retail Subsector for many of the goods purchased by manufacturing companies to operate facilities. The Critical Manufacturing Sector also utilizes the Real Estate Subsector to provide office space.
Defense Industrial Base (DoD)	The Defense Industrial Base Sector relies on the CF Sector's Retail Subsector for many of the goods purchased by DoD to operate its facilities and installations. The Real Estate Subsector is also utilized heavily by the Defense Industrial Base Sector to provide office space for military services and their support contractors.
Energy (DOE)	The CF Sector is dependent on the Energy Sector for power. An interruption to the power supply would directly affect all commercial facilities located in the region serviced, and that interruption could potentially have cascading effects on other sectors that are dependent on goods provided directly by the affected commercial facilities.
Healthcare and Public Health (HHS)	The CF Sector is dependent on the Healthcare and Public Health Sector to provide services to the public in the event of an attack, natural disaster, or pandemic/large-scale outbreak of illness.
National Monuments and Icons (DOI)	The National Monuments and Icons Sector is dependent on the Lodging Subsector of the CF Sector to provide overnight accommodations for people visiting national monuments and icons. In many instances, the Outdoor Events Subsector conducts activities on the property of, or in relation to, national monuments and icons.
Banking and Finance (Treasury)	In many instances, the administrative offices associated with the Banking and Finance Sector are located in buildings associated with the CF Sector's Real Estate Subsector. The Retail Subsector is highly reliant on the Banking and Finance Sector for financial transactions associated with cash, checks, and credit cards.
Water (EPA)	The Water Sector provides a supply of potable water for and handles the treatment of wastewater produced by the public, who occupy commercial facilities. The Drinking Water and Water Treatment Systems Sector also provides water for fire suppression systems. Without these services, State or local health departments might shut down commercial facilities until services are restored.
Emergency Services (DHS)	The CF Sector is dependent on the Emergency Services Sector to protect lives and property in the event of an accident, natural disaster, or terrorist incident involving commercial facilities. The Emergency Services Sector also works to prevent such events from occurring. The Emergency Services Sector is dependent on the Commercial Facilities Sector to provide facilities for use as shelters during any incident where housing has been damaged or destroyed.
Communications (DHS)	Like all other sectors, the CF Sector depends on the Communications Sector for much of its communications capability. Even though an interruption in communications would not be catastrophic to the CF Sector, damage to the Communications Sector would impact the CF Sector's ability to operate and would probably cause some cascading economic damages.

Sector (Sector-Specific Agency)	Dependency/Interdependency/Overlap with the Commercial Facilities Sector
Postal and Shipping (DHS)	The CF Sector Retail Subsector is dependent on postal and shipping systems for the shipment of goods purchased via internet or catalog orders from the Retail Subsector.
Transportation Systems (DHS)	The CF Sector overlaps with and is dependent on the Transportation Systems Sector with regard to the transportation of retail goods by land, water, and air. Modes of transportation used to ship retail goods in various stages of the value chain include ships, barges, trains, trucks, and airplanes. Additionally, transportation assets and facilities occasionally are used to store retail goods (e.g., sea-land containers, and rail cars). Harm to the Transportation Systems Sector has the potential to seriously hinder the movement of retail goods and cause cascading effects throughout the Commercial Facilities Sector and its subsectors. The CF Sector also relies on public transportation systems to get people to and from work. Many transportation and mass transit systems are in close proximity to commercial facilities. Therefore, an attack on a transportation system would adversely impact neighboring commercial facilities, and vice versa.
Government Facilities (DHS)	In many instances, the offices associated with the Government Facilities Sector are located in buildings associated with the CF Sector's Real Estate Subsector. The Government Facilities Sector relies on the Retail Subsector for many of the goods purchased by the government to operate its facilities and installations.

1.2 CIKR Partners

The term "CIKR partners" encompasses all levels of government (Federal, State, local, tribal, and territorial), regional organizations, international partners, private sector owners and operators, and other partners who have roles and responsibilities in protection activities.

1.2.1 DHS as the Sector-Specific Agency

Pursuant to Homeland Security Presidential Directive 7, DHS was designated as the SSA for the CF Sector. Within DHS, sector-specific responsibilities have been delegated to the Office of Infrastructure Protection. As the SSA for the CF Sector, IP has primary responsibility for coordinating with other Federal, State, local, tribal, and private sector partners. IP executes SSA functions for the CF Sector and five other sectors through the SSA Management Project, which is managed by the SSA Executive Management Office. For additional information on the program management approach for the SSA Executive Management Office (EMO), see Section 8.1.

DHS coordinates with all partners to build and sustain a national, cross-sector program. The CF SSA works with both public and private partners to address security issues and collaborates with public partners who are experts on issues to be resolved. The CF Sector is composed of eight diverse subsectors with differing needs and challenges. As a result, an important function of the CF SSA is to respond to the diverse and changing security and preparedness needs within its eight subsectors.

The CF SSA coordinates with other entities within DHS and other Federal agencies to make their resources and tools available to sector partners and to develop new tools and resources. To perform necessary sector CIKR protection activities in the most efficient and effective manner possible, DHS and these agencies must coordinate their efforts. Historically, numerous formal and informal partnerships between DHS and the various pertinent Federal departments and agencies had maintained this coordination. As part of the NIPP, Government Coordinating Councils (GCCs) were formed for each sector to serve as the formal entity for coordinating government-led sector CIKR protection activities. The Commercial Facilities GCC (CF-GCC) is described further in Section 8.3.

In addition to collaborating with Federal entities that are participants on the CF-GCC, DHS must coordinate with the SSAs and other Federal entities that are engaged in CIKR protection activities for those sectors that have interdependencies or overlap with the CF Sector. These sectors, their respective SSAs, and some of the more significant overlaps and interdependencies are identified in Section 1.1.2.

1.2.2 CIKR Owners and Operators, Including Private and Public Entities

Infrastructure owners and operators play a central role in CIKR protection. Within the CF Sector, most of the owners and operators are private sector entities. As a result, the private sector is an integral partner in efforts to protect the CF Sector. In addition to ownership and management of the vast majority of commercial facilities, the private sector is uniquely situated to provide the following important contributions to CF Sector protection:

- Visibility into CIKR assets, networks, functions, facilities, and other capabilities;
- Ability to take actions to respond to incidents;
- Expertise to address and support cybersecurity efforts through their individual companies, membership in the SCC, and participation in the Cross-Sector Cybersecurity Working Group;
- Implementation of a strong base of existing security initiatives that partners can build on to enhance sector protection; and
- Implementation of existing, robust mechanisms that are useful for sharing and protecting sensitive information regarding threats, vulnerabilities, countermeasures, and best practices.

To carry out the public-private partnership essential to CIKR protection effectively and efficiently, each CIKR sector has established an SCC to serve as a coordinating body for private sector participation in CIKR protection issues. The SCCs are designed to serve as the chief interface among private sector owners and operators, DHS, and other Federal entities. They serve as hubs for communication, coordination, sector-specific expertise, and advice between the government and the private sector during protection, response, and recovery activities. The SCCs also play an important role in sector-wide planning, development of sector best practices, sector-wide promulgation of programs and plans, development of requirements for effective information-sharing, research and development (R&D), and cross-sector coordination. The CF-SCC is composed of representatives from industry associations and companies that represent the eight subsectors. Additional information on the CF-SCC can be found in Section 8.3.

1.2.3 U.S. Department of Homeland Security

DHS programs, tools, and methodologies are critical to sector activities and relationships. Through coordination with other DHS entities, the CF SSA identifies applicable resources and initiatives within the agency that may serve to enable or enhance security programs for CIKR within the CF Sector. The following DHS entities have important roles in sector protective activities:

- Federal Emergency Management Agency (FEMA)
- U.S. Immigration and Customs Enforcement (ICE)
- Federal Protective Service (FPS)
- Transportation Security Administration (TSA)
- Office of Infrastructure Protection
- Office of Policy

- Homeland Infrastructure Threat and Risk Analysis Center (HITRAC)
- Private Sector Office (PSO)
- Science and Technology (S&T) Directorate

1.2.4 Other Federal Departments and Agencies

Under HSPD-7, DHS has been charged with primary responsibility for coordinating security in the CF Sector, but numerous other Federal departments and agencies have responsibilities that are involved with the operations of the sector and have resources and initiatives within their agencies that may serve to enable or enhance security programs within the sector. Coordination with other Federal partners plays a crucial role toward ensuring that private sector security efforts can affect maximum use of the Federal Government resources that are available.

Coordination with other Federal partners also provides a mechanism for fostering cross-sector awareness and information sharing on programs and initiatives that have been successful in other sectors and could be similarly applied in the CF Sector. The following departments and agencies play a supporting role in the CF Sector and are members of the CF-GCC:

- National Telecommunications and Information Administration (NTIA), U.S. Department of Commerce
- National Institute of Standards and Technology (NIST), U.S. Department of Commerce
- U.S. Department of the Interior (DOI)
- U.S. Department of Justice (DOJ)
- U.S. Environmental Protection Agency (EPA)
- Federal Bureau of Investigation (FBI)
- General Services Administration (GSA)
- U.S. Department of Housing and Urban Development (HUD)
- Library of Congress
- National Endowment for the Arts (NEA)
- Smithsonian Institution
- United States Secret Service (USSS)

As the level of activity within the CF Sector has increased, the CF SSA is working to expand the GCC to include additional agencies and offices that can provide resources and expertise to owners and operators throughout the CF Sector.

1.2.5 State, Local, Tribal, and Territorial Governments

State, local, tribal, and territorial governments are the first line of defense for implementing the homeland security mission, protecting public safety and welfare, and ensuring the provision of essential services to communities and industries within their jurisdictions. State governments are accountable for establishing CIKR partnerships, facilitating coordinated information sharing, and enabling planning and preparedness for CIKR protection within their borders. Local governments provide critical public services and functions (e.g., drinking water, wastewater, law enforcement, and emergency response) in conjunction with private sector owners and operators (e.g., electric utilities and telecommunications providers). Tribal governments' roles and responsibilities mirror those of the State and local governments and include accountability for the public health, welfare, and safety of tribal members, as well as the protection of CIKR and the continuity of essential services under their jurisdiction.

Many State, local, tribal, and territorial government entities play a valuable role in the CF Sector's security. Tribal governments and organizations, along with the State gaming commissions, are involved in the regulation of casinos and gaming establishments. Each State also has regulations governing the hotel and motel industry, as well as retail establishments. Federal safety and health regulations are further strengthened at the State and local levels.

In order to bring together CIKR protection experts from the private sector and all levels of government, DHS established the State, Local, Tribal, and Territorial Government Coordinating Council (SLTTGCC). The SLTTGCC functions as a forum for State, local, tribal, and territorial government representatives to engage with the Federal Government and the CIKR owners and operators within the sector partnership model. The SLTTGCC has identified three SLTTGCC liaisons to the CF Sector. State, local, tribal, and territorial governments have the opportunity to be involved in the development and implementation of the CF SSP through participation of the designated SLTTGCC liaisons on the CF-GCC.

State Homeland Security Advisors (HSAs) serve as the official coordination point between DHS and State, local, tribal, and territorial government entities for all homeland security matters. The HSAs then coordinate within their governmental structures and with appropriate stakeholders to conduct sector infrastructure protection planning and execution.

Partners at the Federal, State, local, and tribal levels have roles and responsibilities for responding to disasters and emergencies. The National Response Framework details how the Nation conducts all-hazards response—from the smallest incident to the largest catastrophe. The framework identifies the key response principles, as well as the roles and structures that organize national response. It describes how communities, the States, the Federal Government, and the private sector and nongovernmental partners apply these principles for a coordinated and effective national response.

Most owners and operators of commercial facilities have developed strong information-sharing and working relationships with local governments. Local governments exchange security information, including threat assessments, attack indicators and warnings, and advisories with commercial facility owners and operators. Specific examples of this type of information sharing can be found in Section 8.4.1.

At the individual facility level, owners and operators work closely and share information with local emergency response and law enforcement organizations. In the larger cities, facility owners and operators work together to address security issues and cooperative emergency response plans. Additionally, many cities and local jurisdictions have special task forces established to share lessons learned, provide updates on current events, and help prepare for the next manmade or natural incident.

1.2.6 Regional Coalitions

Regional organizations and partnerships enable CIKR protection coordination among partners within and across geographical areas. Two such partnerships involving the CF Sector are the following:

- **Southeast Region Research Initiative (SERRI) and Community and Regional Resilience Initiative (CARRI).** SERRI assists State, local, and tribal leaders in developing the tools and methods required to anticipate and forestall terrorist events and to enhance disaster response. CARRI is a major regional program within SERRI with national implications for how communities and regions prepare for, respond to, and recover from catastrophic events. CARRI works with partner communities to define community resilience and test its emerging resilience framework.

- The **Pacific NorthWest Economic Region (PNWER)** is a regional U.S.-Canadian forum for collaborative, binational planning that involves both the public and private sectors and offers leadership at the State/provincial level. PNWER addresses regional issues through action plans developed by more than 14 working groups corresponding to the region's key priorities. PNWER, through its Pacific Northwest Center for Regional Disaster Resilience, works with key public and private stakeholders to create and implement workable solutions to regional and local infrastructure vulnerability and other related needs.

1.2.7 International Organizations and Foreign Countries

Businesses within the CF Sector are linked, in varying degrees, to global infrastructure. For instance, museums exhibit international items or items having an international theme, and many sporting events include players from foreign countries or foreign teams participating in the competition. Many of the companies represented in the sector own international properties and, in some instances, properties in the United States are owned by foreign companies or individuals. Companies may also have regional offices in foreign countries that are responsible for properties in different parts of the world. In many instances, international call centers, help desks, and catalog services are located in foreign countries.

The CF Sector, in coordination with the U.S. Department of State and other DHS components, has ongoing plans to conduct international outreach activities to promote the adoption of best practices designed to improve the protection of the CF Sector. IP has developed a U.S.-U.K. Engagement Plan that includes efforts to increase understanding of approaches for securing commercial assets, such as soft target facilities that draw significant crowds (e.g., shopping malls and stadiums), and to share experiences and learning in terms of reducing risk related to commercial facilities and crowded places. The Engagement Plan offers the opportunity to share risk assessment and training tools that are applicable to commercial facilities.

In response to an information-gathering trip, the CF SSA and Gaming Subsector council members met with a delegation from the Singapore Ministry of Home Affairs in Atlantic City and Las Vegas to share information on the NIPP Partnership Model and to discuss how agencies engage with hotels, casinos, and other types of commercial facilities. At this meeting, partners also discussed information on security measures, emergency response plans, and the types of interface that these measures and plans have with State and local agencies.

1.3 Sector Goals and Objectives

One of the fundamental purposes of the CF-SSP is to put processes in place to obtain a specified level of protection for the sector. This level of protection is defined by the sector through the creation of a vision statement describing the steady-state of CIKR protection that the sector wishes to achieve. The sector must also develop goals that address the various components of the vision statement and produce measurable outcomes that would allow the sector to allocate resources and track progress toward achieving these goals. The subsectors can use this steady-state view to determine which specific risk reduction and protection strategies most significantly enhance protection within each subsector and within the sector as a whole.

Figure 1-1: Set Goals and Objectives

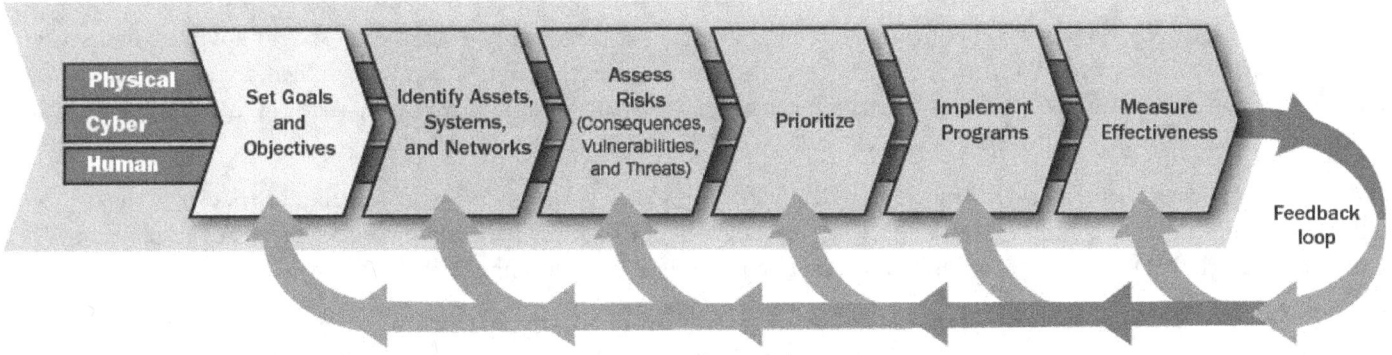

Continuous improvement to enhance protection of CIKR

The SSA met with goal development facilitators provided by DHS to obtain input on the formulation of sector-wide protection goals. As a result, the SSA created a vision statement and protection goals for the CF Sector based on discussions with members of the eight subcouncils.

The CF-SCC has had the opportunity to review and refine the vision statement and goals on an annual basis and in preparation for the 2010 SSP. The vision statement and goals identified below remain the same as in the 2007 CF-SSP, with the addition of a goal related to cybersecurity.

Commercial Facilities Sector Vision Statement

The CF Sector envisions a secure, resilient, and profitable sector in which effective and non–obstructive risk management programs instill a positive sense of safety and security among the public and sustain favorable business environments conducive to attracting and retaining employees, tenants, and customers.

1.3.1 Commercial Facilities Sector Goals

The CIKR protection goals for the CF Sector are as follows:

- Enable trusted and protected information sharing between public and private sector partners at all levels of government;

- Ensure that the public sector partners disseminate timely, accurate, and threat-specific information and analysis throughout the sector;

- Preserve the open-access business model of most commercial facilities while enhancing overall security;

- Maintain a high level of public confidence in the protection of the sector;

- Provide security that meets the needs of the public, tenants, guests, and employees while ensuring the continued economic vitality of the owners, investors, lenders, and insurers;

- Have systems in place (e.g., emergency preparedness, training, crisis response, and business continuity plans) to ensure a timely response to and recovery from natural or manmade incidents;

- Institute a robust sector-wide R&D program to identify and provide independent third-party assessments of methods and tools for sector protective program activities; and

- Implement the appropriate protective measures to secure cyber systems that are vital to the daily operations of the sector.

1.4 Value Proposition

The CF-SSP is a plan for the protection of the CF Sector and its eight subsectors. It outlines the CF Sector's approach to asset identification, risk assessment, and implementation of protective measures that address adversary-specific/manmade and natural threats to the sector's facilities. It becomes a path forward for achieving the protective steady-state described in the sector's vision statement.

The CF-SSP provides a roadmap for the future as Federal, State, and local governments work together to allocate funds to enhance the protection of commercial facilities. The various types of risk assessment and protective measures employed by the CF Sector and detailed in the CF-SSP will play a strong role in these types of funding decisions.

The CF-SSP places a strong emphasis on the communication of timely and accurate information between the Federal Government and subsector owners and operators, between subsectors, and between the 18 CIKR sectors. This emphasis carries strong weight in DHS budgeting allocations and the decisions made by State and local governments. Therefore, the input provided by each subsector ensures that multiple perspectives are heard during CF-SSP implementation.

The CF-SSP and its eight annexes identify best practices and other policy recommendations that help to improve protection throughout the CF Sector. The CF-SSP will influence future decisions at the Federal, State, and local government levels when it comes to addressing the threats to commercial facilities. Therefore, it is in the interests of the CF Sector membership to work with the CF SSA in the implementation of the CF-SSP to carry out an all-hazards risk management framework throughout the sector.

Owners and operators of commercial facilities are the most qualified individuals to offer first-hand expertise on the protective needs of the sector and each subsector. Without this specialized knowledge of routine operating procedures and threat-related concerns, the CF-SSP will be neither accurate nor effective. It also must be stressed that owner/operator cooperation is essential to effectively protect the sector. Because the private sector owns nearly all commercial facilities, it is impossible for the Federal Government to protect the sector unilaterally. The optimal implementation of this CF-SSP ultimately depends on the active engagement of the CF-SCC; the eight subsectors; Federal, State, and local partners (including those represented on the CF-GCC); and individual facility owners and operators.

2. Identify Assets, Systems, and Networks

The CF SSA has been working aggressively with its partners to effectively manage the CF Sector's protective efforts by using the NIPP's risk-based approach to identify what infrastructure (i.e., assets, facilities, systems, and networks) make up the sector. IICD maintains information on the sector's infrastructure through the Infrastructure Data Warehouse (IDW). The CF SSA continues to work with the sector's CIKR partners to populate the IDW with information regarding each facility's functionality within the sector and to refine the sector's taxonomy terminology to categorize the various commercial facility infrastructure elements maintained in the IDW as accurately as possible.

Figure 2-1: Identify Assets, Systems, and Networks

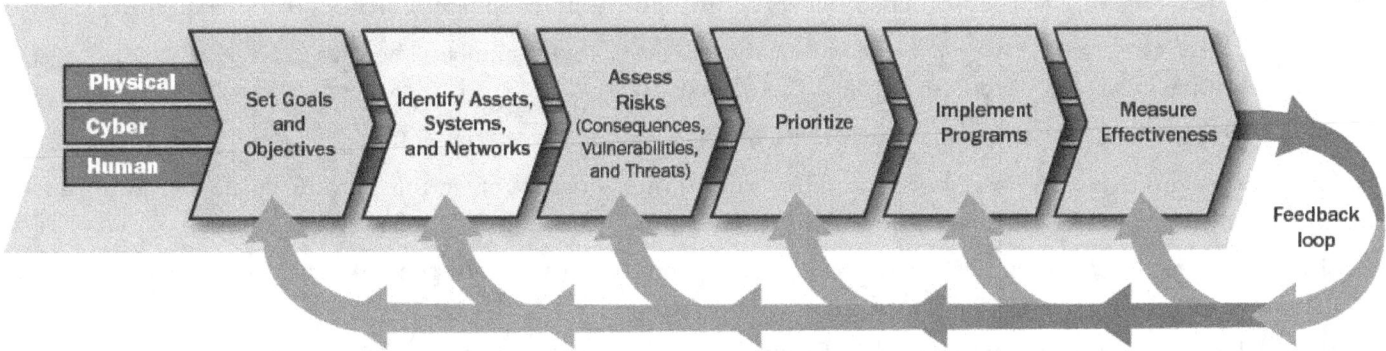

Continuous improvement to enhance protection of CIKR

While some individual companies and subsector organizations have provided infrastructure information to IICD, the CF-SCC has not participated in a sector-wide submission of information to support the IDW's inventory, functionality, and screening processes. For the most part, infrastructure information that is submitted voluntarily to IICD from trade associations includes inventories of their facilities and/or members. Traditionally, industry associations collect this data for various reasons, such as marketing and financial purposes. In line with the collaborative effort employed through the implementation of the CF-SSP, the CF SSA has been working with subsector councils and individual companies to explain the value and benefit to the sector partners and DHS of supporting IICD's CF Sector infrastructure information collection process.

The CF SSA serves as a conduit in the data collection process between the sector and DHS for the identification of specific data elements requested by IICD and the validation of data elements submitted by State and local authorities and sector partners. The CF SSA does not initiate sector data collection on its own, but provides input to the IICD data collection process based on knowledge and experience in implementing the sector's risk management program. The CF SSA does not perform independent data analysis, but utilizes the data analysis capabilities available through DHS.

2.1 Defining Information Parameters

Through the implementation of the CF-SSP, the CF SSA has been working with its sector partners and IICD to identify those data infrastructure elements necessary for understanding the sector's infrastructure dependencies and interdependencies, as well as enabling national, regional, local, and sector-based risk assessments, prioritization, and management. The CF SSA has defined the specific types of data categories that it seeks to collect with regard to the sector's infrastructure and its physical, cyber, and human elements. These selected data categories have become data fields contained within the IDW. In defining the infrastructure protection data utilized by the IDW, the CF SSA has taken a comprehensive, integrated view of the sector's infrastructure, including all of its characteristics and the dependencies necessary for it to function. This is necessary because the functionality of many infrastructure is dependent on multiple elements and systems (e.g., people, physical, information technology (IT), and telecommunications), and it is these attributes of interest (as well as interdependencies with other assets, systems, and networks) that provide the basis for assessing potential consequences, vulnerabilities, threats, and risks, and when developing protective strategies.

The CF Sector has identified the following Attributes of Interest that better define an individual asset:

- **Facility Location.** General geographic situation (e.g., financial district, industrial park, etc.);

- **Facility Proximity.** Proximity to high-risk enterprises (e.g., adjacency to an iconic landmark or important Federal building);

- **Facility Size.** Height, footprint, number of floors, hotel rooms, apartments, public areas, and exhibition/retail space;

- **Facility Capacity/Attendance.** Design population annual attendance (e.g., the number of tenants in an office building, spectators at a sporting event, and visitors/participants at an outdoor event);

- **Facility Type.** Purpose or use of the facility (e.g., office building, stadium, hotel, amusement park, etc.);

- **Geographical Area.** Defined by local government, this includes prestigious commercial (e.g., retail, hotels, and office buildings) and residential assets that are nationally recognized as a tourist destination and unified economic entity;

- **Facility Functions.** Types of events held in the facility (e.g., national sporting events, political conventions, and controversial exhibitions); and

- **Facility Value.** Iconic and economic status of the facility (e.g., historical status, owner, tenants, and clientele).

The CF SSA continues to work with each subsector to identify and refine the categories of information sought for different commercial facility Attributes of Interest. This information is then provided to IICD for inclusion into the IDW.

The CF SSA and IICD employ many processes for collecting, verifying, and updating CF Sector infrastructure information. Voluntary data submissions include direct facility submission (e.g., the Risk Self Assessment Tool (RSAT) assessment process); studies and assessments (e.g., Site Assistance Visits (SAVs), Buffer Zone Plans (BZPs), and the Infrastructure Survey Tool (IST)) performed by DHS; annual DHS data calls (e.g., Level 1/ Level2); and State and local government data collection (e.g., the Automated Critical Asset Management System (ACAMS)). CF Sector data verification is accomplished through data review by sector partners and sector subject matter experts, the comparison of data across various government and sector databases, and analysis of data associated with individual assessments and studies. Annual data calls (e.g., Level 1/ Level 2, taxonomy revisions) and the results from recent DHS assessments and studies are all used to ensure that IICD's CF Sector infrastructure database is up to date.

As discussed in Chapter 1, the sector is divided into the following eight subsectors as a means to help facilitate coordination among those CF Sector infrastructure assets with common characteristics and business models:

- Entertainment and Media
- Gaming
- Lodging
- Outdoor Events

- Public Assembly
- Real Estate
- Retail
- Sports Leagues

Furthermore, the CF Sector is categorized by the DHS Infrastructure Taxonomy, which defines the mutually exclusive categories needed to outline all infrastructure types within all 18 CIKR sectors. The taxonomy is based broadly on the North American Industry Classification System code to allow comparison of business statistics and to help define the type or purpose of an asset and to annotate the infrastructure categorization. The Infrastructure Taxonomy was created to provide a detailed categorization of all CIKR in the following descending order: sector, subsector, segment, subsegment, and asset type. Each SSA provides input to the summary descriptions that represent the types of assets that fall within each of the five categories. The aforementioned Attributes of Interest are also utilized by the taxonomy to better define specific asset types. Table 2-1 contains a portion of the CF Sector Infrastructure Taxonomy for the Public Assembly and Sports Leagues subsectors.

It should be noted that the Infrastructure Taxonomy was created to establish a consistent lexicon for use in domestic CIKR partnership communications by defining the mutually exclusive industrial sectors and outlining all infrastructure types within a given sector. The Infrastructure Taxonomy is not intended to displace common industry terminology and it is not intended to provide any qualification or level of criticality or significance to a particular asset or infrastructure. The taxonomy does not represent the areas of responsibility for the SSAs under the NIPP. The NIPP and this SSP are the guiding documents for outlining the CF Sector's authorities and responsibilities.

The Infrastructure Protection Taxonomy is the foundation for multiple DHS programs that focus on CIKR, such as the IDW and the National Threat Incident Database, and provides the foundation for the lexicon used in the CF-SSP. This common framework allows for more efficient integration and transfer of information, as well as a more effective analytical tool for making comparisons.

Table 2-1: Taxonomy for the Public Assembly and Sports Leagues Subsectors

Subsector	Description	Attributes
Public Assembly		
	Facilities where large numbers of people congregate to pursue business activities, conduct personal transactions, or enjoy recreational pastimes.	
Sports Leagues		
Motor Racetracks	A racetrack built for racing automobiles or motorcycles, which features grandstands, concourses, an infield, pit lanes, and garages. Racetracks can be either open circuit or closed circuit.	• Attendance (number/year) • Capacity (number of people) • Event Frequency (number/year) • Types of Events Held
Horse and Dog Tracks	A race track built for racing horses and dogs, which features grandstands, concourses, an infield, paddocks, and stables.	• Attendance (number/year) • Capacity (number of people) • Event Frequency (number/year) • Types of Events Held

Subsector	Description	Attributes
Arenas	Large indoor facilities in which events are held for large audiences. Generally designed primarily for spectator sports, but also with the ability to host concerts, lectures, rallies, circuses, and other events with large audiences.	• Attendance (number/year) • Capacity (number of people) • Event Frequency (number/year) • Types of Events Held
Stadiums	Large outdoor facilities in which events are held for large audiences. May or may not have a retractable dome for dealing with inclement weather. Generally designed primarily for spectator sports, but also with the ability to host concerts, lectures, rallies, circuses, and other events with large audiences.	• Attendance (number/year) • Capacity (number of people) • Event Frequency (number/year) • Types of Events Held
Cultural Properties		
Amphitheaters	An open air venue for spectator sports, concerts, rallies, or theatrical performances.	• Attendance (number/year) • Capacity (number of people) • Event Frequency (number/year) • Types of Events Held
Museums, Planetariums	Facilities engaged in the preservation and exhibition of objects, sites, and natural wonders of historical, cultural, and educational value.	• Attendance (number/year) • Capacity (number of people) • Event Frequency (number/year) • Types of Events Held
Performing Arts Centers and Auditoriums	Indoor facilities in which performing arts are presented to audiences. Includes concert halls, live theatrical production theaters, dance theaters, community theaters, and other such facilities. Generally smaller than arenas (see below).	• Attendance (number/year) • Capacity (number of people) • Event Frequency (number/year) • Types of Events Held
Zoos, Aquariums, Botanical Gardens	Establishments primarily engaged in the preservation and exhibition of live plant and animal life displays.	• Attendance (number/year) • Capacity (number of people) • Event Frequency (number/year) • Types of Events Held
Other Facilities		
Convention Centers	Facilities where large groups of people (e.g., political party, professional organization, civic group, etc.) meet to exchange information and where trade shows displaying products are held. May also host other events, such as concerts, theater performances, and sporting events. May be attached to other facilities such as hotels.	• Attendance (number/year) • Convention Space (square feet) • Meetings (number/year)
Golf Courses and Country Clubs	Establishments primarily engaged in operating golf courses. May include dining facilities and other recreational facilities that are known as country clubs.	• Membership (number/year) • Types of Events Held
Movie Theaters	Facilities in which motion pictures are shown. May have multiple screens.	• Attendance (number/year) • Capacity (number of people)

Subsector	Description	Attributes
Arenas	Large indoor facilities in which events are held for large audiences. This category is focused on facilities not normally used for spectator sporting events.	• Attendance (number/year) • Capacity (number of people) • Event Frequency (number/year) • Types of Events Held
Stadiums	Large outdoor facilities in which events are held for large audiences. May or may not have a retractable dome for dealing with inclement weather. This category is focused on facilities not normally used for spectator sporting events.	• Attendance (number/year) • Capacity (number of people) • Event Frequency (number/year) • Types of Events Held
Other		
Entertainment Districts	Areas with a concentration of different types of entertainment facilities in close proximity. May include restaurants, nightclubs, and other such establishments.	
Fitness and Recreational Facilities	Establishments primarily engaged in operating fitness and recreational sports facilities featuring exercise and other active physical fitness conditioning or recreational sports activities, such as swimming, skating, or racquet sports.	
All Other Amusement and Recreational Facilities	Not elsewhere classified.	

Along with the designation of the eight subsectors and the taxonomy categorization, the CF SSA also breaks down the sector into two functional groupings. One is composed of national professional organizations and associations, and national corporate headquarters. The other is composed of individual asset owners and operators. These national organizations make up the CF-SCC membership and serve as a conduit to the individual asset owners and operators.

The Sports League Subsector can be used as an example of the CF Sector's use of infrastructure data elements. Individual assets such as stadiums or arenas are either privately owned by the sports team or publically owned by a municipality or public authority. The sports teams themselves are also considered to be subsector assets. The facility assets are associated with professional organizations such as the International Association of Assembly Managers (IAAM) and the Stadium Managers Association (SMA). The human assets are associated with individual sports leagues. Attributes of Interest associated with the facility assets include attendance per game, the capacity of the facility, the frequency of events, the types of events held in the asset (e.g., nationally televised professional sports), and the geographical area (e.g., a cluster of multiple sports venues). The cyber element is tied to the Internet as the conduit for ticket and merchandise sales and the offering of Webcasts of games.

2.1.1 Infrastructure Data Warehouse (IDW)

DHS maintains a national inventory of the assets, systems, and networks that make up the Nation's CIKR. The Nation's infrastructure includes assets, systems, and networks that are nationally significant, as well as those assets that may not be as significant on a national level, but are, nonetheless, important to State, regional, or local CIKR protection, incident management, and response and recovery efforts. The principal national inventory of CIKR systems and assets is the IDW. The IDW comprises a federated data architecture that provides a single virtual view of one or more infrastructure data sources. DHS uses this data to provide all relevant public and private sector CIKR partners with access to the most current and complete view of the Nation's infrastructure information allowed under applicable Federal, State, or local regulations.

The goal of the IDW is to provide access to relevant information for natural disasters, industrial accidents, and other incidents, as well as maintain basic information about the relationships, dependencies, and interdependencies among various assets, systems, and networks, including foreign CIKR on which the United States may rely. The inventory will also eventually include a cyber data framework to characterize each sector's unique and significant cyber assets, systems, or networks.

This information is needed not only to help manage CIKR protection and resilience approaches, but also to inform and support the response to a wide array of incidents and emergencies. Risk may change based on many factors, including damage resulting from a natural disaster; seasonal or cyclic dependencies; and changes in technology, the economy, or the terrorist threat. The inventory supports domestic incident management by helping to prioritize and focus preparedness planning; inform decision-making; establish strategies for response; and identify priorities for restoration, remediation, and reconstruction.

Currently, the inventory and associated attributes are maintained through the Infrastructure Information Collection System (IICS), a federated IDW, accessible in a geospatial context using the capabilities provided by the Integrated Common Analytical Viewer (iCAV) suite of tools, including the iCAV and DHS Earth viewers. The SSAs and DHS work together and in concert with State, local, tribal, and territorial governments and private sector partners to ensure that the inventory data structure is accurate, current, and secure. DHS provides guidelines concerning the information needed to develop and maintain the inventory. Within this inventory, the set of nationally and regionally significant infrastructure is maintained and constantly updated and refined.

All data maintained on DHS systems must adhere to DHS Sensitive Systems Policy (Management Directive 4300). This policy addresses the required management, operational, and technical information security policies that are necessary to secure data such as access control and auditing. DHS also provides guidelines concerning the information needed to develop and maintain the inventory. Within this inventory, the set of nationally and regionally significant infrastructure is maintained and constantly updated and refined. Information in the IDW comes from a variety of sources and takes advantage of work already completed, such as the following:

- **Sector inventories:** The CF SSA maintains a close working relationship with facility owners and operators, the SCC, and other sources that maintain the inventories necessary for the sector's business or mission. CF Sector partners provide relevant information to the CF SSA upon request in order to update it on a periodic basis and to ensure that sector inventories and associated critical functions are adequately represented and that sector and cross-sector dependencies and interdependencies can be identified and analyzed.

- **Voluntary submittals from CIKR partners:** Owners and operators; State, local, tribal, and territorial governments; and Federal departments and agencies voluntarily submit CF Sector information and have previously completed inventories and analyses for DHS and the CF SSA to consider for the IDW.

- **Results of studies:** Various government or commercial databases developed as a result of studies undertaken by trade associations, advocacy groups, and regulatory agencies may contain relevant CF Sector information.

- **Annual data calls:** DHS, in cooperation with the CF SSA and other CIKR partners, conducts a voluntary annual data call to Federal, State, and territorial partners. This data call process allows Federal, State, and territorial partners to propose CF Sector data input that meets specified criteria developed by DHS and the States.

- **Ongoing reviews of particular locations where risk is believed to be higher:** DHS and the CF SSA initiate site assessments to provide information on vulnerability; help identify assets, systems, and networks and their dependencies, interdependencies, and critical functionality; and provide information that will help quantify their value in risk analyses. DHS, in coordination with the CF SSA, State and local governments, private sector owners and operators, and other partners, works to build on and update existing inventories at the State and local levels to avoid duplication of past or ongoing complementary efforts.

DHS recognizes the sensitive, business, or proprietary nature of much of the CF Sector infrastructure information accessed through the IDW. DHS is responsible for protecting this information from unauthorized disclosure or use. CF Sector information in the IDW is protected from unauthorized disclosure or misuse to the maximum extent allowed under applicable Federal, State, or local regulations, including For Official Use Only (FOUO) document classification for venues that are owned by the Federal Government, as well as Protected Critical Infrastructure Information (PCII) and security classification rules. Additionally, DHS ensures that all data and licensing restrictions associated with the IDW are strictly enforced. DHS is also implementing important resilient and redundant security measures that apply to the IDW and provide enhanced systems integrity and security, software security, and data protection.

State and local government agencies play an important role in understanding the CF Sector infrastructure elements by enabling the identification of assets, systems, and networks at the State and local levels. State and local first responders, emergency managers, public health officials, and others involved in homeland security missions frequently interact with CF Sector owners and operators in their jurisdictions to plan for and respond to all manner of natural and manmade hazards. These relationships form the core of the public-private partnership model and translate into first-hand knowledge of the CF Sector infrastructure elements at the State and local levels, as well as an understanding of those CF Sector infrastructure elements that are considered critical from a State and local perspective.

DHS provides a number of tools and resources to help State and local officials leverage their knowledge to create infrastructure inventories that contribute to the IDW. This includes ACAMS, which helps State and local officials leverage their knowledge to create infrastructure inventories, implement practical CF Sector protection programs, and facilitate information sharing within and across State and local boundaries, as well as with DHS and other Federal partners.

2.1.2 CF SSA Role in Inventory Development and Maintenance

The CF SSA has a leading role in several development and maintenance phases of the CF Sector inventory. The CF SSA's role includes nominating infrastructure assets and the adjudication of those high-risk assets proposed by the States and territories in response to the annual data call. The emphasis is on making data collection efforts more manageable and less burdensome by doing the following:

- Prioritizing the approach for data outreach to different partners;
- Identifying assets, systems, networks, or functions of potential national, regional, or sector-level importance; and
- Identifying, reviewing, and leveraging existing sector infrastructure data sources.

The process of ensuring that the CF Sector infrastructure data that is collected is both current and accurate is a continual process overseen by IICD. Data updates and currency are largely dependent on the sources of the data and the frequency of the updates that the CF SSA and State (e.g., the HSAs) and local partners provide to IICD. Efficiency and reliability are maintained by IICD through the implementation of various data quality control techniques. Verification and validation efforts by contracted companies or Federal employees also play a role in ensuring that CF Sector infrastructure information is accurate and current.

The key to IICD's data collection process is the establishment of straightforward and concise collection requirements that help ensure that the CF SSA and State HSAs provide accurate infrastructure data. Because IICD collects data for a variety of customers and for a variety of purposes, asset information needs to be identified in varying levels of granularity. IICD's collection requirements ensure that the collected data is criteria adaptable. This is advantageous because it allows the criteria to change without requiring additional data calls, ensures that the data remain relevant beyond the actual data call time frame, and allows the data to be utilized for multiple purposes.

Key data parameters used by IICD to provide comprehensive information to DHS about the CF Sector's infrastructure assets include the CF Sector's Attributes of Interest and Infrastructure Taxonomy, as well as the sector's subsector organization, which is structured around common characteristics and business models. To identify those CF Sector assets that are most critical to the sector, HITRAC collects consequence-based information (e.g., loss of life, economic impact, and mission disruption) for the National Critical Infrastructure Prioritization Program (NCIPP). The NCIPP program comprises four groups of lists (i.e., the Level 1 list, the Level 2 list, the18 distinct Sector lists, and the State lists (State-specific lists of critical infrastructure, including the Level 1, Level 2, and Sector list infrastructure) and foreign lists, which include foreign infrastructure that is critical to the Nation's public health, economic, and/or national security). HITRAC establishes the Level 1/Level 2 consequence criteria, the CF SSA and the CF-SCC establish the sector's criteria, and the States and Territories establish their criteria, which include information about how the list is used for risk and incident management purposes at the State and local levels. The Level 1/Level 2 lists are used to support eligibility determinations for the Urban Area Security Initiative, State Homeland Security, and Buffer Zone Protection grant programs.

2.1.3 Identifying Cyber Infrastructure

The NIPP addresses the protection of the cyber elements of CIKR in an integrated manner rather than as a separate consideration. As a component of the sector-specific risk assessment process, cyber infrastructure components for the CF Sector are being identified and included as a cyber element of the larger asset, system, or network's description if they are associated with one. The identification process includes information on international cyber infrastructure with cross-border implications, interdependencies, and cross-sector ramifications. Cyber infrastructure that have been identified as existing in the CF Sector include business systems, control systems, access control systems, and warning and alert systems.

The Internet has been identified as a key resource for the CF Sector, comprising the domestic and international assets within both the Information Technology and Communications sectors. While the availability of the Internet is the responsibility of both the Information Technology and Communications sectors, the need for access to and reliance on the Internet is paramount to the daily business functions of the CF Sector.

DHS supports the CF Sector and its partners by developing tools and methodologies to assist in identifying cyber assets, systems, and networks, including those that involve multiple sectors. As needed, DHS works with all sector representatives to help identify cyber infrastructure within the NIPP risk management framework.

Additionally, the DHS National Cybersecurity Division (NCSD), in collaboration with CF Sector partners, is working to provide cross-sector cyber methodologies that, when applied, will enable the CF Sector to identify those cyber assets, systems, and networks within the sector that may have nationally significant consequences if destroyed, incapacitated, or exploited. These methodologies will also help to characterize the reliance of the sector's business and operational functionality on cyber infrastructure components. Once an appropriate cyber identification methodology is defined for the sector, DHS will work with the sector to ensure alignment of that methodology with the NIPP risk management framework.

Since the preparation of the 2007 CF-SSP, the CF SSA has been working with CF Sector partners to identify the sector's cyber infrastructure, the risks to that infrastructure, and ways to mitigate those risks. Progress has been made in the CF SSA's understanding of the various types of cyber systems employed at sector facilities; the impact such systems have on individual facility operations, as well as their corporate organization; and the sector's dependency on the Internet for marketing, merchandising, ticket sales, and reservations. The CF SSA has worked with other DHS components to develop cyber data criteria that will provide a more complete understanding of the Sector's cyber infrastructure. Various DHS assessments (e.g., SAVs and the Buffer Zone Protection Program (BZPP)) collect information on cyber systems and functions at CF Sector facilities. RSAT, developed by the CF SSA in conjunction with IAAM and IICD in 2009, contains a cyber risk assessment section that makes sector partners aware of the importance of their cyber systems and suggests protective programs that can be implemented to respond to cyber threats. Cyber information submitted to DHS through the RSAT process increases DHS's knowledge of the CF Sector's cyber infrastructure.

The CF Sector's cyber infrastructure is composed of business systems, control systems, access control systems, and warning and alert systems. Business systems include lodging reservations, supply chain management, order processing, and sporting and entertainment ticketing. Control systems are represented by HVAC, print media production systems, elevator/escalator systems, gaming systems, property management systems, and life safety systems. Swipe key card readers and electronic hotel key cards are examples of access control systems. Warning and alert systems include facial recognition systems, active and passive detectors/monitors, and CCTV. While all of these cyber infrastructure systems can utilize the Internet for access and operation, the failure of any or all of these systems at a particular asset would not likely affect a broader group of similar assets within the same subsector. However, because of the CF Sector's business system's dependency on the Internet; the failure of that cyber system would create a significant negative economic impact on the sector.

As part of the CF SSA's implementation of the CF-SSP, the sector is working with NCSD to develop a comprehensive CF Sector cyber plan and facilitating cross-sector cyber analysis to understand and mitigate cyber risk to the sector. Working with NCSD, the CF SSA and sector partners will identify and collect cyber data. NCSD will provide guidance to the CF SSA and sector partners to identify gaps, vulnerabilities, and mitigation strategies related to the four cyber systems discussed above, as well as identifying opportunities to improve sector coordination around cyber issues, highlighting cyber dependencies and interdependencies, and sharing government and private sector cybersecurity products and findings.

2.2 Collecting Infrastructure Information

Collecting the necessary information to coordinate a national strategy for the security and protection of the CF Sector requires willingness and a collaborative effort on the part of DHS and sector members. The CF SSA and IICD must develop appropriate processes to encourage and facilitate voluntary data submittals and address information protection concerns.

In addition to collecting data from the States and other Federal entities, DHS collects some asset data by working directly with asset owners and operators. During the implementation of various protective program initiatives, such as the BZPP, SAVs, ACAMS, and RSAT, DHS learns valuable information concerning high-risk critical infrastructure directly from asset owners and operators or local law enforcement and other emergency response personnel. Likewise, the CF SSA partners with the sector subcouncils when creating criteria for use in the NCIPP Level 1/Level 2 process and HITRAC's Strategic Homeland Infrastructure Risk Analysis (SHIRA) report. Similar information is garnered when DHS and the CF SSA work with asset owners and operators when specific threat intelligence causes DHS to respond and possibly provide assistance in securing select facilities. All of this information is catalogued and maintained in the IDW.

Most of the CF Subsector councils have varying degrees of information on the facilities that compose their respective subsectors. Over the past three years, some of this information has been shared with DHS; however, much has not been shared. The sector partners are still hesitant to share the information needed for risk management purposes because it is sensitive security or business proprietary information. Therefore, fostering appropriate protection mechanisms for private sector information remains an essential requirement for the successful implementation of a national strategy for critical infrastructure protection.

The amount and types of information possessed by the subsector councils are described below:

- The **Public Assembly Subsector** has current and comprehensive information on facilities that are members of IAAM. This information is updated on an annual basis and there are methods in place to make the necessary changes as facilities join or leave this association. The majority of the facilities used by the Sports Leagues Subsector are also part of the Public Assembly Subsector. Because the **Sports Leagues Subsector** leases the majority of the facilities utilized for sporting events from the Public Assembly Subsector, the Public Assembly Subsector has not seen any need to create a subsector-wide inventory of facilities that the sports leagues do not own or for which they have operational control. The Public Assembly Subsector, through IAAM, is willing to provide information to DHS for inclusion in the IDW, and a specific process is in place to collect data and information on subsector facilities. The subcouncil has submitted significant information to the IDW.

- Within the **Gaming Subsector**, the American Gaming Association (AGA) and the National Indian Gaming Association (NIGA) collect information on the number of gaming establishments and other industry-related statistics. However, that information does not include an identification of assets or any information pertinent to risk management. Individual casino owners and operators share specific information with their local government and emergency responders, but this is done on a case-by-case basis.

- In the **Real Estate Subsector**, owners and operators are willing to share facility information on an informal basis with trusted and known local first responders and law enforcement agencies. However, the formal disclosure of information in a facility-specific format across the subsector has not yet happened due to information protection concerns. The CF SSA has been working with the subsector to address potential liability issues over the content of the information and to place restrictions (i.e., PCII) on who can access such information.

- Like the Real Estate Subsector, individual companies and associations within the **Retail Subsector** maintain inventories of their facilities for various reasons (e.g., marketing and financial purposes), but not for security or protective programs. Many owners and operators of buildings in the Retail Subsector are willing to share facility vulnerability information on an informal basis with trusted local first responders. The subsector is reasonably confident that key State and local officials are aware of the "critical" retail assets within their jurisdictions. This same understanding applies to DHS's knowledge of "nationally critical" real estate facilities. The CF SSA has been obtaining asset information on a case-by-case basis from those building owners and operators who are willing to submit asset information to DHS.

- Within the **Lodging Subsector**, each hotel company has an inventory of its properties. The American Hotel and Lodging Association (AH&LA) also receives comprehensive and current information on the hotel industry from its members. However, AH&LA uses this information solely to promote the hotel and tourist industry, not for infrastructure protection. Some hotel companies have provided information to DHS for inclusion in the IDW.

- The **Entertainment and Media Subsector** is able to define the types of assets within the subsector, primarily through experience-based knowledge. Subcouncil members have not estimated the size or scope of these assets, although they have acknowledged that DHS may need that information for threat assessments or for warnings involving a specific type of subsector facility.

- Associations representing different venues within the **Outdoor Events Subsector** have records of membership information, but not necessarily an inventory of facilities. While many fairs and carnivals utilize land set aside for their use, other small carnivals use properties designated for other uses. Therefore, it is very difficult to identify all assets associated with this subsector. Individual owners and operators share specific asset information with their local emergency responders on a case-by-case basis. The CF SSA has been working with asset owners and operators within the subsector to determine what asset information would be useful to DHS.

Concern over public disclosure plays a significant role in determining what type of facility information each subsector will provide to DHS. The sector as a whole has emphasized that public disclosure without prior consent from the owners and operators remains a real concern. DHS utilizes the PCII program and the Critical Infrastructure Partnership Advisory Council (CIPAC) to address this concern and to facilitate information sharing from the private sector.

The IICD will continue to work through the CF SSA to reach individual commercial facility companies and subsectors to collect or obtain access to the infrastructure information desired by DHS. This data collection process will continue to be criteria adaptable to ensure that the collection efforts are manageable and less burdensome on the sector partners. Concurrently, the CF SSA will work within DHS and with the sector to maintain and enhance mechanisms already in place to ensure that submitted information is protected.

The CF SSA submits its infrastructure data through the IP Data Call Application, an initiative of the IICD, which provides a front-end solution for the IDW. This federated suite of user interfaces allows IP components and mission partners within the homeland security and homeland defense missions the ability to provide infrastructure data and related information to the rest of the partners. The IP Data Call Application enables SSAs to perform five actions regarding CIKR data list submissions to DHS:

1. Submit CIKR for inclusion on individual 2010 Sector Lists, including CIKR that were previously submitted in 2009 and new CIKR;

2. Review matching data records found in the CIKR submissions;

3. Submit additional information and files related to the CIKR data submissions;

4. Nominate CIKR for inclusion on the 2010 Level 1/Level 2 Lists; and

5. Recommend CIKR for high-priority consideration by DHS.

The Homeland Security Infrastructure Program (HSIP) will serve as the primary data source for the IDW. The major supporting elements within HSIP are data collection, data management, and data dissemination. HSIP Gold is a unified infrastructure geospatial data inventory assembled by the National Geospatial-Intelligence Agency (NGA) in partnership with DHS, the U.S. Department of Defense (DoD), and the U.S. Geological Survey. HSIP Gold is for use by the Federal homeland security and homeland defense community to increase readiness and knowledge about potential threats and vulnerabilities to the Nation, and to reduce response and recovery times in the event of a natural or manmade disaster within the United States. HSIP Freedom will make license-free data available to the SLTTGCC partners. While HSIP collects, manages, and stores information about the Nation's infrastructure, its infrastructure data collection and management ensures that critical infrastructure information is available when needed.

All of this infrastructure information is maintained in multiple Federal, State, and DHS databases. DHS hopes to integrate existing databases using a federated framework to provide a dynamic common operating interface of infrastructure and vulnerability information through a cross-flow of data among separate databases or linked access to other databases. Currently, the IP Taxonomy and associated attributes are maintained within the IDW. DHS is considering integrating the iCAV, National Threat Incident Database (NTID), DHS Earth viewers, and the Linking Encrypted Network System—all databases that contain information sets pertinent to the NIPP's risk management approach—into the IDW. Infrastructure data used by State and local entities via ACAMS can be shared with IDW through the instantiation of Web services, system-to-system interconnect, or other technical means.

As the CF Sector partnership relationship continues to evolve and DHS and sector partners identify infrastructure data needs, new DHS databases (e.g., RSAT Performing Arts module), data collection programs, and associated data calls will be developed and implemented to close risk mitigation gaps.

2.2.1 Commercial Facilities Sector Partners Contribution

The CF Sector infrastructure information accessible through the IDW is highly dependent on the participation and support of the CF SSA, sector partners, State HSAs, and private sector entities. Their contributions include the following:

- The CF SSA has the primary responsibility of validating sector information provided to DHS for inclusion in the IDW.

- Some State governments have already developed infrastructure databases and others have begun the process to identify and assess CF Sector infrastructure data within their jurisdictions. State HSAs work closely with DHS and the CF SSA to ensure that data collection efforts are streamlined, coordinated, and reflect the most accurate data possible.

- CF Sectors owners and operators have the best knowledge of the most current and accurate infrastructure data. Thus, private sector entities are encouraged by the CF SSA to be actively involved in the development of the sector's infrastructure information.

- The ability to expand the Level 1/Level 2 List to include sector, State, Territory, and foreign infrastructure criteria. The addition of the State and Territory lists will help ensure that those CF Sector assets that do not qualify under the Level 1/Level 2 thresholds remain on the infrastructure protection community's radar and are available to Federal, State, and local partners as a standing resource for risk and incident management purposes.

The CF Sector is considered a non-regulatory sector. Private companies own and operate the majority of the facilities in the CF Sector and they have minimal interaction with the Federal Government or other regulatory agencies. There is no regulatory obligation that requires sector owners and operators to submit infrastructure information to DHS, State, and local governments. Therefore, it is the goal of the CF SSA and the State HSAs to educate the facility owners and operators of the importance of identifying critical infrastructure data sets that need to be captured in a DHS and/or State database, and to produce relevant risk management products that benefit CF Sector owners and operators. CF Sector infrastructure information that is provided by the CF Sector partners can be protected from unauthorized disclosure and misuse to the maximum extent allowed under applicable Federal, State, or local regulations, including PCII and security classification rules.

Completing and submitting an RSAT is an example of a non-regulatory data submission program developed by IICD and the CF SSA. Facility data collected during the RSAT process provides the owner and operator with the identification and management of security vulnerabilities to reduce the risk to their facilities. The owners and operators may also choose to have their facility data incorporated into the IDW. RSAT incorporates PCII protections into the self-assessment process to ensure that the information entered into RSAT will be protected from public disclosure under the Freedom of Information Act and similar State and local disclosure laws, and from use in civil litigation or as the basis for regulatory action.

CF Sector infrastructure data collection is an ongoing process implemented by IICD, the CF SSA, CF Sector partners, and other Federal agencies. Sources of infrastructure information include the individual facility owners and operators, State and local governments, industry and professional associations, and commercial sources. Those ongoing data collection efforts include RSAT, ACAMS, the Enhanced Critical Infrastructure Program (ECIP), SAVs, and BZPs. The Level 1/Level 2 process is an annual data call.

The IICS, which includes the federated IDW and uses the capabilities provided by the iCAV suite of tools, will be updated in Fiscal Year 2010. Once completed, the IICS will fuse data records and generate new, comprehensive composite infrastructure data set(s) that contain accurate and merged infrastructure attributes and metadata information, which expose that data to various tools and systems through a Service-Oriented Architecture developed to meet DHS enterprise architecture standards. IICS will provide a single virtual source of spatially and contextually accurate infrastructure data that can be fully analyzed and quickly and efficiently disseminated. This information will provide CF Sector decision makers, through the iCAV Common Operating Picture application and other tools, with the key information that they need to guide a variety of programs, such as disaster relief, national risk management, and infrastructure protection.

2.3 Verifying Infrastructure Information

The CF SSA will work with those subsectors and individual companies that are submitting information to DHS to identify and put into place quality control processes, protocols for reviewing infrastructure information, and methods for addressing incomplete or inaccurate infrastructure data. These verification processes will be shared with other companies and subsectors as they agree to participate in the information-sharing process.

Within IICD, the Infrastructure Data Management (IDM) Branch provides infrastructure data management in the areas of standards development, information sharing, and security policy and oversight. IDM leads DHS's efforts to provide standardized, relevant, customer-focused and protected authoritative infrastructure data to homeland security partners. This Quality Assurance (QA) Plan outlines all of the information necessary to implement quality assurance activities for the infrastructure data collected via the data call. The QA Plan for infrastructure data has been developed to promote the accuracy and accessibility of the record holdings in the IDW. The ability to provide accurate and useable data to mission partners depends on the following:

- Accurate, descriptive, and complete attributes;
- A single record for each asset that holds a copy of all current information related to that facility; and
- Precise geographical data.

The IDW provides the capability for similar data sets from multiple data sources to be viewed and compared in aggregate. This information is used by the CF SSA and IICD to verify the quality, accuracy, and so forth of infrastructure information across applicable systems. Data inaccuracies identified through the IDW must be corrected in the source system from which the IDW obtained the data.

2.4 Updating Infrastructure Information

The IDW stores and maintains data from original data source systems/owners. Updates to the data stored on the IICS occur through predetermined, recurring manual data updates or through an automated mechanism such as a Web service. The accuracy and currency of the data itself is determined by the original data source system/owner because the IICS/IDW aggregates data from various sources and does not create the data itself.

Updates to the information in the IDW are conducted on an as-needed basis determined by the owner or operator (e.g., DHS, Federal agencies, and State and local governments) of the source applications/systems. Information is managed and input into the source systems or application and then provided to the IDW via predetermined technical means, such as Web services, system-to-system interconnects, scheduled data deliveries, and via updates made to connected applications. One example of an "as needed" update is RSAT. It is recommended that the assessment tool be used when there is a change in the threat/hazard or when a change in protective measures has taken place at the facility. However, updates to RSAT are at the discretion of the user.

The CF SSA will work with sector partners to develop a process for updating commercial facility infrastructure information. This process will define the frequency of updates, processes for maintaining the updated data, how the data will be shared with DHS, and any information protection mechanisms needed to facilitate information sharing.

Data concerning commercial facilities must be updated routinely so the CF SSA and CF Sector partners will be able to leverage the most up-to-date information when making decisions concerning the sector's security and protection strategies. For example, the Public Assembly Subsector will continue its collaboration with IICD representatives by performing an annual review of the Public Assembly Subsector infrastructure data contained in the IDW and by providing information on new and deleted facilities on an annual basis.

3. Assess Risks

The cornerstone of the NIPP is its risk management framework. The CF SSA has prepared this CF-SSP to complement the NIPP and describe the processes and methodologies used by the sector to carry out an all-hazards risk management framework throughout the sector. The risk management framework is an important means of prioritizing mitigation efforts within the sector at individual facilities, subsector companies and organizations, and cross-sector organizations. This framework is applicable to threats such as natural disasters, manmade safety hazards, and terrorism. The CF SSA is responsible for leading sector-specific risk management programs and for ensuring that the tailored, sector-specific application of the risk management framework is implemented through the CF-SSP.

Figure 3-1: Assess Risks

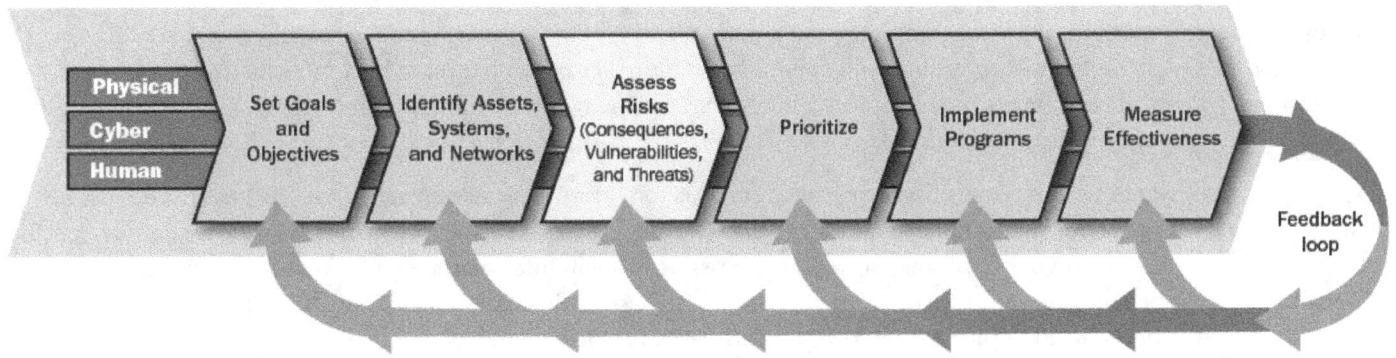

Continuous improvement to enhance protection of CIKR

Because the risk environment is dependent on many variables, it is imperative for a comprehensive risk assessment to be conducted at the facility, regional, and national levels. Many companies, corporations, and professional associations within the CF Sector perform their own internal risk assessments based on their individual business models (e.g., loss prevention, security, safety, and natural hazards; cyber attack; and potential foreign or domestic terrorist attacks). The results of these assessments are not usually shared with entities outside of the corporate structure due to the sensitive, business, liability, or proprietary nature of the information associated with the risk assessment. In an effort to collect risk information and create a CF Sector-wide risk assessment process, the CF SSA has been working with sector partners to develop several risk assessment tools and assessment reports that address the risks that are of concern to the sector.

An example is the CF SSA's partnership with IAAM to create a risk assessment model for use by stadium and arena owners and operators. RSAT assists stadium and arena managers with the identification and management of vulnerabilities (adversary-specific/manmade and natural) to reduce the risk to their facilities. It is the goal of the CF SSA to create risk management tools (e.g., RSAT modules or assessment methodologies based on the FEMA Risk Management Series) for facility types across all eight subsectors.

DHS, with input from the CF Sector, conducts an annual assessment of the key risks to the CF Sector from a national perspective. The SHIRA report identifies those hazards (adversary-specific/manmade and natural) that create the greatest risk on the CF Sector as a whole or which would produce a national impact (e.g., significant loss of life, economic impact, psychological impact, etc.).

Information sharing, with regard to risk, continues to be a challenge within the CF Sector. Owners and operators remain reluctant to share risk information outside of the corporate construct because of potential liability reasons, as well as the potential for public disclosure. DHS and the CF SSA continue to demonstrate the benefits of the PCII program in protecting infrastructure (e.g., assets, facilities, systems, and networks) information shared with DHS from public disclosure. DHS does collect and utilize CF Sector risk assessment data that DHS generates because of the various protective programs implemented throughout the sector. An example is the risk assessment information on individual stadiums and arenas that can be submitted through RSAT. DHS also obtains information that is important to risk analysis through the sharing of data that is required for the SHIRA process, ECIP's enhancement, IST, and various risk assessment programs (e.g., SAVs and BZPs).

DHS, through IICD and the CF SSA, collaborated with IAAM to develop RSAT, a sector-specific risk assessment methodology for stadiums and arenas. RSAT assists stadium and arena managers identify and manage vulnerabilities to reduce the risk from selected hazards (e.g., a bomb or tornado) as the result of the interaction of three components: the threat (adversary-specific/manmade or natural) to a facility, the facility's vulnerability to the threat, and the consequences of a successful attack or natural disaster.

RSAT uses estimated values for the three components of risk to calculate a risk value for each hazard/threat scenario evaluated. RSAT utilizes facility manager input regarding vulnerabilities and estimates of some threats, in combination with DHS threat (HITRAC) and consequence estimates, to provide a stadium or arena manager with information on methods for mitigating and increasing protection against the greatest risks facing the facility.

For those instances where sector partners have reached out to DHS to perform risk assessments, DHS has initiated the development of risk analysis methodologies and the definition of the resulting data sets. The sector partners provide the facility-specific information needed to perform these risk analyses. CF Sector risk assessment information that is provided to DHS by the CF Sector partners is protected from unauthorized disclosure and misuse to the maximum extent allowed under applicable Federal, State, and local regulations, including PCII and security classification rules.

3.1 Cyber Risk

NCSD is the lead organization within DHS for securing cyberspace and the Nation's cyber assets and networks. NCSD has developed guidance and tools to assist critical infrastructure owners and operators in assessing and managing their cyber risks. One of these tools, the Cyber Security Evaluation Tool (CSET), provides users with a systemic and repeatable approach for assessing the risk posture of their cyber systems and networks. CSET is a desktop software tool that guides users through a step-by-step process to assess their cyber systems and network security practices against recognized industry standards. The output from CSET is a prioritized list of recommendations for improving the cybersecurity posture of the organization's business and industrial control systems.

While NCSD addresses cyber issues and risks across all sectors, there are also additional sector-specific approaches for addressing the cyber risk. For example, RSAT has a set of cyber questions that are directed specifically at the assessment of cyber risks at stadiums and arenas. With the increased emphasis on cybersecurity, IAAM's Academy for Venue Safety and Security offers a cybersecurity module as part of their risk management curriculum.

3.2 Use of Risk Assessment in the Sector

As mentioned above, many owners and operators of commercial facilities assess the risks to their facilities with respect to loss prevention and safety. The risk assessments performed by owners and operators of commercial facilities generally have been focused on property, merchandise, and information theft (e.g., credit cards), and on how safe their facilities are, often with regard to natural disasters (e.g., earthquakes) and life safety (e.g., the National Fire Protection Association code). It is important for the CF SSA to understand the risk profile by facility type, across the subsectors, and from a cross-sector perspective.

With the issuance of the NIPP and the 2007 CF-SSP, an all-hazards approach to risk management (e.g., adversary-specific/man-made terrorist attacks and natural disasters) has been embraced by the sector in addition to loss prevention and life safety. Many individual facility owners and operators within the CF Sector have continued to voluntarily assess the various risks associated with their facilities; however, there are still many owners and operators of potentially medium- and high-risk commercial facilities that have yet to perform appropriate risk assessments. There are various reasons for the reluctance of owners and operators to assess risk at their facilities, which may include concern over public disclosure and potential liability issues. The performance of such risk assessments is necessary for owners and operators to make informed decisions about the risk posture and needs of their individual facilities, share assessment data for other purposes (e.g., developing protective programs), and for use in screening and comparing facilities' risks.

Facility-specific risk assessments have helped to better secure specific assets against an attack and prepare for a natural disaster, as well as define the risk profile of the subsector as a whole. Facility-specific risk assessments, unfortunately, are of limited value in helping to compare the risks across the eight subsectors. Additionally, the utility of facility-specific assessments are diminished further when attempting to compare the risks associated with a specific facility type to those risks associated with critical infrastructure in other sectors (e.g., nuclear power plants, airports, hydroelectric dams, chemical facilities, etc.). DHS has been performing these in-sector and cross-sector risk assessment comparisons in order to inform the proper allocation of the limited national resources, both public and private, that are available for the protection of the Nation's CIKR.

To facilitate the development or evolution of methodologies that allow cross-subsector and cross-sector comparisons, the CF-SSP utilizes the basic principle that assessing risk involves analyzing three separate components: consequence, vulnerability, and threat.

Risk (R) = f (Consequences (C) x Vulnerability (V) x Threat (T))

Despite the variety of risk assessment methodologies currently used internally within the sector, the same widely accepted steps are used in virtually all of them to create a reproducible, defensible, and complete risk assessment. The risk assessment steps are as follows:

1. Initial **screening** of facilities or infrastructure to determine which assets warrant a detailed risk assessment (Section 3.3);

2. Determination of the potential **consequences** of a successful attack (Section 3.4);

3. Identification of the **vulnerabilities** related to the specific infrastructure (Section 3.5);

4. Determination of the **threat** to or attractiveness of the specific infrastructure (Section 3.6); and

5. Combining consequence and vulnerability information with threat or attractiveness information to determine a piece of the infrastructure's **overall risk** level or score (Section 3.7).

Whenever possible, DHS seeks to use information from individual facility risk assessments to contribute to an understanding of risk across all 18 sectors. To do this consistently, the disparity in the risk assessment approaches must be addressed through a set of core criteria. These criteria include both the analytic principles that are broadly applicable to all parts of a risk methodology and specific guidance regarding the information needed to understand and address each of the three components of the risk equation—consequence, vulnerability, and threat. The CF Sector employs these criteria in its RSAT program to ensure that RSAT risk assessments are as follows:

- **Documented.** The RSAT risk methodology and follow-on assessment documents what information is used and how it is synthesized to generate a risk estimate. Any assumptions, weighting factors, and subjective judgments are transparent to the RSAT user, its audience, and others who are expected to use RSAT results. The types of decisions that RSAT is designed to support and the time frame of the assessment (e.g., current conditions versus future operations) are identified by the methodology.

- **Reproducible.** The RSAT risk methodology produces comparable, repeatable results, even though assessments of different subsector facilities will be performed by different facility managers. RSAT minimizes the number and impact of subjective judgments, allowing policy and value judgments to be applied by the infrastructure owners and operators.

- **Defensible.** The RSAT risk methodology is technically sound, making use of professional disciplines relevant to the analysis, as well as being free from significant errors or omissions. RSAT identifies the uncertainty associated with consequence estimates and provides confidence in the vulnerability and threat estimates.

- **Complete.** The RSAT risk methodology assesses consequence, vulnerability, and threat for every defined risk scenario and follows the guidance for each of these risk components given in the sections that follow.

3.3 Screening Infrastructure

In light of the large and diverse number of commercial facilities spread throughout the Nation, it is neither practical nor financially responsible to ask that comprehensive risk assessments be performed on every infrastructure within the sector. Thus, the first step of the CF Sector risk assessment process is a screening that identifies which commercial facilities warrant the expenditure of resources necessary for a detailed risk assessment.

In accordance with the 9/11 Commission Act, DHS is the lead coordinator in the national effort to identify and prioritize the country's CIKR. DHS executes this responsibility through the NCIPP, which includes the Level 1/Level 2 Program, a national screening process to identify domestic infrastructure that if disrupted could critically impact the Nation's public health and safety, economy, and national security. The Level 1/Level 2 Program utilizes an annual data call to refine selection criteria and update the various infrastructure lists. A consequence-based criterion (e.g., loss of life, economic impact, mission disruption, etc.) is utilized for developing the various Level 1/Level 2 screening lists to capture the true criticality of the nominated infrastructure.

The CF SSA has been working with the CF-SCC, CF-GCC, Protective Security Advisors (PSAs), State HSAs, and other sector partners to develop CF Sector national-level criteria based on the unique attributes and considerations of the sector. These criteria are used to develop the CF Sector List of CIKR that do not meet the Level 1/Level 2 threshold criteria, but are still deemed critical to the ability of the sector to fulfill its mission at the national or regional level. In addition to the Level 1/Level 2 Lists and the Sector List, NCIPP has created guidelines for the development of a State/Territory screening list.

The State/Territory Lists will help ensure the inclusion of those CF Sector facilities that do not qualify under the Level 1/Level 2 thresholds or are not included in the Sector List, but are nonetheless critical at the State and Territory levels due to the public health and safety or economic consequences that would result from their disruption. The State/Territory Lists allow facilities to remain on the infrastructure protection community's radar and available to Federal, State, and local partners as a standing resource for risk and incident management purposes.

Each State and Territory faces unique circumstances and possesses unique attributes. As such, no one set of screening criteria would be appropriate for all State and Territory partners. While the consequences of a lost asset may not have a national impact, the impact on the State or the region may have a profound effect on the local economy; therefore, NCIPP has developed guidance that allows each State and Territory to build their own screening criteria for developing their individual lists. As with the Level 1/Level 2 and Sector Lists, NCIPP recommends the use of consequence-based criteria, which are more defensible and allow partners to more reliably identify critical infrastructure. No limit is placed on the number of qualifying infrastructure that may be nominated to the State/Territory Lists. These lists will not be used in the DHS grant allocation formula for State Homeland Security and other grants historically assembled by the Level 1/Level 2 process; however, they will be a critical element of the Federal incident response, recovery, and reconstitution process, and will offer a vehicle to elevate State infrastructure priorities to the national CIKR protection dialogue.

The Level 1/Level 2 List is utilized by many DHS programs (e.g., the State Homeland Security Program, the Preparedness Grant Program, etc.) during incidents as a tool for prioritizing Federal, State, and local response and recovery efforts. In addition, the list is used for follow-on detailed assessments and studies (e.g., ECIP) and to develop tools for those facilities that are not included on the Level 1/Level 2 List (e.g., RSAT).

The primary screening criteria employed by the CF Sector involve addressing concentrations of people and population density within commercial facilities. This screening process for the sector focuses on identifying facilities that if attacked, as in a prescribed set of scenarios, or damaged by a natural incident could result in a significant loss of life. A secondary screening criterion is the economic impact in the form of lost business and structural losses. The economic impact of attacks against commercial facilities are likely to be comparatively low for direct effects (e.g., loss of real estate), although they could potentially be very high in indirect effects due to changes in consumer behavior (e.g., no longer shopping at malls). These behavior changes are tied to fears related to loss of life. As a result, screening of the sector focuses predominantly on the potential for loss of life, with direct and indirect economic consequences given significant consideration.

DHS has developed other screening tools for use by the CF Sector. FEMA's soon-to-be-released *Handbook for Rapid Visual Screening of Buildings to Evaluate Terrorism Risk* (FEMA 455) is a procedure that has been developed for use in assessing the risk of terrorist attacks on standard commercial buildings in urban or semi-urban areas. Additionally, it is intended to be applicable nationwide for all conventional building types. It can be used to identify the level of risk for a single building or the relative risk among buildings in a portfolio, community, or region as a prioritization tool for further risk management activities. The information gathered as part of this screening procedure can also be used to support and facilitate higher-level assessments by expert investigators performing building-specific evaluations of consequence, vulnerability, and threat.

Once the broad consequence Level 1/Level 2 screening has been completed for the sector, NICCP will work with sector CIKR partners to facilitate the implementation of assessments (e.g., SAVs, IST) at all potentially critical commercial facilities.

3.4 Assessing Consequences

There are many consequence assessments that can assist a CF Sector facility owner or operator in assessing the consequences and, ultimately, the risks associated with their facility. These assessments must have certain characteristics in order to be useful to support sector risk analyses and DHS resource allocations. The details of the consequence criteria that such assessments contain are described in Chapter 3 of the NIPP. These criteria can be divided into four main categories:

- **Public Health and Safety:** The effect on human life and physical well-being (e.g., fatalities, injuries/illness, etc.).

- **Economic:** Direct and indirect economic losses (e.g., the cost to rebuild an asset, the cost to respond to and recover from an attack, downstream costs resulting from the disruption of a product or service, and the long-term costs due to environmental damage).

- **Psychological:** The effect on public morale and confidence in national economic and political institutions. This encompasses those changes in perception that emerge after a significant incident that affect the public's sense of safety and well-being and can manifest in aberrant behavior.

- **Governance/Mission Impact:** The effect on the ability of government or industry to maintain order, deliver the minimum essential public services, ensure public health and safety, and carry out national security-related missions.

The Level 1/Level 2 Program utilizes a consequence assessment approach in all of the above categories to support all three levels of protection efforts (i.e., cross-sector; sector- or subsector-specific; and asset, system, or network-specific). As described above, the CF Sector focuses its consequence assessments on the two most fundamental impacts—human health and safety and relevant economic impacts. Because the impacts of the four consequences detailed above are difficult to quantify, the CF SSA and NICCP provide estimates in a coordinated process with the sector partners. However, the owner and operator should identify any unique considerations that would increase the psychological or any other impact of an attack or natural disaster against a particular commercial facility (e.g., iconic value).

Many commercial facility assets, systems, and networks are dependent on elements of other assets, systems, and networks to maintain functionality. In some cases, a failure in one sector will have a significant impact on the ability of another sector to perform necessary functions. This reliance on another sector for the functionality of certain infrastructure is called a dependency. If two pieces of infrastructure are dependent on one another, they are interdependent. It is extremely important to identify dependencies and interdependencies, both at the CF Sector level and at the asset, system, or network level in order to fully understand the consequences of a successful attack on a piece of CF Sector infrastructure and to identify the manner in which attacks on other sectors' infrastructure could impact the CF Sector.

The CF Sector is dependent on many other sectors to maintain full functionality. For instance, it relies on technology solutions from the Communications Sector to support operations and communications. The CF Sector is also highly dependent on the Transportation Systems Sector to provide rail, shipping, and trucking services for the secure transport of its retail products. Conversely, many sectors are reliant on the CF Sector. The National Monuments and Icons Sector is dependent on the Lodging Subsector of the CF Sector to provide overnight accommodations for people visiting national monuments and icons. The Defense Industrial Base Sector depends on retail products purchased by the Federal Government to operate military services. Government agencies and banking and finance companies may rely on the Real Estate Subsector for office space.

The CF Sector cyber infrastructure systems include business systems, control systems, access control systems, and warning and alert systems. These cyber systems are utilized for day-to-day operations such as ticketing; reservations; property management; human resources and financial management; controlling HVAC systems; elevator and escalator controls; lighting; and CCTV. The consequences of a cyber-related security event against a commercial facility asset, system, or network would only affect the operations of a limited number of sector infrastructure associated with the attack (e.g., hotel guest financial information). However, the sector as a whole would be affected by any sort of mass communications failure, including a mass disruption of the Internet. The Internet is widely used by the sector to provide information on sector facilities (e.g., marketing, merchandising, ticket sales, and reservations).

Many CF Sector partners conduct risk assessments to meet their own decisionmaking needs, using a broad range of methodologies. Whenever possible, DHS seeks to use information from stakeholders' assessments to contribute to an understanding of risks across all sectors. To do this consistently, the following set of core criteria have been developed by DHS that describe the desired attributes of consequence assessment methodologies:

- Document the scenarios assessed, tools used, and any key assumptions made.

- Estimate the number of fatalities, injuries, and illnesses, where applicable and feasible, keeping each separate estimate visible to the user.

- Estimate the economic loss in dollars, stating which costs are included (e.g., property damage losses, lost revenue, and loss to the economy) and what duration was considered.

- If monetizing the human health consequences, document the value(s) used and the assumptions made.

- Consider and document any protective or consequence mitigation measures that have their effect after the incident has occurred, such as the rerouting of systems or hazardous materials, or fire and rescue response.

- Describe the psychological impacts and mission disruption, where feasible.

3.5 Assessing Vulnerabilities

DHS employs vulnerability assessments (VAs) to identify potential weaknesses in an asset, system, or network that could be exploited through a particular type of threat (e.g., adversary-specific/manmade or natural) and would, if successful, result in consequences of national significance or loss of a critical functionality. A VA can be a stand-alone process or part of a full risk assessment. VAs are performed by DHS, as well as owners and operators, to support three levels of risk reduction efforts: cross-sector; sector- and subsector-specific; and asset, system, and network-specific.

Once a consequence assessment, including physical, cyber, and human scenarios, is completed on a commercial facility and it is determined that a successful terrorist attack or natural hazard could result in significant consequences, the next step is the performance of a VA to determine the likelihood that an attack or incident could be successful. A variety of VA methodologies are currently available, either as stand-alone methodologies or as parts of programs being implemented by DHS or other Federal CIKR partners. Some of the federally sponsored programs and methodologies employed by DHS across all 18 sectors include the following:

- **Site Assistance Visits:** SAVs are visits to critical CF Sector facilities that are led by DHS protective security professionals in conjunction with subject matter experts and local law enforcement to assist owners and operators in assessing and characterizing vulnerabilities. These visits, which typically last from one to three days, facilitate vulnerability identification and mitigation discussions between DHS and the facility's owner or operator. In addition to identifying vulnerabilities at a specific facility, these visits assist DHS in identifying vulnerabilities that are common to specific facility types, facilities within different subsectors, and facilities within sectors. At the conclusion of these visits, DHS representatives brief the facility's owner or operator on identified vulnerabilities and provide a list of options for consideration. The SAV team also authors a SAV report for distribution to the facility, the facility's owner or operator, and possibly the appropriate State HSA, local law enforcement, and first responders. To date, SAVs have been performed at 305 commercial facilities across the Nation.

  Information learned via SAVs is also used to develop three types of educational reports for facilities within each sector and subsector. They can be used by infrastructure owners and operators in those sectors or subsectors as a starting point for identifying infrastructure vulnerabilities. These three types of reports are Characteristics and Common Vulnerabilities (CV), Potential Indicators of Terrorist Activity (PI), and Protective Measures (PM). Historically, SAVs have focused primarily on vulnerabilities. Recently, SAVs have begun to incrementally move toward implementation of a broader risk-based assessment by analyzing consequences in addition to vulnerabilities and incorporating threat scenarios in their assessments.

- **Buffer Zone Protection Program (BZPP):** The BZPP is a national grant program aimed at providing local law enforcement and emergency responders with resources to enhance security "outside the fence" at CF Sector sites. The enhanced security capabilities make it more difficult for terrorists to conduct surveillance or successfully launch an attack from the immediate vicinity of CF Sector targets. As part of the BZPP, DHS staff trains State and local law enforcement, as well as private industry, on how to develop BZPs. A BZP is a facility-specific document that accomplishes the following:

  – Defines a buffer zone outside the security perimeter of a specific CF Sector target;

  – Identifies specific threats and vulnerabilities associated with the CF Sector target type and the buffer zone; and

— Recommends corrective measures for application in or related to the buffer zone that will reduce the risk of a successful terrorist attack.

Local law enforcement develops the BZP and, upon DHS approval, funds are dedicated to local jurisdictions to address shortfalls. In conjunction with the BZP, grants are provided to the local law enforcement that is responsible for the protection of commercial facilities. To date, more than 876 commercial facility BZPs have been conducted, with awarded grants totaling more than $40 million.

- **Maritime Transportation Security Act (MTSA) Facility Security Assessments:** Pursuant to the MTSA, owners of facilities located along waterways are required to conduct Facility Security Assessments to identify their facility's maritime transportation vulnerabilities, develop Facility Security Plans (FSPs) that detail the steps necessary to mitigate those vulnerabilities, submit the FSPs to the United States Coast Guard (USCG) for review and approval, and implement the steps outlined in the FSPs. USCG personnel have reviewed all commercial facilities that are subject to the MTSA.

- **Federal Emergency Management Agency (FEMA) Risk Management Series:** FEMA has published the Risk Management Series, a collection of publications that provide design guidance on reducing the risks from adversary-specific/manmade and natural disasters to infrastructure, with a particular focus on the types of buildings that fall within the CF Sector. FEMA's publications have historically focused on the threat posed by floods, wind, and earthquakes, but they were expanded following the September 11th attacks to include specific activities that may reduce the vulnerability to potential terrorist attacks. One publication in the FEMA Risk Management Series, *Methodology for Preparing Threat Assessments for Commercial Buildings* (FEMA 452), is designed to assist commercial facility owners and operators in assessing the vulnerabilities, threat, and risks associated with their facilities. The objective of this how-to guide is to outline methods for identifying the critical assets and functions within buildings, determining the threats to those assets, and assessing the vulnerabilities associated with those threats. The methods presented provide a means to assess risks and make decisions on mitigation efforts. The scope of the methods include a reduction in the physical damage to structural and nonstructural components of buildings and related infrastructure, and a reduction in the number of casualties that would occur during conventional bomb attacks and attacks involving chemical, biological, and radiological (CBR) agents. FEMA 452 has been used to assess hundreds of buildings within the CF Sector.

- **Cyber Security Evaluation Tool (CSET):** The DHS NCSD has developed CSET, a desktop software tool that guides users through a step-by-step process to assess their cyber systems and network security practices against recognized industry standards. The output from CSET is a prioritized list of recommendations for improving the cybersecurity posture of the organization's business and industrial control systems.

- **Infrastructure Survey Tool (IST):** During an ECIP visit, PSAs document information on a CF Sector facility's current protection posture and overall security awareness using IST, a security survey. The tool has more than 1,000 variables covering six major components, such as physical security, and 42 subcomponents, such as access control. The data collected are used in a framework consistent with the NIPP, incorporating consequence, vulnerability, and threat components in an all-hazards approach.

To make use of this data source and to be able to make comparisons among critical assets across sectors, a procedure has been developed to estimate a Vulnerability Index, which represents the overall level of vulnerability of a specific facility based on the results obtained during the ECIP visit. The resulting information is used to assist DHS in analyzing CF Sector and subsector vulnerabilities, identify potential ways to reduce vulnerability, and assist in preparing sector risk estimates. The analysis for a specific asset is provided to the owner or operator, as well as appropriate sector/subsector comparisons, to give an indication of the strengths and weaknesses of that asset's contributing factors to vulnerability.

Additionally, there are numerous robust VA methodologies, independent from Federal involvement, that are being used by owners and operators of commercial facilities. Additional VA methodologies include the following:

- **American Society for Industrial Security (ASIS) International General Security Risk Assessment Guidelines:** ASIS International, with more than 34,000 members, is the largest international organization for professionals who are responsible for security, including managers and directors of security. ASIS International released the General Security Risk Assessment Guidelines, a seven-step process that creates a methodology by which security vulnerabilities and risks at a specific location can be identified and communicated. Appropriate solutions are also offered.

- **The CARVER Methodology:** The CARVER methodology (Criticality, Accessibility, Recuperability, Vulnerability, Effect, Recognizability), whose original use was to examine a facility based on the effects of a planned attack, can be used to identify strengths and weaknesses in security at a site. There are many variations of the CARVER methodology in use by owners and operators across all 18 CIKR sectors. A CARVER analysis focuses on six distinct elements:

    - Criticality (the impact of losing the asset);

    - Accessibility (the ease with which the asset can be reached);

    - Recognizability (the degree to which a target can be identified under various conditions);

    - Vulnerability (the ease with which the asset can be damaged);

    - Effect (the consequences of a successful attack on the asset); and

    - Recoverability (the amount of time and resources required to repair or replace the asset).

The CF SSA and sector partners are in the process of collecting and documenting the VA approaches used within the sector. The CF SSA is also working with sector partners and DHS to compile VA results for use in sector and national risk analysis efforts. In addition, the CF SSA works with DHS to review the results of assessments for assets, systems, and networks that are of greatest concern from the CF SSA's perspective. DHS works to ensure that appropriate VAs are performed on CF Sector infrastructure that are considered nationally critical. DHS also works with CF SSA, appropriate State and local authorities, and CF Sector owners and operators to perform the VA or to verify the adequacy and relevance of previously performed assessments to support risk management decisions.

DHS and the CF SSA collaborate to support VAs that address the specific needs of the NIPP's approach to CIKR protection and risk management. Such assessments may accomplish the following:

- More fully investigate dependencies and interdependencies;

- Serve as a basis for developing common vulnerability reports that can help identify strategic needs for protective programs or R&D across sectors or subsectors;

- Fill gaps when sectors or owners and operators have not yet completed assessments and decision making requires such studies immediately; and

- Test and validate new methodologies or streamlined approaches for assessing vulnerability.

In order to increase the number of VAs performed in the CF Sector, DHS works with the CF SSA, facility owners and operators, and other CF Sector partners to provide the following:

- VA tools that may be used as part of self-assessment processes;

- Informative reports for CF subsectors, classes of activities, and high-consequence or at-risk special event sites;

- Generally accepted risk assessment principles for major classes of CF Sector activities and high-consequence or at-risk special event sites;

- Assistance in the development and sharing of "industry" based standards and tools;

- Recommendations regarding the frequency of assessments, particularly in light of emergent threats;

- SAVs and VAs of specific CF Sector assets as requested by owners and operators, when resources allow; and

- Cyber vulnerability assessment best practices. (DHS works to leverage established methodologies that have traditionally focused on physical vulnerabilities by enhancing them to better address cyber elements.)

Some VAs will include both vulnerability and consequence analyses for specified scenarios.

3.6 Assessing Threats

The third variable in the risk equation is threat. In the context of a terrorist risk assessment, the threat component of the analysis is calculated based on the likelihood of a terrorist attack method being used against a particular CF Sector asset, system, or network. The estimate of this likelihood is based on an analysis of the intent and capability of a defined adversary, such as a terrorist group. Accurately estimating such a threat, however, is beyond the scope of most CF Sector owners and operators. Consequently, most CF Sector facility owners and operators must rely on threat input from DHS or other Federal, State, or local government agencies to accurately calculate the risk associated with a given facility.

HITRAC conducts integrated threat and risk analyses for all CIKR sectors, including the CF Sector. HITRAC is a joint intelligence center that spans both the DHS Office of Intelligence and Analysis (I&A)—a member of the intelligence community—and IP. HITRAC brings together intelligence and infrastructure specialists to ensure a sufficient understanding of the risks to the CF Sector from foreign and domestic threats. HITRAC works in partnership with the U.S. intelligence community and national law enforcement to integrate and analyze intelligence and law enforcement information in threat and risk analyses products. HITRAC also works in partnership with the CF SSA and infrastructure owners and operators to ensure that their expertise on infrastructure operations is integrated into HITRAC analyses.

HITRAC develops analytical products by combining threat assessments based on all-source information and intelligence analysis with vulnerability and consequence assessments. This process provides an understanding of the threats, CIKR vulnerabilities, and potential consequences of attacks and other hazards. Analyses may also include potential options for managing risk. This combination of intelligence and practical CIKR knowledge allows DHS to provide products that contain strategically relevant and actionable information. It also allows DHS to identify intelligence collection requirements in conjunction with CIKR partners so that the intelligence community can provide the type of information necessary to support the CIKR risk management and protection missions. HITRAC coordinates closely with partners outside the Federal Government through the SSAs, SCCs, GCCs, Information Sharing and Analysis Centers (ISACs), State and local fusion centers, and State Homeland Security Offices to ensure that its products are relevant to partner needs and are accessible.

HITRAC serves as a national center for the integration, analysis, and sharing of information regarding the threat of terrorist attack against the CF Sector. HITRAC coordinates threat information with CF Sector partners through discussions, briefings, conference calls, and bulletins. HITRAC may also brief the CF-SCC, CF-GCC, subcouncils, sector professional organizations, and individual sector corporations and facility owners and operators. This information sharing utilizes threat information from a variety of classified and unclassified sources to provide an overview of the particular risks facing the CF Sector. HITRAC prepares seasonal and regional bulletins and an annual unclassified Strategic Sector Assessment of the terrorist threat to the CF Sector for dissemination to State, local, tribal, and private sector entities to help them manage risk. HITRAC updates the Strategic Sector Assessment as the threat environment warrants.

In addition to the provision of both classified and unclassified general threat information to CF Sector partners, HITRAC will share, upon receipt, specific threat information regarding particular commercial facilities with the targeted facility owners and operators. This allows DHS; the facility owner and operator; and other Federal, State, and local entities to implement an appropriate, coordinated response to the threat.

HITRAC leverages intelligence and operations monitoring and reporting from multiple sources to provide analyses based on the most current information available on threats, incidents, and infrastructure status. The timely analysis of information provided by HITRAC is of unique value to the CF Sector and helps determine whether changes are needed in a sector's steady-state and threat-based risk management measures.

Using a broad range of methodologies, many CF Sector partners conduct risk assessments to meet their own decision making needs. Whenever possible, DHS seeks to use information from stakeholders' assessments to contribute to an understanding of risks across all sectors. To do this consistently, the following set of core criteria have been developed by DHS that describe the desired attributes of threat assessment methodologies:

- For adversary-specific/manmade threat assessments:
  - Account for the adversary's ability to recognize the target and the deterrence value of existing security measures.
  - Identify attack methods that may be employed.
  - Consider the level of capability that an adversary demonstrates with regard to a particular attack method.
  - Consider the degree of the adversary's intent to attack the target.
  - Estimate threat as the likelihood that the adversary would attempt a given attack method against the target.
  - If threat likelihoods cannot be estimated, use conditional risk values (consequence multiplied by vulnerability) and conduct sensitivity analyses to determine how likely the scenario would have to be to support the decision.
- For natural disasters and accidental hazards:
  - Use best-available analytic tools and historical data to estimate the likelihood that these events would affect CIKR.

A CF Sector Risk Profile has been derived from the HITRAC-managed SHIRA process. This Unclassified/For Official Use Only (U/FOUO) profile is available for those with a need to know. Please contact the CF Sector team at **CFSTeam@hq.dhs.gov**.

3.7 Calculating Risk

As described above, the ultimate purpose of assessing the consequences, vulnerabilities, and threats associated with specific commercial facility assets is to determine the overall level of risk associated with the sector. By assessing the level of risk associated with different CF Sector infrastructure, DHS and its CIKR partners can make better-informed decisions regarding the allocation of resources for sector protection. The CF SSA is implementing a common risk model within the CF Sector using RSAT. The CF SSA will continue to collaborate with the sector in the design, development, production, and implementation of RSAT to quantify the risk data variables necessary for the comparative risk assessment required by the NIPP.

HITRAC conducts risk analyses for each of the 18 CIKR sectors, working in close collaboration with the SSAs, State and local authorities, and private sector owners and operators. This includes execution of the SHIRA data call that provides input to risk analysis. SHIRA involves an annual collaborative process conducted in coordination with interested members of the CIKR protection community to assess and analyze the risks to the Nation's infrastructure from terrorism, as well as from natural and adversary-specific/manmade hazards. The information derived through the SHIRA process feeds a number of HITRAC analytic products, including the National Risk Profile, the foundation of the National CIKR Protection Annual Report, and the CF Sector Risk Profile.

HITRAC uses risk analysis and other approaches to aid the CF SSA's effort to identify, assess, and prioritize risk management approaches. HITRAC also develops specialized products for strategic planning that directly support the NIPP and SSPs. In addition to these specific products, HITRAC produces strategic assessments and trend analyses that help define the evolving risk to the CF Sector. Examples of HITRAC programs include the following:

- The National Infrastructure Risk Analysis Program utilizes risk analyses and assessments to aid decision makers with planning and prioritizing risk reduction measures within and across the CIKR sectors. These analyses and assessments leverage a number of analytical approaches, including the SHIRA process, which are tailored to particular decisions.

- The Infrastructure Risk Analysis Partnership Program (IRAPP) assists partners interested in pursuing their own CIKR risk analysis, regardless of whether they are in the Federal, State, local, or private sector CIKR protection communities. IRAPP provides customized support to interested partners and the sharing of best practices across the CIKR protection community.

- The Critical Infrastructure Red Team Program focuses its analysis on high-risk sectors and subsectors and high-risk attack methods from the perspective of our Nation's adversaries by conducting open-source analysis, developing operational plans, and exercising these scenarios through tabletop exercises and developing lessons learned from those activities. These efforts identify gaps in current strategies and risk reduction programs for the Nation's CIKR and support the development of recommendations for closing or managing identified gaps.

4. Prioritize Infrastructure

The CF-SCC and the CF SSA have found that it is not appropriate to develop a single overarching prioritized list of assets for the CF Sector. Instead, sector assets, including cyber assets, are categorized using a consequence methodology that allows the CF SSA to drive sector-wide protection efforts. Facilities are categorized based on consequence as follows: facilities that have a national impact, facilities that are significant to the sector, and facilities that have a State and regional impact.

Figure 4-1: Prioritize Infrastructure

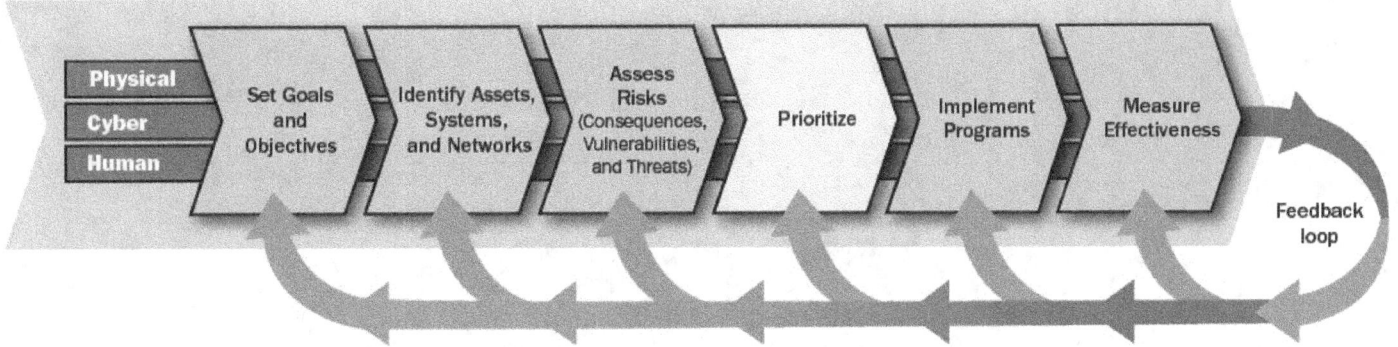

Continuous Improvement to enhance protection of CIKR

However, it has been determined that rapid restoration of retail centers (a subsector of the CF Sector) following a disaster is vital to community revitalization and resilience. Prioritization during an incident can help to focus planning, foster coordination, and support effective resource allocation and incident management decisions. Resource identification and prioritization support the sector's goal of having systems in place to ensure a timely response to and recovery from natural or manmade incidents.

Within the CF Sector, owners and operators on more than one level perform infrastructure prioritization in order to support national CIKR protection. Some owners and operators may prioritize their assets by function (including physical or cyber), while others may prioritize by location. The CF SSA places importance on owner/operators' prioritizations as they are in the best position to determine the importance of their own infrastructure.

5. Develop and Implement Protective Programs and Resilience Strategies

As the CF Sector is largely unregulated and extremely diverse, individual owners and operators apply the effective implementation and evaluation of protective programs and resilience strategies. The CF SSA facilitates risk management decisions and the tasks of assessing, prioritizing, and implementing security and preparedness measures by promoting the implementation of protective programs that are in line with the NIPP risk management framework (i.e., deter threats, mitigate vulnerabilities, and minimize consequences). Owners and operators recognize that the desired outcome of protective programs is to reduce the risk profile by preventing, deterring, and mitigating potential threats; reducing vulnerability to an attack or other disaster; minimizing consequences; and enabling timely, efficient response and restoration in any post-event situation, whether it is a terrorist attack, natural disaster, or other incident.

Figure 5-1: Develop and Implement Protective Programs and Resilience Strategies

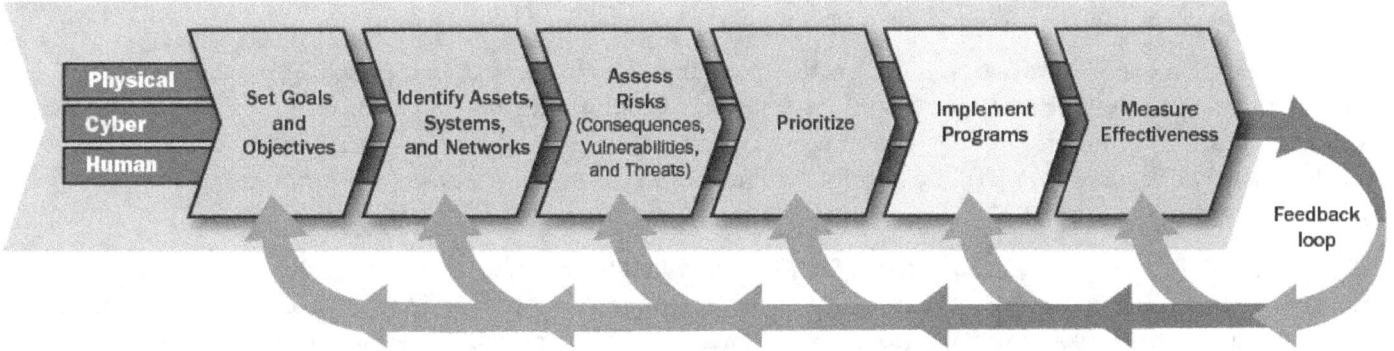

Continuous improvement to enhance protection of CIKR

5.1 Overview of Sector Protective Programs and Resilience Strategies

The protective measures implemented within the CF Sector are as diverse as the sector itself. The majority of the sector has an open-access business model and spans the elements of the NIPP risk management framework to address the physical, cyber, and human dimensions of vulnerability. DHS protective programs guide facility owners and operators toward implementing the most effective strategies for protecting their physical, cyber, and human assets.

Protective measures implemented by the CF Sector may include deploying equipment and new technologies, personnel, awareness and threat-specific training, and executing policies and procedures designed to protect a facility against threats and

---

to mitigate the consequences of an attack or natural disaster. Protective measures are designed to meet one or more of the following objectives:

- **Devalue:** Lower the value of a facility to a potential adversary; decrease the target's attractiveness.

- **Detect:** Spot the presence of adversaries and dangerous materials and provide responders with the information needed to mount an effective response.

- **Deter:** Make the facility more difficult to attack successfully.

- **Defend:** Respond to an attack to defeat adversaries, protect the facility, and mitigate any effects of an attack.

The development of a viable protective program will maintain the capability of implementing protective measures that are sustainable throughout the steady-state, as well as the ability to implement additional protective measures when the threat environment changes. Throughout the CF Sector, owners and operators use a wide variety of protective measures, which are applicable to a wide range of facilities and against a number of threats. However, given the diverse nature of the sector, additional unique solutions may need to be implemented to support the needs of a specific facility or a specific threat.

5.1.1 Implementation

As previously stated, the CF Sector is largely unregulated, extremely diverse in business activity, and primarily privately owned. Because of this, risk management decisions can be made at either the corporate or the facility level. The CF Sector represents diverse assets with different functions and scopes. The majority of these assets are privately owned; designed to be easy to identify; open to public access; and traditionally have had limited interaction with Federal, State, and local governments. Given the nature of the sector, there is no universal solution to the implementation of protective security measures. Vulnerability varies widely across the sector because each facility owner or operator has distinct assets with different operational procedures, business environments, and risk management strategies in place. The common security concern of the CF Sector is to protect its facilities and the public from all hazards without compromising accessibility and profitability.

The implementation of protective measures involves the commitment of resources, namely personnel, equipment, materials, time, and funds. Facility owners and operators may coordinate and consult with local law enforcement, emergency responders, and State and local government agencies to determine which measures to implement, how extensive they should be, and how long they should be continued to maximize security and preparedness. However, the responsibility for execution remains with facility management.

Following the NIPP sector partnership model, the CF SSA works with the CF-SCC to identify gaps, assess risks, implement protective programs, and measure the effectiveness of the protective programs. The CF SSA has worked extensively with sub-sector councils and has developed working groups to create materials and programs designed to fill the gaps identified by the sector. The *Active Shooter: How to Respond* awareness materials are an example of these efforts. When the Retail Subsector identified a gap in the educational materials that address the threat of an active shooter in a public place, the CF SSA partnered with the Emergency Services Sector (ESS) SSA and the Retail Subsector to create a program that would fill the identified gap across all 18 CIKR sectors.

5.1.2 SSA Programs

Through the NIPP Partnership, the CF SSA has developed several programs designed to meet the objectives of detect, deter, devalue, and defend against an array of threats. Some of these CF SSA programs are as follows:

- *Active Shooter: **How to Respond** Awareness Materials*

  In spring 2008, the Retail Subsector determined that due to a recent number of active shooter situations, there was a need for materials to raise the level of awareness and to detail how the retail community should respond to the threat of an active shooter. The CF SSA developed a working group made up of the ESS SSA, representatives of the law enforcement community, and retail partners to develop guidance materials.

The *Active Shooter: How to Respond* materials are designed to address how employees, managers, training staff, and human resources personnel can mitigate the risk of and appropriately react to the situation in the event of an active shooter. The final products include a desk reference guide, a reference poster, and a pocket-sized reference card that provide guidance to managers, employees, and human resources departments. The materials are written for a general audience and are applicable to a variety of facility types, in addition to retail establishments. The *Active Shooter: How to Respond* publications were launched in October 2008.

- **Evacuation Planning Guides and Templates**

Both the Public Assembly and Sports Leagues subsectors identified a need for an evacuation guide that will assist owners and operators of public assembly venues with preparing an Evacuation Plan. The CF SSA has developed two separate documents: the National Association for Stock Car Auto Racing (NASCAR) *Mass Evacuation Planning Guide and Template* and the *Evacuation Planning Guide for Stadiums*. Both documents were developed by a working group composed of the CF SSA, members of the CF-GCC, CF subsector council members, industry subject matter experts, and academia.

The purpose of both documents is to increase the level of preparedness, respond to an incident quickly and appropriately, and ensure the safety of the public by determining when and how to evacuate, conduct shelter-in-place operations, or relocate stadium spectators and participants. The guide includes a template that can be used to create an evacuation plan that will represent the unique policies and procedures of State and local governments, surrounding communities, and specific stadium characteristics.

- **Protective Measures Guides**

Protective Measures Guides provide an overview of best practices and protective measures designed to assist owners and operators in planning and managing security at their facilities or events. The measures identified in the guides reflect the special considerations and challenges posed by specific types of facilities or events. With input from sector partners, the guides are tailored to the needs and special characteristics of different types of facilities and events. The guides also provide examples of successful planning, organization, coordination, operations, and training activities that enhance safety and security at a facility or event.

The Sports League Subsector identified a need for a guide that addresses protective measures tailored to sporting events. Development of the guide provided the mechanism for the professional sports leagues to share measures and best practices across all leagues to the benefit of all stadium and arena owners and operators. In January 2008, the *Protective Measures Guide for U.S. Sports Leagues* was published and distributed to participating Sports Leagues and Public Assembly Subcouncil members, as well as other stadium and arena owners and operators.

The success of the *Protective Measures Guide for U.S. Sports Leagues* sparked an interest in developing similar guides focused on other subsector facilities and activities. The CF SSA plans to continue the development of applicable guides in partnership with the various subsector councils as required.

- **Risk Self Assessment Tool (RSAT)**

The Public Assembly Subsector identified the need for a simplified method of assessing risk and identifying viable protective measures to reduce the risk at public assembly venues. The CF SSA, IICD, and IAAM have developed a comprehensive and user-friendly assessment tool. RSAT provides facility managers with the ability to balance resilience with focused, risk-informed prevention, protection, and preparedness activities so that they can be managed to reduce their most serious risks. RSAT, a Web-based module for stadiums and arenas, was made available in March 2009. Additional modules are currently under development.

- **The SAVER Program**

  DHS developed the System Assessment and Validation for Emergency Responders (SAVER) Program to assist emergency responders in making procurement decisions; this program was found to meet the needs of the CF Sector.

  Located within the DHS S&T Directorate, the SAVER Program conducts objective assessments and validations on commercial equipment and systems. It then provides those results, along with other relevant equipment information, to the emergency response community in an operationally useful form. The SAVER Program provides information on equipment that falls within the categories listed in the DHS Authorized Equipment List. The SAVER Program mission includes the following:

  - Conducting impartial, practitioner-relevant, and operationally oriented assessments and validations of emergency responder equipment; and

  - Providing information that enables decision makers and responders to better select, procure, use, and maintain emergency responder equipment.

    The SAVER Program is supported by a network of technical agents who perform assessment and validation activities.

For further information on protective programs being implemented throughout the CF Sector, please refer to the Commercial Facilities Sector Annual Report (SAR).

5.1.3 Cybersecurity

Because commercial facilities are privately owned, cyber assets are managed in a similar manner as physical assets. Owners and operators have distinct assets and cybersecurity risk management strategies, which drive their individual decisions. In the CF Sector, owners and operators independently identify cybersecurity gaps, determine needs, and subsequently complete a cost-benefit analysis at the facility level. Because cost can be a prohibitive factor in the decision making process for CF owners and operators, the CF SSA encourages a strategy that promotes security upgrades as an investment against a variety of cybersecurity threats.

DHS cybersecurity programs provided to the CF Sector include the following:

- **Control Systems Security Program (CSSP)**

  The CSSP coordinates activities among Federal, State, local, and tribal governments, as well as control systems owners, operators, and vendors to reduce the likelihood of success and the severity of the impact of a cyber attack against CIKR control systems through risk mitigation activities.

- **Industrial Control Systems Joint Working Group (ICSJWG)**

  The CSSP established the ICSJWG to facilitate information sharing and to reduce the risk to the Nation's industrial control systems. The ICSJWG provides a vehicle for communicating and partnering across all CIKR sectors among Federal agencies and departments, as well as among private asset owners and operators of industrial control systems.

- **Critical Infrastructure Protection Cyber Security Program (CIP CS)**

  In partnership with the public and private sectors, CIP CS helps improve the security of the IT Sector and cyberspace across the domestic CIKR sectors by facilitating risk reduction through infrastructure identification, vulnerability assessment, and protective measures initiatives.

- **Cross-Sector Cybersecurity Working Group (CSCSWG)**

  The CSCSWG was established to improve cross-sector cybersecurity protection efforts across the Nation's CIKR sectors by identifying opportunities to improve public and private sector coordination on cybersecurity issues and topics, highlighting cyber dependencies and interdependencies, and sharing government and private sector cybersecurity products and findings.

- **Cyber Exercise Program (CEP)**

  CEP improves the Nation's cybersecurity readiness, protection, and incident response capabilities by developing, designing, and conducting cyber exercises and workshops at the Federal, State, regional, and international levels. CEP employs scenario-based exercises that focus on the risks to cyber and information technology infrastructure.

- **The United States Computer Emergency Readiness Team (US-CERT)**

  US-CERT is a partnership between DHS and the public and private sectors. The partnership coordinates defense against and responses to cyber attacks across the Nation and is responsible for analyzing and reducing cyber threats and vulnerabilities, disseminating cyber threat warning information, and coordinating incident response activities.

- **Cyber Security Evaluation Tool (CSET)**

  CSET provides users with a systematic and repeatable approach for assessing the risk posture of their cyber systems and networks. CSET is a desktop software tool that guides users through a step-by-step process to assess their cyber systems and network security practices against recognized industry standards. The output from CSET is a prioritized list of recommendations for improving the cybersecurity posture of the organization's business and industrial control systems.

- **Software Assurance Program (SAP)**

  SAP seeks to reduce software vulnerabilities, minimize exploitation, and address ways to improve the routine development and deployment of trustworthy software products. These activities enable more secure and reliable software that supports the Nation's CIKR.

Additionally, the CF SSA has developed the following materials to guide the sector in implementing cybersecurity protective measures.

- **Protective Measures Guides**

  The CF SSA has developed Protective Measures Guides that provide an overview of best practices and protective measures, including cybersecurity best practices, designed to assist owners and operators in planning and managing security at their facilities or events. The *Protective Measures Guide for U.S. Sports Leagues* was published in 2008 and Protective Measures Guides are planned for the Outdoor Events and Lodging subsectors.

- **Training Guide**

  The CF SSA has developed and distributed a guide throughout the sector that recommends training from the following:

  - **Cyberterrorism Defense Initiative (CDI)**

    CDI is a national counter-cyberterrorism training program developed for technical personnel and managers who monitor and protect our Nation's critical infrastructure.

  - **ACT Online**

    ACT Online provides a unique combination of expertise and capabilities and leverages the background of a successful academic program in information assurance that is uniquely recognized by DHS. The nationwide program uses a comprehensive approach to prepare professionals to identify assets, recognize vulnerabilities, prioritize assets, and implement protective measures in cyber infrastructure.

5.2 Determining the Need for Protective Programs and Resilience Strategies

Protective programs must meet a legitimate need in order to be considered for implementation. In the CF Sector, owners and operators independently identify gaps, determine needs, and subsequently complete a cost-benefit analysis at the facility level.

Because cost can be a prohibitive factor in the decision making process for many owners and operators, the CF SSA encourages a strategy that promotes security upgrades as an investment against a multitude of threats.

Most facilities within the CF Sector operate under the open-access business model with the business function of attracting attention and visitors in order to generate revenue. As such, many considerations must be taken into account during the development and implementation of protective measures and programs that may be used by the CF Sector. Due to the operational environment, protective programs need to be unobtrusive and considerate of the business model while also providing enhanced security.

The cost of modern security programs is usually a significant deterrent for commercial facility owners and operators. With the continuous changes in the economic climate, it is a growing challenge for owners and operators to dedicate resources for costly protective security measures. Additionally, the profitability of the business is a significant concern. When developing programs, the CF SSA must consider the operational environment of the sector by balancing the need for security and ensuring profitability.

Aside from some building code-mandated items that are primarily focused on structural integrity, safety, and basic emergency response issues (e.g., emergency exits, evacuation plans, fire prevention, and mitigation), implementation of protective programs in the CF Sector is mainly voluntary. Programs are usually implemented based on needs assessments conducted by individual owners and operators; however, DHS utilizes programs to assist owners and operators in assessing risk within the CF Sector.

SAVs are visits to critical infrastructure facilities that are led by DHS protective security professionals, in conjunction with subject matter experts and local law enforcement, to assist CIKR owners and operators in assessing and characterizing vulnerabilities at their respective sites. Information based on comparative statistics, feedback, lessons learned, and effective security practices is shared with facility owners and operators. These visits are designed to facilitate vulnerability identification and mitigation discussions in the field between DHS and the facility. In addition to this primary function, participants assist DHS in identifying vulnerabilities that are common to specific facility types, overall sectors, and subsectors. At the conclusion of the visit, DHS representatives brief the facility's owner or operator on identified vulnerabilities and provide a series of options for consideration.

The SAV collects consequence and vulnerability information to support risk analysis, taking into account both the dynamic and static vulnerabilities of a site or system. The methodology also includes elements of asset-based approaches (identifying and discussing critical site components and current risk posture) and risk-based approaches by using the factors of vulnerability and attractiveness based on threat streams. This methodology provides the opportunity to conduct visits across all CIKR sectors and collects information to be used by DHS Protective Security Coordination Division (PSCD) risk models. Specific elements or tasks associated with each phase of the SAV are tailored to meet the specific company, infrastructure, and resource objectives.

The CF SSA, CF-SCC, and CF-GCC have worked to identify and validate protective program needs to identify the types of protective actions to be taken to fill the gaps and evaluate existing programs that could be used to fill those gaps. This is an ongoing process as the sector continues to grow.

The protective programs created by the CF SSA are designed to manage risk by minimizing consequences, mitigating vulnerabilities, and deterring threats. When creating these programs, the private sector partners identify needs and provide significant input during the development of the protective programs. Once developed and implemented, the use of such protective programs allows commercial facilities to reduce their vulnerability; minimize consequences; and enable timely, efficient response and restoration in a post-event situation. These risk management activities are the cornerstone of most protective programs instituted by private sector partners within the CF Sector.

5.3 Protective Program/Resilience Strategy Implementation

A variety of factors influence how programs may be implemented, including the fact that the CF Sector comprises a wide array of distinct assets, operational processes, business environments, and risk management approaches. Because the CF Sector is unregulated, the majority of the protective programs implemented in the sector are not compulsory. In addition, funding for protective programs is most commonly obtained from the individual owners and operators of commercial facilities. As numerous protective programs are underway across the CF Sector, it is not practical for the CF SSA to attempt to monitor implementation of all programs.

The CF Sector has increased its participation with the CF SSA to identify gaps in programs and available resources in order to develop protective programs. This has increased information sharing among sector partners and the CF SSA ensures that the protective programs created meet the needs of the CF Sector and are practical and viable security solutions. Increased trust and communication demonstrate the considerable progress that the CF SSA, CF-SCC, and CF-GCC have made in strengthening public-private partnerships.

5.4 Monitoring Program Implementation

Prior to the creation of the CF-SCC and CF-GCC, there had been no formal attempt at the national level to assess protective programs across the CF Sector. Although industry associations and individual asset owners and operators had implemented a variety of coordinated protective programs and individual protective measures, a system for monitoring the implementation of such programs was not in place.

As discussed further in Chapter 6, the CF SSA works with the CF-SCC and CF-GCC to monitor protective program implementation. Sector goals are used as guiding principles when considering risk management activities and investments. Aligning activities with sector goals allows for the tracking of progress over time in achieving the vision of a secure, resilient, and profitable sector.

Working collaboratively, DHS, the CF-SCC, CF-GCC, and industry associations use methods for information sharing to monitor and evaluate protective program performance. Monitoring helps determine whether programs are effective, whether they have closed an identified protective program gap, and whether they can be improved. The effectiveness of protective programs is assessed via metrics progress indicators as discussed in Section 4 of the SAR.

One of the most essential benefits of the public-private partnership is the flow of information that allows for feedback on program implementation. The typical methods of communication include regular meetings with representatives of the leading industry associations, outside events with industry associations, annual conventions, the Homeland Security Information Network (HSIN) program, and information posted on special Web sites.

Coordination within and across the sector is critical because owners and operators are responsible for implementation of CIKR protection activities. Because the CF Sector is largely unregulated and made up of unique, competitive organizations, it is left up to each individual owner and operator to assess, prioritize, and implement security and preparedness at their respective facilities. The CF SSA relies on voluntary feedback to determine the success of a program.

6. Measure Effectiveness

CF SSA activities are driven by a number of determining factors, including sector goals, the current threat environment, needs demonstrated by the private sector, and the implementation of the NIPP.

The NIPP sets forth a comprehensive approach that is used to establish national priorities, goals, and requirements for CIKR protection so that Federal resources are applied in the most effective and efficient manner to minimize the consequences of attacks and other incidents, reduce vulnerability, and deter threats. The NIPP is based on developing strong public-private partnerships that foster relationships and facilitate coordination within and across the Nation's CIKR sectors. The sector partnership model is the public-private sector coordination structure under the NIPP.

The sector partnership model has been an important contributor to collaboration among private sector CIKR partners. Utilizing the strength of the sector partnership model, the CF SSA works with the CF-SCC and CF-GCC to identify gaps, implement protective programs, and measure the effectiveness of protective programs.

Because the CF Sector is largely unregulated, the tasks of assessing, prioritizing, and implementing physical and cybersecurity and preparedness measures is the responsibility of individual or corporate owners and operators at their respective facilities.

Figure 6-1: Measuring Effectiveness

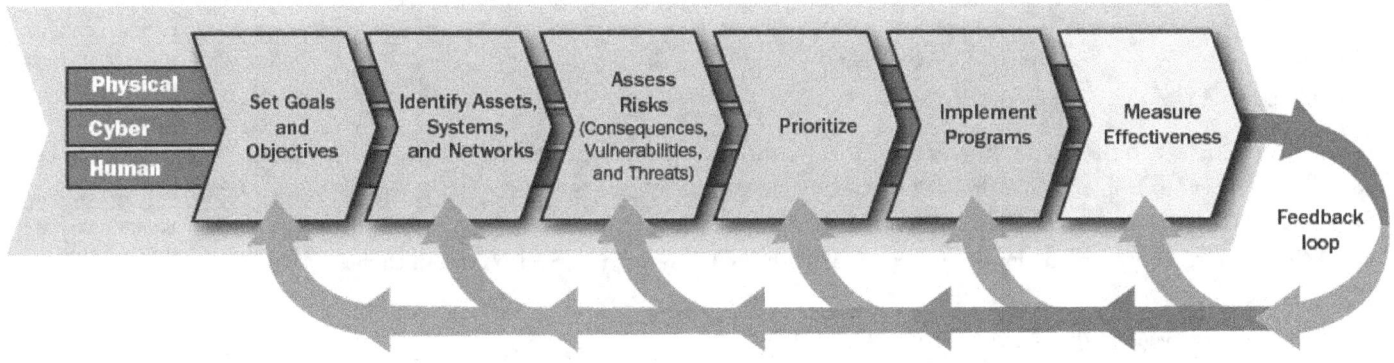

Continuous improvement to enhance protection of CIKR

6.1 Risk Mitigation Activities

Following the NIPP sector partnership model, the CF SSA works with the CF-SCC, CF-GCC, and private sector partners to collectively identify gaps and obtain feedback from sector partners. Over time, as the partnership has become more established, there has been an increase in information sharing and an ongoing dialogue with the CF SSA regarding sector needs.

In order to ensure that practical protective measures are developed for commercial facility owners and operators, an important function of the CF SSA is to respond to the changing risk environment and needs within its eight subsectors. The CF SSA places much value on input from sector partners and the needs identified by the sector to guide the consideration of risk mitigation activities and investments. Feedback is collected from a variety of sources, including, but not limited to, the CF-SCC; subsector councils; industry associations; corporate entities; owners and operators; Federal, State, local, tribal, and territorial government entities; and identified industry subject matter experts.

Many collaborative programs and key risk mitigation activities (as described in the 2009 SAR) are developed collaboratively and are based on needs identified by the sector. For example, in spring 2008, members of the Retail Subsector requested that the CF SSA develop materials to provide guidance to individuals who may be caught in an active shooter situation, including discussion of how one should react when law enforcement responds to an active shooter. As a result, in October 2008, the CF and Emergency Services SSAs worked closely with the Retail Subsector and law enforcement to develop the *Active Shooter: How to Respond* training materials (as discussed in Section 4, *Key Risk Mitigation Activities* of the Commercial Facilities SAR).

Increased trust and communication from the private sector, as demonstrated through collaboration in the creation of materials such as the *Active Shooter: How to Respond*, demonstrate the considerable progress that the CF SSA, CF-SCC, and CF-GCC have made in strengthening public-private partnerships.

The demand for SSA-produced protective programs has only increased with recent changes in the economic climate because funding for protective programs is most commonly provided by the individual or corporate owners and operators of commercial facilities. Examples of this would be the lodging protective measures guide, the lodging advisory poster, and technology connections. While funding for security has become a greater challenge, the sector owners and operators have increased participation levels with the SSA to identify gaps in programs and available resources.

6.2 Process for Measuring Effectiveness

In addition to sector feedback, the CF SSA uses goals as guiding principles when considering risk mitigation activities and investments. Aligning activities with sector goals allows for the tracking of progress over time in achieving the vision of a secure, resilient, and profitable sector.

Because the CF Sector is not regulated, one major challenge faced by the CF SSA is tracking the application and effectiveness of protective programs. The CF SSA works with private sector partners to develop and implement protective programs. Relationships with trade associations and sector owners and operators are the main source of the distribution and measurement of the effectiveness of the CF SSA's programs.

The sector has identified the need to increase awareness about available cybersecurity protective programs. A new goal has been added by the sector to implement appropriate protective measures to secure cyber systems that are vital to the daily operations of the sector. The goal has led to increased awareness about National Cyber Security Division protective programs (see chapter 5) and CF progress indicators to identify functions within the CF Sector (see Section 5.4 in the CF SAR).

6.2.1 Process for Measuring Sector Progress

The CF SSA works with the sector to develop and implement programs. It uses the partnership model and relationships with trade associations to distribute the programs. Given the vast size, the diversity of the sector, and the non-regulatory nature, it is very difficult to measure whether materials are being utilized by the intended audience.

Because of these challenges, descriptive progress indicators are most effective for the CF Sector and offer the most meaningful approach to measuring the progress of sector protection and resilience activities.

The CF SSA will continue to work with the private sector to obtain information and feedback on SSA and private sector programs. The development of progress indicators by owners and operators for specific risk mitigation activities and programs is also underway.

The CF SSA will work with the CF-SCC, associations, and others involved in sector risk mitigation initiatives to identify and improve the type and quality of the progress indicators that are used to assess the progress of programs and activities that are underway across the sector.

6.2.2 Information Collection and Verification

As the CF Sector is non-regulatory, information about protective measures undertaken at the facility level is maintained by the owners and operators. A challenge faced by the CF SSA is tracking the accuracy of the information collected annually as progress indicators. Additionally, the sheer size and diversity of not only the sector, but of each of the subsectors, increase the challenge of collecting data at the facility level. A more meaningful approach would be to track and collect data at the corporate level. This would be consistent with how the CF SSA develops programs by working with senior corporate security or crisis management personnel.

While the CF SSA uses its relationship with private sector partners and trade associations to collect information and assist in creating sector metrics, information is shared only on a voluntary basis.

Private sector programs are measured by the developers and shared as metrics with the SSA exclusively through the SAR. Facility owners and operators continue to express concern over sharing sensitive or proprietary information on assets or security measures with the Federal Government. This concern is specific to the identification of asset vulnerabilities due to potential legal liabilities. In order to address this concern, the CF SSA is working with the PCII Program Office to widely advertise the PCII among the sector.

6.2.3 Reporting

The CF SSA works with the CF-SCC and CF-GCC to gather information on protective programs throughout the sector on an annual basis. The CF SSA reports the sector's progress indicators through the metrics portal; and subsequently they are shared only in the SAR.

6.3 Using Metrics for Continuous Improvement

The CF SSA relies completely on voluntary feedback in order to measure the effectiveness of its programs and support the development, refinement, and reporting of sector progress indicators. By receiving this feedback, the CF SSA is better able to tailor existing programs to meet the ever-changing needs of the private sector partners and to create programs that benefit the CF Sector.

The CF SSA has been using a metrics system that includes understanding the output of a protective program, as well as the outcome of that program. Understanding the outcome and the effectiveness of protective programs in the absence of an attempted terrorist attack remains a challenge. Identifying improvements in the protective posture at the facility or industry level is a successful means for determining areas for continuous improvement.

The CF SSA works closely with associations and trade groups to obtain feedback on sector protective programs. Although these associations and partners provide the CF SSA with access to a wide variety of private sector owners and operators, they do not provide a complete representation of the CF Sector as a whole because of the sheer size and diversity of the sector. However, their feedback is crucial to assisting the CF SSA in developing future programs.

A recently developed program based on subsector feedback is the *Evacuation Planning Guide for Stadiums*. In April 2008, the Public Assembly and Sports Leagues subsectors requested an evacuation guide to assist stadium owners and operators with preparing an evacuation plan. The existing NASCAR guide was modified into an *Evacuation Planning Guide for Stadiums* (as discussed in Section 4, *Key Risk Mitigation Activities* of the Commercial Facilities Sector Annual Report) by a working group composed of various Federal agencies, members of the CF-SCC, and other interested private sector partners.

Voluntary participation in protective program development and implementation presents a challenge for developing and using outcome-based metrics to measure continuous improvement. The CF Sector will continue to use descriptive data and feedback from the subsectors as the primary source of information on how to improve sector activities and decision making processes on a continuous basis.

7. CIKR Protection Research and Development

Although the CF Sector comprises diverse subsectors with differing needs and challenges, the common security concern is to protect the facilities and the public from all hazards without compromising accessibility and profitability. The CF Sector primarily operates on the principal of open public access without the deterrent of highly visible security barriers. The facilities are usually easily identifiable and may host large crowds of people in public spaces. Therefore, a significant focus for the sector includes R&D initiatives related to preserving the open-access model for most facilities while enhancing overall safety and security in response to all hazards. The development of more effective and efficient detection and surveillance technologies geared toward preventing an attack, as well as initiatives related to minimizing the effects of manmade or natural hazards (e.g., public-private sector emergency response coordination, efficient and effective evacuation strategies, building and glass structural reinforcement strategies and technology, etc.), address the sector's need to ensure the safety and security of facilities and the public, as well as to sustain a viable business environment.

Under the leadership of the SSA, each sector is responsible for determining what new technical capabilities need to be developed to achieve the sector's desired security end state and national goals, formulating R&D plans to develop these new technologies, and executing a coordinated R&D effort to mature these technologies to benefit the sector. Individual commercial facilities owners and operators employ new technologies, but only a very few have the resources to engage in their own R&D.

The CF Sector R&D plan aligns with the overall mission for CIKR that is outlined in Chapter 6 of the NIPP and the roles and responsibilities outlined in the IP R&D Charter.

7.1 Sector R&D Requirements

HSPD-7 establishes the requirement for a National Critical Infrastructure Protection Research and Development Plan (NCIP R&D Plan). The plan identifies nine technology themes that are applicable to all sectors and specifies three strategic R&D goals. The three strategic goals are used to guide Federal R&D investment decisions and to provide a coordinated approach to the overall Federal research program. The nine R&D themes cut across all sectors and are used by SSAs in developing sector-specific R&D requirements.

Table 7-1: National Critical Infrastructure Protection R&D Plan

R&D Technology Themes	Strategic R&D Goals
1. Detection and Sensor Systems	A. A common operating picture to continuously monitor the health of CIKR
2. Protection and Prevention	
3. Entry and Access Portals	B. A next-generation Internet architecture with designed-in security
4. Insider Threats	
5. Analysis and Decision Support Systems	C. Resilient, self-diagnosing, self-healing infrastructure systems
6. Response and Recovery Tools	
7. New and Emerging Threats and Vulnerabilities	
8. Advanced Infrastructure Architectures and Systems Design	
9. Human and Social Issues	

For the 2007 SSP, general issues related to R&D activities were identified through informal discussions with individual subsector members. These general issues are still valid and include the following:

- **Cost of the Technology:** There is a need to improve the affordability of surveillance and detection technologies. Many methods and devices are commercially available; however, the cost is a deterrent to implementation, particularly at smaller facilities.

- **Integration with Existing Systems:** There is a need for increased attention to making upgraded and new technologies compatible with existing surveillance, detection, and access control systems. This would allow improvements to be made as technology advances without replacing entire systems.

- **Commercial Viability:** Commercial facilities generally need a commercial off-the-shelf (COTS) technology that works effectively under a range of operating conditions rather than exclusively in a controlled environment.

- **Product/Vendor Validation:** The public and private sectors need to implement a joint process that validates the credibility of new technologies and the vendors that distribute them.

R&D topics of interest were first identified in the 2007 CF-SSP. R&D needs were subsequently refined and communicated through conversations and communications with the informal CF R&D Working Group, conversations with individual members of the sector, the SAR process, and participation in the Capstone Integrated Product Team (IPT) management process and the October 2008 S&T Technology Game. The S&T Directorate established the Capstone IPT management process to prioritize capability gaps, consider technology options, and oversee the execution of projects that show promise for addressing the capability gaps of DHS components; State, local, tribal, and territorial emergency responders; NIPP partners; government at all levels; and private sector owners and operators. To support these goals, the S&T Directorate sponsored a series of broad-based technology transition process games. The games focused on enhancing the Capstone IPT process and assisting the professional workforce of the DHS S&T community and DHS S&T customers in developing concepts for technologies that can close validated capability gaps and successfully transition new and emerging technologies to customers. The CF SSA and members of the CF Sector participated in such a game in October 2008, to refine several existing capability gaps.

To date, the massive size and diversity of the CF Sector have prevented the CF SSA from developing a comprehensive picture of sector R&D requirements, thereby making comprehensive prioritization impossible. However, a continuing, strong public-private partnership will be the mechanism for continuing to identify and refine capability gaps. The gaps listed below have been commonly identified by our private sector partners:

- **Integrated, Wide-Area Explosive and Chemical/Biological/Radiological (CBR) Detection Devices:** The CF Sector is seeking to quickly and effectively detect and alert against chemical, biological, radiological, and explosive (CBRE) hazards inside and outside of commercial facilities, including large numbers of people and large volumes of vehicles, trucks, and delivery items. The CF Sector is also seeking HVAC systems with CBR detection capability.

- **Image Recognition Systems (Identification, Verification, and Cross-Referencing Capabilities):** A need exists for Image Recognition Systems that build on biographic and biometric collection and allow for real-time automated identification, verification, and cross-referencing with suspected terrorist watch lists. Current image recognition systems are not widely available and do not allow for real-time operations and automated identification, verification, and cross-reference with suspected terrorist lists.

- **Uniform Blast Effects Tool for Buildings and Facilities:** Current research activities are focused on blast dynamics in urban canyons (i.e., areas where streets cut through dense blocks of structures, causing a canyon effect). Research on the urban canyon model is important for downtown properties; however, many commercial facilities are not located in a metropolitan environment, and therefore it is unclear whether this research and these tools would be applicable or would satisfy the needs of those types of properties. A tool that accommodates a variety of structural configurations in a variety of environments is needed.

- **Modeling, Simulation, and Strategies to Address the Handling and Evacuation of Large Crowds:** This gap addresses modeling and simulations to further refine strategies for quickly evacuating large crowds (e.g., 50,000–130,000 individuals).

- **Economic Impact Analysis of Disruptions to Interdependent Sectors:** There is a high demand for, but little understanding of, the ways in which the private sector is resilient to large-scale infrastructure disruptions (in particular, the private sector's sensitivity/vulnerability to the disruption).

- **Modeling and Analysis Study of the Economic, Social, and Political Impacts of Major Incidents:** A modeling and analysis study of the economic, social, and political impacts of a major natural disaster and a major terrorist attack against commercial assets would provide the necessary information to fill the recognized gap.

The CF Sector has not currently identified an attack to cyber systems as a top threat concern. As such, the decision to implement protective programs within facilities is left up to owners and operators. The CF SSA is increasing outreach at the corporate level to identify sector cybersecurity gaps, guide sector cybersecurity priorities, and identify resources to fill the identified gaps. The CF SSA is re-introducing an effort to expand an existing Cybersecurity Working Group. Current membership of the working group includes sector Chief Information Officers and IT Directors representing each subsector. NCSD will assist with outreach to grow the Cybersecurity Working Group, provide subject matter expertise, and share protective programs with the sector.

7.2 Sector R&D Plan

The DHS S&T Directorate has identified ongoing projects related to the technology requirements identified by the sector; however, these ongoing projects are not focused specifically on the needs identified by the sector. Out of the seven capability gaps identified by the sector, three were determined to be needs that cannot be met through R&D (Technology Connection for Security Systems, Technologies, and Devices; Economic Impact Analysis of Disruptions to Interdependent Sectors; and Modeling and Analysis Study of the Economic, Social, and Political Impacts of Major Incidents), three were referred to the Capstone IPT program, and one was submitted by the S&T Directorate for the National Institute for Homeland Security.

The three gaps that were referred to the IPT Capstone process are Integrated, Wide-Area Explosive and CBR Detection Devices; Image Recognition Systems; and Modeling, Simulation, and Strategies to Address the Handling and Evacuation of Large Crowds. The Uniform Blast Effects Tool for Buildings and Facilities gap was submitted to the S&T Directorate for the National Institute for Homeland Security. The CF SSA will still pursue solutions to meet the other capability gaps identified by the sector that are not deemed pure R&D.

The SSA, together with sector partners, will review possible solutions recommended by the S&T Directorate to determine whether they are viable. The DHS SAVER Program was initially recommended as a solution for the Commercial Facilities Technology Connection for Security Systems, Technologies, and Devices gap. The DHS SAVER Program identifies emergency responder equipment information needs (including the needs of private sector security and facilities managers), uses a network of technical agents to assess commercial off-the-shelf equipment using realistic emergency response operational environments and scenarios, and then provides unbiased comparative assessments. To date, this is the only initiative that has been presented to the sector for review. At the time, it did not meet sector needs, but the tool has evolved and merged with the Responders Knowledge Database, which may provide a more workable solution. Although the Technology Connection is no longer considered an R&D gap, the CF SSA and subsector members are continuing to work with the DHS SAVER Program Manager and the Responders Knowledge Base (where the DHS SAVER Program technical reports are housed) to make this resource more useful to the sector by identifying and incorporating operational parameters that make a technology operationally feasible for practitioners at commercial facilities.

7.3 R&D Management Processes

Implementation and maintenance of a sector R&D plan require management processes to identify and prioritize technology requirements on an ongoing basis, coordinate with the ongoing NCIP R&D Program and other sectors that share similar technology requirements, and monitor the progress of existing and new initiatives.

DHS IP is actively engaged with the S&T Directorate in the management and prioritization of R&D capability gaps. The SSA EMO has supported these initiatives via SSA participation in the S&T Capstone IPTs. General issues and topics of interest for R&D activities have been obtained through discussions with individual subsector members, the informal R&D Working Group, and exercises such as the S&T game held in October 2008.

The sector coordinates with the ongoing NCIP R&D Program and with other sectors that share similar technology requirements through the Capstone IPT process. The sector relies on the IPT Capstone process to pair its capability gaps with gaps in other sectors, to capitalize on any redundancies, and to identify cross-cutting gaps.

The sector monitors the progress of existing and new initiatives and the impact of R&D toward sector goals through a review of the R&D gaps submitted annually in the SAR. The sector does not monitor technology developments as a whole. Commercial facilities are extremely diverse and they are responsible for identifying their own vulnerabilities, as well as investigating and researching existing or emerging technologies that meet their needs.

No formal processes have been established for technology transition; however, the CF SSA is currently recommending a potential solution to the sector's Technology Connection capability gap—the DHS SAVER Program. The CF SSA is advertising the program as a potential solution to the sector at large; however, the SSA EMO cannot direct anyone to implement any solution sector-wide.

8. Managing and Coordinating SSA Responsibilities

This chapter of the CF-SSP describes how the CF SSA will administer its responsibilities as the sector lead for coordinating protective programs and resilience strategies in partnership with CIKR stakeholders. It also details how the CF SSA will manage CF-SSP development, maintenance, and implementation; the processes used for identifying and managing budgetary and resource needs for critical infrastructure key resources protection and resilience; and the processes used for establishing and tracking CF-SSP implementation milestones. In addition, this chapter describes how the sector is implementing the NIPP sector partnership model; describes sector training and education initiatives; and discusses how the sector protects and shares information among sector partners, across sectors, and with other relevant stakeholders.

8.1 Program Management Approach

Each of the 18 CIKR sectors develop and implement their own coordinated and unified security strategy to mitigate risk, increase resilience, and protect against all hazards, whether naturally occurring or manmade. DHS is the SSA for 11 of the 18 CIKR sectors. The Secretary of Homeland Security has designated IP to carry out the SSA mission for six of those CIKR sectors: the Chemical, Commercial Facilities, Critical Manufacturing, Dams, Emergency Services, and Nuclear sectors.

IP executes SSA functions for these six CIKR sectors through the SSA Management Project, which is managed by the SSA EMO. SSA EMO is one of seven divisions within IP, and contains six branches. Each of the six SSA EMO branches is responsible for implementing the SSA mission for one of the six CIKR sectors.

The CF Sector is widely diverse in both scope and function, and represents a wide range of asset categories. To help facilitate coordination among those commercial facilities with similar functions and operations, the CF Sector has been divided into the following eight subsectors: Entertainment and Media, Gaming Facilities, Lodging, Outdoor Events, Public Assembly, Real Estate, Retail, and Sports Leagues. The CF SSA, therefore, implements the SSA mission for eight different subsectors, which requires a concomitant level of effort and resources.

As a component of the DHS National Protection and Programs Directorate, IP is responsible for managing the coordinated national program to reduce all-hazards risk to the Nation's CIKR and for strengthening national preparedness, timely response, and rapid recovery in the event of an incident or emergency. IP manages this broad mission through three broad program areas:

- Identifying and analyzing threats and vulnerabilities;
- Coordinating nationally and locally through partnerships with both government and private sector entities that share information and resources; and
- Mitigating risk and effects (encompassing both readiness and incident response).

Seven IP divisions develop and implement projects that support these program areas. The CF SSA carries out its function by coordinating with IP divisions to ensure that sector partners can take advantage of IP projects. For example, the CF SSA works with PSCD to nominate commercial facilities for vulnerability assessments, establish contacts between commercial facilities and their PSAs, and deliver awareness and training programs. Additionally, the CF SSA, as part of the SSA EMO, has access to the combined resources and integration efforts of the SSA Management Project in its coordination with other IP divisions.

The success of the SSA Management Project is highly dependent on integration with other IP divisions and associated projects within DHS, as well as ongoing engagement with external government and private sector partners. The SSA EMO oversees the SSA Management Project and implements the SSA mission of leading the unified public-private sector effort to coordinate, develop, and implement a comprehensive security strategy for the six CIKR sectors under its authority.

To execute its mission, SSA EMO has established five primary program areas through which to support implementation of the SSPs and the NIPP risk management framework, and through which to build and mature SSA functionality. These program areas contain cross-sector and sector-specific initiatives that allow SSA EMO to manage the overall process for building CIKR partnerships and for implementing the SSP by leveraging CIKR security expertise, relationships, and resource investments, prioritized as a result of effective risk management:

Planning and Project Integration: While CIKR sectors exhibit unique characteristics and maintain different security priorities and needs, SSAs share certain common processes that can be efficiently executed under a single organizational structure (e.g., SSP development, SAR development, SHIRA, the National CIKR Prioritization Program, participation in the IP Capstone IPT process, participation in national-level exercises, and metrics development). The coordination of common SSA functions under one organizational umbrella within IP facilitates cohesive and coordinated budgetary, acquisition, personnel, and programmatic planning.

Education and Training: To raise security awareness and increase the cadre of trained individuals across SSA EMO sectors, SSA EMO has developed and collaborated with sector partners to develop a wide range of training and security awareness initiatives. These programs help to raise the security bar within CIKR sectors and provide easy-to-use, accessible tools that enable sector partners to share best practices across the entire range of CIKR protection activities.

Partnership and Information Sharing: The cornerstone of effective CIKR protection, resilience planning, and program implementation, is the voluntary public-private partnership established under CIPAC. Each SSA is ultimately reliant on strong public-private partnerships and coordination to implement meaningful security programs that reduce all-hazards risk across the six CIKR sectors. Timely, accurate, and actionable information sustains educated decisionmaking for the implementation of programs and initiatives across the entire spectrum of critical infrastructure protection activity. Effective information sharing is particularly important in a fluid risk environment such as during incident conditions and with respect to cybersecurity, where new threats and vulnerabilities evolve daily and require new mitigation strategies. With respect to cybersecurity initiatives, the SSAs work most closely with the DHS Office of Cybersecurity and Communications (CS&C) to support broad sharing of cybersecurity information, bring awareness to issues of concern, share leading cybersecurity practices, and participate in cyber-related exercises.

Exercises and Incident Management: The SSAs are responsible for providing DHS, other government decision makers, and private sector partners with a clear and accurate picture of the potential or real impact of an incident on the sector and the potential cross-sector, regional, and international consequences resulting from the incident. SSA EMO is responsible for carrying out the following core incident management functions in the Chemical, Commercial Facilities, Critical Manufacturing, Dams, Emergency Services, and Nuclear sectors: Situational Awareness, Analyses and Assessments, Information Sharing, and Requests for Information (RFIs).

Assessment and Mitigation: Each CIKR sector contains its own unique characteristics and risk landscape. Accordingly, each SSA works with partners to develop sector-specific security improvements designed to deter, mitigate, or neutralize potential attacks. Where possible, the SSA leverages SSA EMO's integration functions to develop and pilot cost-effective tools and programs that can be replicated across CIKR sectors. As the risk landscape changes, the SSA works with Federal, State, local, tribal, and territorial governments and private sector partners to develop and implement security practices that build resilience within its sector and exploit SSA EMO's cross-sector capabilities to drive risk downward.

8.2 Processes and Responsibilities

Maintaining the relevance of the CF-SSP and reporting on progress in meeting goals are among the responsibilities of the SSA. Implementing the CF-SSP and supporting the sector's goals will require sufficient resources and budgets, as well as training and education.

8.2.1 SSP Maintenance and Update

The SSP is the primary planning document for each CIKR sector, so it is essential that the document be kept current and that it reflect substantive changes to sector priorities, goals, dynamics, and programs. As one of its core competencies, the SSA is accountable for coordinating the development and maintenance of the sector's SSP.

Each SSA undertakes a comprehensive triennial review of its SSP in close cooperation with its sector partners. In addition, the SSA completes and updates its SSP as necessary. While specific processes and required levels of effort vary across sectors—depending on that sector's priorities, needs, and preferences—both the annual updates and the more comprehensive triennial revisions follow the same general drafting and development procedures, including rigorous technical and substantive review.

The CF SSA works with its CF-GCC, CF-SCC, and other CIKR partners, as appropriate, to assess the requirements for updating and amending the CF-SSP (based on changes to sector priorities, NIPP Program Management Office guidance, etc.). Prior to initiating the triennial CF-SSP revision, the CF SSA organized conference calls with sector partners to solicit their input on changes and updates. The conference calls were held on a chapter-by-chapter basis. The CF SSA developed a draft CF-SSP based on these conference calls. The CF SSA provided the draft CF-SSP to CF-GCC and CF-SCC members for review and, in the case of the CF-SCC, for further distribution to subsector council members and other interested partners. A copy of the draft was also posted on the CF HSIN to ensure that sector interests were broadly represented in the review of the document; the leadership of the SSA EMO and IP were also asked to review the document and provide substantive input. Subsequent to revising the draft CF-SSP based on partner comments, the CF SSA provided a copy of the revised CF-SSP for final review. The revision process also included final review by the Homeland Security Council's Interagency Policy Committee.

8.2.2 SSP Implementation Milestones

The implementation milestones set forth in the SSP enable sector partners, the SSA, and DHS to gauge progress toward verifying, validating, and realizing the goals and objectives as defined in Chapter 1 of the SSP. The NIPP risk management framework provides a logical basis for describing the broad activities that the SSA and its partners will undertake in implementing the SSP.

Milestones for the specific programs and activities that are the responsibility of the six SSAs within IP/SSA EMO are tracked and managed through the SSA Project Management Plan (PMP). The PMP is a comprehensive business-planning document that describes how IP will administer and resource SSA activities within its six sectors and how it will gauge the progress of internal business processes and SSA programmatic activities.

SSA EMO leadership meets regularly with IP and DHS senior leadership to discuss the status of various SSA initiatives; this includes formal IP quarterly reports that track budget, acquisition, personnel, and SSA Management Project execution. These internal reporting and management mechanisms better enable SSA EMO to plan for and meet the needs of the SSA and the sector, and to address DHS, congressional, and White House reporting requirements.

The CF SSA continues to work with sector partners to achieve the following sector-level implementation milestones, which are complementary to the progress reports issued each year through the CF SAR:

- Review and refine sector goals to ensure that they provide a clear direction for the sector's CIKR protection efforts;

- Ensure that the CF Sector data utilized in the IDW accurately represents the sector's taxonomy and are relevant to the sector's risk management framework;

- Identify, develop, and promote risk assessment tools;

- Develop protective programs and highlight private-sector programs to show risk mitigation activities in the sector; and

- Identify capability gaps and technology needs and communicate them to the DHS S&T Directorate.

8.2.3 Resources and Budgets

The SSA is responsible for leading the effort to coordinate protection and resilience initiatives and strategy across the sector. However, it is important to note that the private sector and numerous Federal, State, local, tribal, and territorial governments carry out critically important programs in support of the greater critical infrastructure protection mission, based on assessed risk and priorities. Accordingly, it is beyond the SSA's capability and scope of mission to account for all resources devoted to CIKR protection in the sector, or to direct allocation of resources beyond its control.

Resourcing and budget for the six SSAs under the authority of IP are managed through the SSA EMO. As described in Section 8.1, SSA EMO has developed the SSA PMP, a comprehensive five-year planning document that describes budget, personnel, acquisition, and programmatic strategies for the six IP SSAs and the Interagency Security Committee Program Management Office.

Using the PMP to guide and prioritize its business processes, SSA EMO works within the IP budget process to submit personnel and program requirements in accordance with the needs of each of the SSAs for which it is responsible. Each SSA within SSA EMO is responsible for outlining SSA personnel needs, sector-specific programmatic priorities, and associated cost estimates in alignment with overarching SSA EMO and sector goals, objectives, and priorities.

The CF SSA identities and prioritizes sector-specific investments through engagement with sector partners. Owners and operators and other sector partners share information on crucial CIKR protection gaps and needs, and the CF SSA relies on this close involvement with partners to identify and prioritize CIKR protection and resilience projects. The CF Sector competes with other sectors for available funding. Budget allocation decisions are made based on the stated priorities of each SSA within SSA EMO and through a consultative process among SSA EMO and IP leadership.

8.2.4 Training and Education

Training, education, and outreach are a key focus of IP and the SSA. Within the organizational construct of SSA EMO, one of the SSA's core goals is to enhance sector-specific critical infrastructure protection capabilities through the coordinated development of education and training programs.

Training and education initiatives are critical for ensuring the continual improvement of CIKR preparedness efforts across both government and the private sector. To support broad situational awareness across CIKR sectors, SSA EMO is currently developing a voluntary Web-based, interactive training program designed to assist CIKR sector employees across sectors to identify suspicious activities at their facilities. This voluntary training is appropriate for any CIKR employee and will be freely available online. Based on cross-sector industry best practices, the interactive program augments an organization's existing security training.

In addition to SSA EMO training initiatives, the CF SSA has developed the following programs in cooperation with sector partners:

- *Active Shooter: How to Respond* materials
- Evacuation Planning Guide for Stadiums
- Training Resources pamphlet

The CF SSA also works in close coordination with other organizational elements within IP to develop training and education products across CIKR sectors and to participate in conferences, workshops, and other outreach and educational events. Additionally, the CF SSA leverages the expertise of government and private sector stakeholders to develop and participate in sector-specific training and education initiatives, including the development of leading physical and cybersecurity practices to complement existing private sector security, preparedness, and resilience training programs. Private sector expertise has yielded the following programs for the CF Sector:

- International Association of Arena Managers Academy for Venue Safety and Security
- University of Southern Mississippi National Center for Spectator Sports Security Management
- Shopping Center Security Terrorism Awareness Training Program

Training offered by DHS generally focuses on increasing competencies in risk analysis and implementation of protective measures and strategies. Sector partners have participated in the following DHS training programs:

- Soft-Target Awareness course
- Protective Measures course
- Private Sector Counterterrorism Workshop

The CF SSA-, private sector-, and DHS-sponsored training programs identified above are more fully discussed in Section 4 of the 2009 CF SAR.

8.3 Implementing the Sector Partnership Model

Chapter 1 of the SSP describes the specific organizational entities and participants involved in the coordinated development and implementation of a robust and comprehensive security strategy for the sector. The SSA works with these partners to support more focused initiatives targeting specific subsectors or issues of concern, as well as broader initiatives and strategies that foster partnership, coordination, information sharing, and risk management activities across the sector. In addition, each SSA works with public and private sector partners to ensure that international physical and cybersecurity issues with implications for the sector are properly addressed and coordinated. The NIPP sector partnership model is the overarching framework within which the broad CIKR partnership operates.

DHS established CIPAC in 2006 to facilitate effective coordination among Federal, State, local, tribal, and territorial governments, and between government and the private sector. CIPAC provides a forum that allows CIKR partners to engage in a broad range of critical infrastructure protection and resilience activities. CIPAC membership includes the following:

- **CIKR Cross-Sector Council:** Comprises the leadership from each SCC and is currently represented by the Partnership for Critical Infrastructure Security (PCIS).
- **Federal Senior Leadership Council (FSLC):** Comprises the leadership from each SSA, which serves as the chair for its respective GCC.

- **Sector Coordinating Councils (SCCs):** CIKR owners and operators make up the SCCs, which are self-organized, self-run, and self-governed.

- **Government Coordinating Councils (GCCs):** The GCCs are the government counterpart to each SCC and are made up of the SSA and representatives from Federal, State, local, tribal, and territorial government entities, as appropriate, which have security equities in a CIKR sector.

- **State, Local, Tribal, and Territorial Government Coordinating Council (SLTTGCC):** The SLTTGCC is made up of State, local, tribal, and territorial partners who coordinate across jurisdictions on State and local government-level CIKR protection guidance, strategies, and programs.

- **Regional Consortium Coordinating Council (RCCC):** The RCCC brings together regional representatives and organizations to enable CIKR protection coordination across geographical areas and sectors.

As the chair of the GCC, the CF SSA holds quarterly GCC meetings or teleconferences, supplemented by working group meetings and consultations as circumstances warrant. The SCC holds semi-annual meetings. In addition, the CF SSA works with CF-SCC and CF-GCC members to hold joint meetings. The CF SSA has also convened temporary working groups to review and provide input on key sector reports and documents. Both the CF-SCC and CF-GCC continue to examine which new entities should be represented on their councils in order to improve representation and communication within and among groups that have a stake in the CF Sector.

As sector needs drive the development of protective programs and education and training products, an important function of the CF SSA is to ensure that feedback is received from representatives from all subsectors. Therefore, the CF SSA continues to engage in an active outreach program in order to connect with additional partners. The ongoing communication and coordination enabled by this broad public-private partnership are critical to the SSA's mission to manage its responsibilities for leading the unified effort to manage risk to the sector.

The CF SSA has engaged with members of the CF Sector by presenting and hosting information booths at the various conferences, trade shows, workshops, and seminars held by private sector partners. Information on the services and resources offered by DHS and the CF SSA, handout materials, and reference documents are made available to conference attendees, and an unclassified HITRAC threat briefing is provided when appropriate.

The CF SSA has collaborated with partners to develop guides and other tools for use by sector partners. The outreach program has resulted in the development of the following collaborative key risk management activities: Protective Measures Guides, RSAT, Active Shooter: How to Respond training materials, and the Evacuation Planning Guide for Stadiums and Arenas.

To foster preparedness and increase effective response during an incident, the CF SSA works with the sector to develop and participate in sector-specific, as well as national level, cross-sector exercises. These initiatives provide critically important measures for the state of preparedness, information sharing, and incident management procedures and protocols. Examples of cross-sector exercises that the CF SSA has participated in include the Top Officials Exercise Series (TOPOFF) 4, the 2009 National Level Exercise, and Cyber Storm II.

8.4 Information Sharing and Protection

8.4.1 Information Sharing

Development and maintenance of a robust public-private partnership requires routine and comprehensive information sharing among all sector partners. The ability to efficiently share information with government and owners and operators within the sector and across sectors is vital to efficient steady-state infrastructure protection activity and to effective incident management. Timely information provides broad situational and specific tactical awareness, and enables risk-informed decisionmaking for the implementation of programs and initiatives during normal and incident management operations. The SSA has made information sharing, including the sharing of threat information, open-source data, and biannual classified briefings to appropriate stakeholders, a core component of its critical infrastructure protection strategy. The SSA uses a variety of information-sharing mechanisms—including ad hoc means (e.g., e-mail, conference bridges, Webinars, etc.)—to share information with its sector partners.

Information sharing flows both ways. DHS gains new information on effective security practices, general industry standards, and patterns of suspicious behavior from both industry associations and individual CIKR partners. The result is a partnership wherein the U.S. Government and private industry work together to share information.

8.4.1.1 Homeland Security Information Network Critical Sectors (HSIN-CS) and Homeland Security Information Network Commercial Facilities (HSIN-CF)

HSIN-CS facilitates information sharing with and across critical infrastructure sectors and actively encourages all sector partners to utilize HSIN to share practices and coordinate through sector portals. HSIN-CS is designed to enable communication within a given sector, between multiple sectors, and between a sector and governmental entities. HSIN-CS offers four major components to network participants:

- **Alerts Broadcasting/Narrowcasting from DHS:** This is a secure medium in which DHS and sector leaders can transmit actionable alerts and warnings about threats to critical infrastructure to a vetted audience.

- **HSIN-CS Portal:** The portal can store sensitive documents, including sophisticated imaging and maps. The portal also enables real-time analysis of data and reporting tasks.

- **Collaboration Tools:** These tools support a peer-to-peer collaboration space in which members can engage in real-time dialogue.

- **HSIN-CS Infrastructure:** HSIN-CS provides an underlying technology platform and network on which additional infrastructure can be added.

The HSIN-CF portal is open to all HSIN users with direct affiliation with commercial facilities CIKR. Within the CF Sector portal there are 10 subportals—one for each of the eight subsectors and one each for the CF-SCC and CF-GCC. Examples of information posted include notes from the monthly suspicious activity calls, redacted patriot reports, incident updates, workshop notifications, and other important documents.

Nomination and validation of users for each CF subportal are based on direct correlation with their work function and the specific subsector. Some HSIN-CF users may have access to multiple subsector portals due, in part, to their role within their organization, the type of facilities that they work in, and the events that they host. For example, the hotel manager with management responsibility for a large conference space adjacent to a convention center that hosts sporting events, concerts, political events, and large association conferences may desire access to the Lodging, Public Assembly, and Sports Leagues subsector portals.

In all cases, approval for HSIN-CF subportal access comes from the subsector chair/co-chair. Affiliation alone is not enough to be validated. The information contained and maintained on each subportal is managed directly by the group dedicated to that subportal, thus access is restricted to that group, unless access is granted by the chair/co-chair.

8.4.1.2 National Infrastructure Coordinating Center (NICC)

The NICC serves as IP's focal point for coordination across the 18 CIKR sectors during normal operations and incident management activities. The NICC is both an operational component of IP and a watch operations element of the DHS National Operations Center (NOC). The NICC operates 24 hours a day, 7 days a week, 365 days a year to facilitate coordination and information sharing with CIKR sectors. The NICC produces consolidated CIKR reports for incorporation into the Federal

Interagency DHS Common Operating Picture. During an incident, the NICC provides situation reports to the CF SSA through the Executive Notification Service (ENS); the CF SSA, in turn, contacts their respective CIKR owners and operators and related government agencies to develop impact assessments.

8.4.1.3 Cybersecurity Information Sharing

United States Computer Emergency Readiness Team (US-CERT): A public-private partnership established in 2003 to protect the Nation's Internet infrastructure, US-CERT coordinates defenses against and responses to cyber attacks across the Nation. As part of this responsibility, US-CERT interacts with Federal agencies, industry, the research community, State and local governments, and others to disseminate reasoned and actionable cybersecurity information to the public.

Cross-Sector Cybersecurity Working Group (CSCSWG): This working group provides a forum to bring government and the private sector together to collaboratively address risk across all CIKR sectors under CIPAC. The CSCSWG addresses a wide variety of cybersecurity issues and enables comprehensive planning and sharing of information across the community of interested stakeholders.

Critical Infrastructure Warning Information Network (CWIN): CWIN is the critical, survivable network connecting DHS with the vital sectors that are essential in restoring the Nation's infrastructure during incidents of national significance, including Electricity, Information Technology, and Telecommunications; the States' HSAs; and the SSAs, as well as sector-specific resources for each of the critical infrastructure sectors. CWIN provides voice and data connectivity using voice over Internet Protocol phones; thin client computing devices; and, in select locations, videoconferencing capabilities. In addition, CWIN connects the emergency operations centers of the 50 States and the District of Columbia to the NOC. CWIN's backbone is used to provide classified connectivity among DHS, the States, and select law enforcement sites via HSIN-CS.

While the CF SSA is continuing to expand cybersecurity information-sharing and outreach efforts, the CF Sector has not currently identified an attack to cyber systems as a top-threat concern. The CF SSA is providing assistance to sector partners by reintroducing an effort to expand an existing Cybersecurity Working Group. Current working group participants include sector chief information officers and IT directors representing each subsector. The CF SSA is increasing information sharing and outreach at the corporate level to identify sector cybersecurity gaps, guide sector cybersecurity priorities, and identify resources to fill the identified gaps. Additionally, the CF SSA continues to share information about DHS NCSD programs and activities with sector partners.

8.4.1.4 Sharing of Threat Information

The SSA hosts unclassified threat briefings as circumstances warrant and classified threat briefings with appropriately cleared CIKR partners. These briefings, which the Critical Infrastructure Threat Analysis (CITA) branch of HITRAC primarily facilitates, are closely coordinated with the intelligence community.

8.4.1.5 Private Sector Clearances

Requests within the CF Sector led the SSA to improve information sharing through the sponsorship of more security clearances for corporate-level officials. These clearances allow officials to gain access to timely and practical threat information.

8.4.2 Protecting Information

Often, the information used by DHS and its CIKR partners to effectively manage risk and protect the Nation's critical infrastructure may contain sensitive security information and sensitive business and proprietary information. As a result, information protection is a significant concern for the SSA and for CIKR partners who provide this sensitive information.

8.4.2.1 Sensitive But Unclassified Information and Classified Information

Information held by the SSA and by sector partners is designated as classified, sensitive but unclassified, or open according to corresponding distribution conditions and classification guidelines. Although the Federal Government maintains a preference for full transparency, the sensitive nature of much of the information obtained by the SSA and its government partners may require classified or restricted access and protection from general public disclosure.

8.4.2.2 Protected Critical Infrastructure Information (PCII)

Pursuant to the Critical Infrastructure Information Act (CIIA) of 2002, the PCII Program was created as an information-protection mechanism that would facilitate information sharing between the private sector and the government. PCII is used by DHS and other Federal, State, and local analysts to accomplish the following:

- Analyze and secure critical infrastructure and protected systems;

- Identify vulnerabilities and develop risk assessments; and

- Enhance preparedness measures.

If submitted information satisfies the requirements of the CIIA, it will be protected from public disclosure to the maximum extent permitted by law. The PCII Program is managed by IICD within IP. The rules governing the PCII Program are located in Title 6, Part 29 of the Code of Federal Regulations. General information on the PCII program, including instructions on how to properly submit information in compliance with the program, can be found on the DHS Web site at **http://www.dhs.gov/pcii**.

8.4.2.3 Critical Infrastructure Partnership Advisory Council (CIPAC)

DHS has exercised its authority under Section 871 of the Homeland Security Act to exempt CIPAC from the Federal Advisory Committee Act.[8] This ensures that CIPAC members can discuss sensitive security issues without the risk that these discussions could become public and jeopardize security. CIPAC can meet as a whole or in the form of joint committees specific to a particular sector.

8.4.2.4 Real Estate Information Sharing and Analysis Center (RE-ISAC)

RE-ISAC is a nonprofit entity that was organized by the Real Estate Roundtable. Structured as a public-private partnership between the U.S. real estate industry and DHS, RE-ISAC seeks to facilitate information sharing on terrorist threats, warnings, incidents, vulnerabilities, and response planning in order to counter potential terrorist acts and to protect commercial and residential buildings and their occupants.

RE-ISAC fulfills three key roles:

- Disseminate information from the Federal Government, including terrorist alerts and advisories, to real estate industry participants;

- Facilitate industry reporting to government authorities of credible threats to real estate assets, enable analysis of the information to detect patterns or trends, and potentially develop coordinated actions; and

- Bring public and private sector experts together to share useful information and to discuss and develop best practices on risk assessment, asset protection, and emergency response planning.

The formation of RE-ISAC was based on a 1998 Presidential Directive. Other industries that have also formed ISACs are found in the Banking and Finance, Energy, Water, Information Technology, Communications, and Agriculture and Food Sectors.

---

[8] Federal Register (FR) 14930, March 24, 2006.

Annex 1: Entertainment and Media Subsector

The Entertainment and Media Subsector comprises movie and television studios, newspaper and other print media publishing/printing facilities, and television and radio transmission facilities (fixed and mobile). The facilities are owned and operated by the private sector, with minimal interaction with the Federal Government or other regulatory entities dealing with security issues. For the most part, facility owners and operators must be responsible for assessing and mitigating their specific facility vulnerabilities and practicing prudent risk management and mitigation measures.

This annex was prepared with input from members of the Entertainment and Media Subcouncil, which comprises 14 members representing the safety and security programs of the entertainment and media industry. Some subcouncil members are involved with multiple elements of the entertainment business. For example, several members are involved with both film and television production, and others may have some degree of security responsibility for television stations or for television networks. Some also are responsible for facilities and personnel at international locations. Although the CF SSA is actively seeking to expand its partnerships beyond the movie and broadcast studios into print and other media, the focus of discussions for input to this annex was primarily on movie and television studio operations.

1. Entertainment and Media Subsector Profile and Goals

1.1 Entertainment and Media Profile

The Entertainment and Media Subsector represents facilities that are involved in the production of movies, television shows, television news, and radio broadcasts. Facilities include sound stages, office buildings, data centers, transmission centers, and television and radio stations. The subsector reaches the general population daily and on a continuous basis through the broadcasting of radio and television news.

The degree of open public access to entertainment and media facilities varies across the subsector. In particular, movie and television studios employ rigorous access control procedures, which screen and limit the number of visitors and employees on the studio lot. Although studio lots may often have public tours or live studio audiences on their grounds, visitors are subject to bag searches or magnetometer screening. General access to an offsite office building may be less rigorous, while some studios may have an associated theme park or entertainment venue where the public can move freely throughout the facilities. There is some overlap between the Entertainment and Media Subcouncil and the other subcouncils. The Outdoor Events Subsector, for example, incorporates entertainment venues, and the Real Estate Subsector oversees commercial buildings with Entertainment and Media Subsector tenants.

1.1.1 CIKR Partners

Facilities in the Entertainment and Media Subsector are mainly regulated at the State and local levels through building codes geared toward life safety requirements. Security concerns have not traditionally played a significant role in these codes. Entertainment and Media Subcouncil members report strong relationships and useful information sharing with local police, fire, and emergency services personnel who are involved with operations on studio grounds, as well as at top media broadcast special events in the local area, such as the Academy Awards and the Emmy Awards. For example, strong partnerships exist among studio security chiefs in the Los Angeles area who are members of the Entertainment and Media Subcouncil. These individuals continually share information on common security issues and problems at their facilities so that their counterparts may be aware of and vigilant toward suspicious incidents or individuals. Subcouncil members consist of industry professionals.

In some cases, relationships exist to share an emergency operations center in the event of an emergency. Local police and intelligence centers provide members with security updates and summaries for the area. State and local law enforcement agencies and task forces have developed terrorism intelligence and antiterrorism plans. Federal partners include DHS and the FBI.

1.1.2 Distinguishing Characteristics

The Entertainment and Media Subsector possesses a number of features that distinguish it from the other CF Subsectors:

- **Access:** Entertainment and media facilities involved in the production of movies, television shows, and broadcast news generally do not operate on the principle of open public access. Visible security barriers and access control measures are in place to prevent the public from entering these facilities and moving about freely once inside. Although studio lots offer tours to the public, these visitors often go through magnetometers and are subject to bag searches.

- **High-Profile Celebrities:** High-profile celebrities with both national and international recognizability are continually present on studio sites. Public fascination with film and television personalities requires that security procedures be put in place to deal with the starstruck public, paparazzi, and stalkers. Stars often have private security details as well.

- **Piracy:** Piracy is a major concern for studios. The distribution of a film prior to its release could cost a studio millions of dollars. Employees use electronic access cards to enter studio sites and are subject to many of the same security measures as visitors (e.g., bag searches).

- **Geographical Area:** There is a concentration of major movie studios within relatively close proximity to each other in the Los Angeles area. These studios also have corporate affiliations with television studios in the New York City area.

- **Self-Contained Services:** The larger movie studios operate like small cities and maintain some of their own emergency services equipment and personnel, although they coordinate closely with both county and city police and fire departments. Several studios have their own fire departments and have local police officers on site. Studio employees may also receive search and rescue, earthquake response, and emergency medical service training.

1.1.3 International Relationships

There is a strong international component to the Entertainment and Media Subsector. Although major movie studios are concentrated in the Los Angeles area, movies are filmed around the world, and set locations are continually changing. Asset owners and operators must be up to date on international threat conditions and special security concerns; they use a variety of databases or reporting services to provide them with this information. Entertainment and media companies also own or lease movie/television production facilities, offices, television and radio stations, transmission facilities, and distribution facilities worldwide. Some companies have print media publishing facilities in multiple international locations

1.1.4 Cyber Systems

Each Entertainment and Media Subsector facility or event has cyber systems related to its operations (e.g., access control, loss prevention systems, fire and intrusion alarms, communications/dispatch centers, HVAC, lighting, CCTV, property management, and human resources and financial management). Production and editing systems, television and radio broadcast systems, print media production systems, and product-tracking systems are also dependent on cyber systems.

1.1.5 Key Issues

Because of the meetings and discussions held with members of the Entertainment and Media Subsector, the following issues emerged as areas of concern for the subsector:

- **The Importance of Response:** Entertainment and media facilities are considered soft targets. Development and testing of emergency plans, public-private sector emergency response coordination, and training are key factors in minimizing the effects of a successful terrorist attack or other manmade or natural disaster. Emergency response plans and procedures are used to maintain safety and security for all personnel onsite, as well as to allow for the resumption of normal business functions. Effective business continuity plans allow for the resumption of business functions in the event of a large-scale emergency.

- **Access to Threat Information:** The Entertainment and Media Subcouncil continues to work with DHS to provide readily available threat information to the owners and operators of subsector facilities regarding potential terrorist threats or other manmade or natural disasters, including cyber threats. The subsector wants the information to be clear, concise, and provided in a timely manner, as well as providing the source of the threat and threat analyses so that the owners and operators can determine an appropriate level of response to individual threat bulletins. DHS is providing the necessary security clearances to key sector members so that the distribution of threat information does not become constrained by the need to classify specific information. The CF SSA is working with US-CERT to share information about cybersecurity threats to all subsectors, including the Entertainment and Media Subsector.

- **Information Sharing With the Federal Government and Legal Liability:** Members of the Entertainment and Media Subcouncil have expressed concern over sharing sensitive or proprietary information on assets or security measures. Facility owners and operators are also concerned with the identification of asset vulnerabilities and potential legal liabilities. DHS will utilize the PCII Program and CIPAC to address these concerns and to facilitate information sharing from the Entertainment and Media Subsector (see chapter 8 for additional details).

- **Clearinghouse for Government Resources and Industry Best Practices:** Entertainment and media facility owners and operators could benefit from knowing what resources are available to them from the Federal Government. DHS is sponsoring partnerships for sharing information within the security industry (e.g., HSIN and SCC/GCC joint meetings) on best practices that would assist owners and operators in implementing effective protective security programs.

1.2 Entertainment and Media Subsector Goals

The Entertainment and Media Subcouncil identified two primary goals for their subsector:

- Develop best practices that apply to all members of the subsector; and

- Receive meaningful and timely intelligence information from DHS and other security agencies that members can use to develop short- and long-term security strategies and to encourage support for those strategies from senior managers.

These goals will continue to be expanded on and updated with the addition of members to the Entertainment and Media Subcouncil and the continued development of relationships among the CF-SCC, CF-GCC, and other CIKR partners. The Entertainment and Media Subcouncil may develop additional goals in the future.

1.3 Authorities

The Entertainment and Media Subsector is almost entirely regulated at the State and local levels through building codes geared toward safety requirements. Security concerns have traditionally not played a significant role in these codes. Federal regulation is mostly limited to safety-related Occupational Safety and Health Administration (OSHA) requirements. Accordingly, the primary partners of the Entertainment and Media Subsector will fall within the parameters of State and local governments instead of those of the Federal Government.

2. Identification of Assets and Facilities

The Entertainment and Media Subsector is able to define the types of assets within the subsector, primarily through experience-based knowledge. Concern over public disclosure plays a significant role in determining what asset information subcouncil members will provide to government agencies. If subcouncil members are confident that the information they provide will not be compromised by public disclosure, they will share what they can with DHS. DHS will utilize the PCII Program and CIPAC to facilitate this information-sharing process in a secure environment.

The subcouncil has identified several criteria for determining which facilities are potentially critical assets. These criteria include the iconic importance of an asset, the financial importance of the asset to the core business, the size of the asset, and the number of people employed by and visiting the asset.

3 and 4. Risk Assessment and Prioritization

Individual asset owners and operators within the Entertainment and Media Subsector conduct VAs internally with their own staffs, with staff from another corporate-owned facility, or with hired private contractors. Subcouncil members did not indicate that they utilize any methodologies that would determine the degree to which a given asset is susceptible to an attack. There is concern over sharing asset information with the Federal Government in order to make formal decisions on the prioritization of assets (e.g., concluding that one asset is more "at risk" than another).

5. Develop and Implement Protective Programs

Protective measures employed by owners and operators of entertainment and media facilities are similar to those employed across the CF Sector. Examples include controlled entrances; access identification; vehicle barriers; CCTV and other surveillance systems; metal detectors; personnel and vehicle inspections; antivirus software and other cyber defense tools; coordination among Federal, State, and local law enforcement; and emergency response plans.

Individual asset owners and operators assess the risk of security vulnerability and employ protective measures to mitigate that risk. Local crime conditions and internal operating procedures, as well as the possibilities of a terrorist incident, can influence security decisions. Individual operators budget for equipment and personnel, and they apply the resources received in accordance with individual plans of action. Individuals might consult with other subsector members or law enforcement agencies based on previously established relationships.

Budget constraints are the primary impediment to security implementation. Technology solutions are usually off-the-shelf items that are readily obtainable if funding is available. A return on investment is usually not a major issue driving security initiatives. In most instances, a return on investment is realized if an incident has been prevented. If no incident occurs, it is difficult to demonstrate that the utilization of a program or piece of equipment has actually deterred an incident from taking place.

Various Federal, State, and local governments and organizations have developed preparedness and protective programs that are available to the subsector. DHS and the FBI issue Joint Special Assessments and Joint Information Bulletins to members of the Entertainment and Media Subcouncil that address possible terrorist activities as they relate to the subsector. Members of the subcouncil will be able to obtain, analyze, and share information through HSIN. DHS HITRAC issues Private Sector Notes that address topical information and offer analyses on current security issues of interest to the subsector. Other protective programs that are available to the Entertainment and Media Subsector include SAVs, the BZPP, and various DHS training programs (e.g., the Soft Target Awareness course).

6. Measure Progress

Each individual facility owner or operator determines a need for protective measures at the facility through the use of in-house assessments. This need is then considered along with other facility needs and, depending on the overall availability of internal resources, is fully funded, partially funded, or not funded by the facility owner or operator. The progress made toward completing a protective measures project may be tracked by the individual facility's owner or operator; it is not currently being tracked by the subsector.

Because many members of the subcouncil are competitors in the business world and in-house funding for assessments and protective programs is specific to a facility or a company/organization, there has not been an immediate development of a subsector-wide methodology for assessing the success or effectiveness of protective programs. Over time, as the Entertainment and Media Subsector evolves, as specific goals and objectives are created, and as communication mechanisms mature, the methods for monitoring the progress of the implementation of protective programs designed to meet goals and objectives should be put into place.

7. Research and Development

Most owners and operators within the Entertainment and Media Subsector rely on trade shows, conferences, recommendations relayed by word-of-mouth, vendors with established products, and associates within the industry to identify technologies to resolve security vulnerabilities. Entertainment and media facilities already employ advanced security and surveillance technologies due to the need to limit access to high-profile entertainers and to prevent the theft and piracy of films. However, owners and operators are always looking for improvements. For example, the evolution of digital technology currently provides high-quality CCTV pictures, but this technology will continue to improve.

Entertainment and Media Subcouncil members have expressed an interest in several areas of new and improved security-related and detection technologies, but they are concerned that the new technologies available today may not be as effective in the near future due to rapid changes in technology. Members have emphasized the need to know what developments are on the horizon and whether they are compatible and integratable with existing systems.

The Entertainment and Media Subcouncil has identified the following R&D areas of interest:

- **Explosives Detection:** Current technologies are too labor intensive and time consuming for inspection of large volumes of vehicles, trucks, and delivery items.

- **Biochemical Detection:** A quick and unobtrusive way to check for biological and chemical items is necessary. Although people move quickly through magnetometers for metal detection, there is nothing similar for biological and chemical agents.

- **Improved Facial Recognition Technology:** Current systems are not widely available. In addition to identifying unwelcome persons, the systems could have other benefits (e.g., assisting in the search for a lost child).

- **Improved Technologies:** These technologies implant radio frequency identification (RFID) chips that will set off alarms during a theft of valuable equipment.

- **Use of Palm Pilots:** Palm Pilots assist in the issuance of photo alerts for suspicious and wanted individuals.

Annex 2: Gaming Facilities Subsector

The Gaming Facilities Subsector represents commercial and tribal casinos along with the associated convention centers, shopping arcades, lodging facilities, nightclubs, theaters, and performing arts centers that make up the entire gaming facility complex. Gaming Facilities Subsector assets overlap with some of the assets found in other CF Subsectors. For example, theaters, convention centers, and exhibition halls are part of the Public Assembly Subsector, hotels are part of the Lodging Subsector, and shopping arcades are part of the Retail Subsector.

This annex was prepared with input from the members of the Gaming Facilities Subcouncil, comprises security professionals in the industry.

1. Gaming Facilities Subsector Profile and Goals

1.1 Gaming Facilities Profile

In 2008, 445 commercial casinos were operating in 12 States. Nevada, with its 266 facilities, is home to the largest number. According to the American Gaming Association (AGA), the top two casino markets in the United States by gaming revenue are Las Vegas and Atlantic City, NJ, followed by Chicagoland (Indiana/Illinois), Connecticut, Detroit, and Tunica/Lula, Mississippi.[9] Casino facilities are often part of a resort complex that includes lodging facilities, convention centers, shopping centers, theaters, nightclubs, and performing arts centers. In major casino markets, some of the facilities that are part of the gaming facilities complex may be huge. Seventeen of the twenty largest hotels in the United States, as well as several large convention centers, are associated with casinos in Las Vegas.

In 2008, U.S. commercial casinos generated more than $32 billion in gross gaming revenue and employed more than 357,000 people. The industry is a major contributor to State and local economies, distributing more than $5.6 billion in direct gaming taxes in 2008.[10]

State gaming commissions regulate the gaming part of casino operations and can establish specific standards for security and surveillance (e.g., the number and type of cameras, pixels of resolution, the number of security guards in the gaming areas, etc.). The commissions can also impose requirements on additional facilities associated with the casino. For example, the State of New Jersey requires that a casino include a hotel with a minimum of 500 rooms. Various States have imposed geographic limitations on casinos. In New Jersey, casinos are limited to Atlantic City. In Illinois, Indiana, Iowa, Louisiana, Mississippi, and Missouri, casinos are limited to locations along waterways.

---

[9] American Gaming Association, State of the States: The AGA Survey of Casino Entertainment 2009.

[10] Ibid.

Tribal governments operate 411 gaming facilities in 28 States. Tribes generated $26 billion in gross gaming revenue and States received $2.5 billion in taxes, regulatory payments, and revenue sharing as a result of State tribal gaming compacts. Tribes produced another $3.2 billion in gross revenue from related resorts, hotels, restaurants, and other lodging or entertainment venues in 2008.[11] The National Indian Gaming Commission (NIGC) is responsible for regulating gaming on Indian lands.

Four associations represent gaming activities in the Gaming Facilities Subsector. The Las Vegas Security Chiefs Association is made up of security chiefs from more than 80 hotel, casino, and resort properties located throughout the Southern Nevada area. Its main mission is to promote security professionalism through training, communication, and service. NIGA represents 184 Indian nations and a number of other members engaged in tribal gaming enterprises across the country. The mission of NIGA is to protect and preserve the general welfare of tribes striving for self-sufficiency through gaming enterprises. AGA represents the commercial gaming industry by addressing legislative issues and serving as a national clearinghouse for gaming industry data. The Casino Association of New Jersey (CANJ) is composed of all 11 Atlantic City casinos. CANJ serves as the collective voice of the industry and concentrates on the betterment of industry employees, government relations, casino-affiliated businesses, and the casino industry itself.

1.1.1 CIKR Partners

The facilities represented by the Gaming Facilities Subsector maintain strong relationships with local governments, first responders, and local law enforcement professionals in the normal course of business operations. Federal partners include DHS, the FBI, and the Drug Enforcement Agency. Gaming facility partners have participated in a pilot of FEMA's Rapid Visual Screening Tool (FEMA 455). CIKR partners in Las Vegas and NIGA have participated in a DHS-sponsored Counterterrorism Workshop. Strong partnerships exist among the security chiefs at both Las Vegas and Atlantic City casinos and resorts. These individuals meet on a regular basis to discuss common security issues and problems at their facilities and they continually share information via phone, fax, and e-mail so that their counterparts can be aware of and watch for a particular problem or individual.

1.1.2 Distinguishing Characteristics

The Gaming Subsector possesses a number of features that distinguish it from the other CF Subsectors:

- **Small City:** A large gaming facility complex is a small city unto itself, with numerous different types of large facilities (e.g., casinos, convention centers, hotels, nightclubs, theaters, restaurants, and shopping centers) under one roof. In addition to the facilities and services provided to customers, gaming facility complexes often house dry cleaners, daycare centers, and other support functions for the employees who work at the facility. In major casino markets, gaming facilities are grouped close together in a "strip" area, creating several small cities in a relatively small geographic area. These gaming facilities employ large staffs and welcome large numbers of visitors.

- **24/7 Operations:** The casino portion of a gaming facility complex operates under an open public access model, 24 hours a day, 7 days a week. Although there may be access control measures in other parts of the complex (e.g., tickets are required in a theater), casino customers enter and exit the resort continually.

- **Sophisticated Surveillance:** Casino gaming complexes are typically a mix of open/unrestricted access (gaming and restaurant areas) and also highly restricted access areas (CCTV, security command, information technology, and currency storage areas). Although access controls are not employed to gain entrance onto a casino floor, a sophisticated array of surveillance measures continuously monitors activities in that area.

- **Cash on the Premises:** The casino portion of the complex retains large quantities of cash on the premises.

---

[11] National Indian Gaming Association, The Economic Impact of Indian Gaming in 2008, **http://www.indiangaming.org/info/pr/press-releases-2009/NIGA_08_Econ_Impact_Report.pdf.**

1.1.3 International Relationships

Although most U.S.-owned gaming facility companies generally have casino properties only in the United States, some companies have international properties as well. In some instances, properties in the United States are owned by foreign companies or individuals.

1.1.4 Cyber Systems

The Gaming Facilities Subsector facilities or events have cyber systems related to facility operations (e.g., access controls, loss prevention systems, fire and intrusion alarms, communication and dispatch centers, HVAC, lighting, CCTV, property management, human resources, and financial management). Gaming facilities employ sophisticated cyber protection measures to prevent unauthorized access to financial information for the resort and its customers. Any cyber event affecting the operations of one facility is not likely to affect cyber assets at other facilities within the sector. However, the Gaming Facilities Subsector would certainly be affected by any sort of mass communications failure.

1.1.5 Key Issues

The Gaming Facilities Subsector possesses a number of features that distinguish it from the other CF Subsectors:

- **The Importance of Response:** Because gaming facilities fall within the category of soft targets, a significant focus is on efforts to minimize the effects of a terrorist attack or any other manmade, natural, or health-related emergency, and to resume normal business operations as soon as possible. Gaming facility owners and operators expect that they may be on their own for at least several days after such an emergency, and they cite effective emergency response and recovery capabilities as being essential to limiting the impact on their facilities and operations.

  Communications, coordination, equipment, and training are cited as key components of the emergency planning process. Emergency plans must be coordinated and tested with local government and first responders. In the absence of established standards and guidance for developing emergency operations and business continuity plans, gaming facility owners and operators must generally take the lead in developing their own appropriate emergency plans and procedures. In the case of a wide-scale emergency, coordination and communication with State and local governments are critical to understanding how food, water, and power will reach the facility. Even for an emergency on a smaller scale, relationships and communication with local law enforcement and fire department representatives are critical.

- **Industry Vulnerability to Public Fears and Perception:** The Gaming Facilities Subsector is primarily supported through the public's discretionary income. As a result, the subsector is particularly sensitive to any incident that causes a downturn in the economy, creates concerns about gatherings in public places, or results in people staying closer to home. In the major casino markets where gaming facilities are clustered together, the economic impact of a downturn in the casino business would create a downturn in the State and local economies as well.

- **Incentives to Harden Targets:** The costs of making physical changes to a building to harden it against a potential terrorist attack are significant. Subcouncil members have identified the need for tax incentives and insurance premium reductions to reduce the economic burden on owners for making these improvements.

- **Access to Threat Information:** The Gaming Facilities Subcouncil continues to work with DHS to provide readily available threat information to the owners and operators of subsector facilities regarding potential terrorist threats or other manmade or natural disasters, including cyber threats. The subsector wants the information to be clear, concise, and provided in a timely manner, as well as providing the source of the threat and threat analyses so that the owners and operators can determine an appropriate level of response to individual threat bulletins. DHS is providing the necessary security clearances to key sector members so that the distribution of threat information does not become constrained by the need to classify specific information. The CF SSA is working with US-CERT to share information about cybersecurity threats with all subsectors, including the Gaming Facilities Subsector.

- **Information Sharing with the Federal Government and Legal Liability:** Members of the Gaming Facilities Subcouncil have expressed concern over sharing sensitive or proprietary information on assets or security measures. Facility owners and operators are also concerned with the identification of asset vulnerabilities and potential legal liabilities. DHS will utilize the PCII Program and CIPAC (see Chapter 8) to address these concerns and to facilitate information sharing from the Gaming Facilities Subsector.

- **Resistance to a "Fortress Mentality:"** The design and construction of gaming complexes is focused on an open-access model where multiple entrances and glass doors welcome visitors. Limited access or security checkpoints may imply a potential security threat. Along with this concern over perceived threats, many owners and operators are concerned about the increased costs incurred by the implementation of security measures and the potentially hostile atmosphere that it creates for visitors. The goal is to implement security measures that are efficient, cost-effective, and as unobtrusive as possible.

1.2 Gaming Facilities Subsector Goals

The Gaming Facilities Subcouncil identified the following goals and objectives:

- Maintain unobtrusive but effective security procedures;

- Resume business functions as soon as possible after any kind of emergency or disaster, including terrorist incidents, natural disasters (e.g., flood, earthquake, etc.), life safety emergencies (e.g., fire, natural gas leak, etc.), and health incidents (e.g., pandemic flu, norovirus, etc.);

- Establish and test effective emergency plans that would help to minimize the damage and disruption caused by a disaster and to facilitate resumption of business operations;

- Establish standards and guidance for development of business continuity plans;

- Establish standards and guidance for security officer training;

- Improve communications methods with local government and other businesses after a disaster through additional equipment and training; and

- Maintain a link between business and government for information sharing (e.g., threat information, best practices documents, trends in R&D, etc.).

The Gaming Facilities Subcouncil may refine its goals in the future as it expands to include different gaming facilities types and locations, and with the continued development of relationships through the CF-SCC, CF-GCC, and other CIKR partners.

1.3 Authority

Commercial gaming facilities have strong ties to State and local governments that are not exclusive to the gaming portion of their operations. Building codes for safety and security are almost entirely regulated at the State and local levels. Federal regulation is mostly limited to safety-related OSHA requirements. Casinos that are defined as vessels or designated waterfront facilities by USCG are subject to MTSA. These facilities are required to conduct Facility Security Assessments to identify vulnerabilities and to develop Facility Security Plans detailing the steps necessary to mitigate these vulnerabilities.

2. Identify Assets and Facilities

AGA and NIGA collect information on the number of gaming establishments and other industry-related statistics; however, that information does not include an identification of assets or any information pertinent to risk management. Individual resort owners and operators share specific information with their local government and emergency responders; however, this is done on a case-by-case basis. The assets and facilities of the Gaming Facilities Subsector are addressed by the NCIPP framework outlined in Section 2.1.2.

3 and 4. Risk Assessment and Prioritization

Gaming Facilities Subcouncil members may use their own in-house safety and security staff to conduct security and vulnerability assessments, or they may contract with commercial vendors for these services. The self-assessments are often informal with no written report. Although there is no shortage of commercial vendors in the security assessment business, subcouncil members cite uncertainty over who is qualified/certified to perform the assessment, what the scope of the assessment should be (e.g., terrorism, natural disaster, health, etc.), and whether detailed facility information should be made available to persons outside of the resort as reasons for not using an outside contractor. However, subcouncil members have expressed an interest in receiving information from DHS on commonly used and accepted self-assessment tools to identify vulnerability and risk.

Assessment tools may be available to resort owners and operators from their State or local governments. For example, the New Jersey State Casino Control Commission and the New Jersey Division of Gaming Enforcement sponsor an Enhanced Threat and Risk Assessment course for casino owners and operators. This course is geared toward large facilities and provides training on the use of a risk assessment model and hands-on assessments.

Gaming Facilities Subcouncil members have expressed concern over sharing assessment information with the Federal Government for any initiative that makes formal decisions on the prioritization of assets (e.g., concluding that one asset is more "at risk" than another).

5. Protective Programs and Resilience Strategies

Protective measures employed by owners and operators of gaming facilities are similar to many of those employed across the CF Sector. Electronic access controls, surveillance cameras, and the use of security personnel are all areas of importance to the Gaming Facilities Subsector. However, additional or significantly more rigorous practices are employed in the casino portion of the complex. Security measures within the casino are dictated by the governing body for gaming operations at each particular resort. State gaming control commissions can dictate security measures, including the number and type of surveillance cameras or the number of security personnel on the floor of the casino. These measures are in place to prevent cheating, to ensure that the customer is getting a fair game, and to protect large quantities of cash. In addition to the stringent security measures in place within casinos, Gaming Facilities Subcouncil members have reported an increased focus on perimeter security within the past eight years. These measures, as opposed to security measures within the casino, are voluntary.

Although easy and open customer access to casinos is the rule, access control measures may exist in other areas of the gaming facility complex. Access card readers are usually required for entry into employee areas and card readers may also be required to access hotel floors. Gaming facility owners and operators have hardened some areas, such as loading docks; however, subcouncil members have cited the need for tax incentives and Federal assistance to undertake major structural changes to any facility.

Common protective measures employed across the Gaming Facilities Subsector include the following:

- An extensive and sophisticated network of CCTV inside and outside the facility, especially on the casino floor;

- Motion detectors;

- Background checks of employees;

- Security staff training;

- Security patrols inside and outside the resort;

- Hotel floor access control;
- Garage access control;
- Stairway access control;
- Loading dock access control;
- Critical utility access control; and
- Emergency response plans and programs.

Cost is the primary constraint on instituting and enhancing protective security measures at resorts. Individual owners and operators are subject to their own operating budgets, and each individual company makes its own decisions with regard to the amount of money spent on mitigating risk.

Gaming Facilities Subcouncil members have suggested that the Federal Government serve as a clearinghouse for information on protective measures and industry practices so that owners and operators would not have to "reinvent the wheel" each time they try to implement or improve a protective program. Members have identified the need for additional guidance on and standards for developing emergency response and business continuity plans and on developing security training programs. Members would like to be provided with access to other security industry standards and practices and to white papers developed by different security-focused associations.

Various Federal, State, and local governments and organizations have developed preparedness and security guides to address protective programs and resilience strategies that are applicable to the Gaming Facilities Subsector. For example, the IAAM Safety and Security Task Force has developed four security planning guides to address the need for selecting security practices based on the levels of threat or the vulnerability matrices associated with the DHS Homeland Security Advisory System (HSAS). These guides were developed through a peer review process among IAAM members. The four security guides are as follows:

- Safety and Security Best Practices Security Planning Guide for Arenas, Stadiums, and Amphitheaters;
- Safety and Security Best Practices Security Planning Guide for Convention Centers;
- Safety and Security Best Practices Planning Guide for Emergency Preparedness; and
- Safety and Security Best Practices Planning Guide for Theaters and Performing Arts Centers.

DHS and the FBI issue Joint Special Assessments and Joint Information Bulletins to members of the Gaming Facilities Subcouncil that address possible terrorist activities as they relate to the subsector. Members of the subcouncil will be able to obtain, analyze, and share information through HSIN. DHS HITRAC issues Private Sector Notes that address topical information and analysis on current security issues of interest to the subsector. Protective programs and resilience strategies offered by DHS include SAVs, the BZPP, and other DHS training programs (e.g., the Soft Target Awareness course).

6. Measure Progress

Each individual facility owner or operator determines a need for protective measures through the use of in-house assessments. This need is then considered along with other facility needs and, depending on the overall availability of resources, is fully funded, partially funded, or not funded. The progress made toward completing the project may be tracked by the individual facility's owner or operator. It is not currently being tracked by the subsector.

Because many members of the subcouncil are competitors in the business world and in-house funding for assessments, protective programs, and resilience strategies is specific to a facility or a company/organization, there has not been an immediate development of a subsector-wide methodology for assessing the success or effectiveness of protective programs and resilience strategies. Over time, as the Gaming Facilities Subsector evolves, as specific goals and objectives are created, and as communication mechanisms mature, the methods for monitoring the progress of implementing protective programs and resilience strategies on an individual program basis will mature.

7. Research and Development

Gaming facilities already employ advanced security surveillance technologies due to the need to maintain the security and integrity of the gaming process and to protect large quantities of cash. Deployment of sophisticated and improved CCTV and card access systems has already had a significant positive impact on security at these facilities. Gaming Facilities Subcouncil members have expressed an interest in new and improved security-related and detection technologies. However, they have emphasized that these technologies must be unobtrusive and convenient for the customer and that they must work under actual operating conditions, as opposed to a controlled environment. Areas of interest include the following:

- Biochemical agent detection;
- Biochemical sensors and automatic shutoffs for HVAC systems;
- Explosives detection for vehicles, persons, and packages;
- Automated CCTV facial recognition capabilities;
- License plate recognition capabilities;
- Methods that do not impede ingress (e.g., data mining, image recognition, etc.); and
- Behavior profiling.

Gaming facility owners and operators generally learn about new technologies from individual vendors, from vendor shows, or from colleagues in the industry. Some vendors may ask a resort facility to test a product at a resort in order to get feedback on what potential customers like or do not like about a product or system. Actual demonstration and operation of products and how they integrate into existing systems are critical to evaluating whether the systems will benefit a gaming facility and be worth the cost. Demonstration of newly developed technologies in areas where gaming facilities are concentrated (e.g., Las Vegas) or in individual gaming facilities would provide an opportunity to test and evaluate a new technology in an operating environment. Subcouncil members point out that some new technologies are most appropriately deployed in the surrounding area (e.g., license plate recognition systems) and not on the gaming facilities property.

Annex 3: Lodging Subsector

The Lodging Subsector comprises hotels and motels that provide travel accommodations generally for short-term stays and may also provide a range of other services (e.g., restaurants, golf courses, conference and convention centers, etc.). Hotels are considered open public access facilities. Hotel lobbies are open to the general public and hotels encourage off-the-street visitors to use their on-site services (e.g., restaurants, shops, etc.). However, access to guest rooms and, in some cases, the floors on which guest rooms are located may be restricted to hotel guests only. The majority of hotels and motels are privately owned and operated with minimal interaction with the Federal Government. Most State and local jurisdictions have regulations applicable to hotel operations, fire safety, and taxes. The hotel owner is responsible for practicing prudent risk management and mitigation measures with respect to manmade or natural incidents.

This annex was prepared based on information obtained from members of the Lodging Subcouncil, which is composed of 25 members representing the safety and security programs for all major hotel brands. This annex provides information on the Lodging Subcouncil's protective programs and will be updated as the protective status of the subsector changes over time.

1. Lodging Subsector Profile and Goals

The Lodging Subsector represents owners and operators of full-service hotels, limited-service hotels, resorts, conference centers, motels, extended-stay hotels, timeshare rentals, and convention hotels.

Information provided on the American Hotel and Lodging Association (AH&LA) Web site indicates that there were 48,062 lodging properties (each with a minimum of 15 rooms) in 2007, totaling approximately 4,476,191 guest rooms across the Nation. The industry generated $139.4 billion in sales. Industry-wide, the average occupancy rate was 63.1 percent in 2007.[12]

Hotels range from stand-alone, multi-story structures located in the downtown business district of a city to structures of only a few stories spread out over many acres in a resort setting. Many full-service hotels have restaurants, shops, and meeting rooms. Convention centers, shopping malls, sports facilities, and public transportation facilities may be adjacent to or integrated into the hotel facility. Hotels can be found in almost all of the other Commercial Facilities Subsectors, and they are an integral part of the Resorts, Outdoor Events, and Entertainment and Media subsectors.

Not only is the Lodging Subsector fully integrated with other commercial facilities, the lodging industry has a significant impact on business in the United States. In 2007, 11 percent of the national gross domestic product, or $1.6 trillion, was

---

[12] http://www.ahla.com/content.aspx?id=23744.

generated throughout the national economic chain by the lodging and hospitality industry. Additionally, 15.1 million jobs are supported in all U.S. industries though the presence of the lodging industry.[13]

Many hotels have been primary targets for terrorists overseas. Recent attacks have included hotels in Jakarta, Indonesia; Peshawar, Pakistan; Mumbai; and Islamabad; and, in some instances, U.S. brand hotels were targets. These attacks have made the Lodging Subsector keenly aware of the importance of security and the implementation of protective programs.

1.1 CIKR Partners

The members of the Lodging Subcouncil have worked to develop relationships with all Federal, State, and local governments. This includes DHS, the FBI, the USSS, ICE, and State and local law enforcement. Many members of the subcouncil are also members of the Overseas Advisory Council (OSAC), a Federal advisory committee with a U.S. Government charter to promote security and cooperation between the U.S. Government and private sector interests worldwide. Subcouncil members and security staff from the various hotel companies also meet on an annual basis as part of the AH&LA's Loss Prevention Committee. Members of the subcouncil utilize HSIN as a way of obtaining, analyzing, and sharing information. Information is also shared by those subcouncil members who belong to the International Security Managers Association (ISMA). Subcouncil members comprise industry professionals.

At the property level, hotel managers and security staff work together closely and share information with local emergency response and law enforcement organizations. In the larger cities, hotel owners cooperate to address security issues, crowd management, mutual-aid agreements, and cooperative emergency response. Many hotels within a specific district or area have a special radio frequency that properties use to communicate with each other. Other cities have special tasks forces established to share lessons learned, provide updates on current events, and become better prepared for the next manmade or natural incident.

1.2 Distinguishing Characteristics

The Lodging Subsector possesses a number of features that distinguish it from the other CF subsectors.

- **Continuous Occupancy:** Unlike many other commercial facilities, hotels and motels are occupied around the clock. People can eat, sleep, conduct business, and take part in entertainment activities within the same facility over multiple days. The average number of guests each night in all U.S. hotels in 2007 was 4.4 million people.[14]

- **Residential Properties:** The lodging industry is expanding into condominiums and timeshare facilities. This will align these properties with the Real Estate Subsector.

- **Emergency Shelters:** Hotels and motels have been used as shelters during times of natural disasters. Hotel companies have collaborated to find rooms for disaster victims and to make their properties available in times of need.

- **Self-Contained:** Some hotels are similar to small cities. They have the capability of generating their own electrical power and they operate their own potable water filtration and wastewater treatment facilities.

- **Just-In-Time Buyers:** Many hotels are "just-in-time" buyers. They often rely on the Internet to place orders and on the transportation and commercial distribution systems to deliver goods and services when needed. This results in fresh foods and supplies being available without the need to store, prepare, or process them onsite. However, this creates a problem for these hotels if they are to be used for shelter-in-place because there may not be sufficient supplies available for the anticipated time frame or number of people being sheltered.

---

[13] http://www.ahla.com/content.aspx?id=27642.

[14] Ibid.

1.3 International

Many of the Lodging Subsector hotel companies have international properties. In some instances, properties in the United States are owned by foreign companies or foreign individuals. Companies may have regional offices in foreign countries that are responsible for properties in different parts of the world. In many instances, international call centers are located in foreign countries.

According to the U.S. Department of Commerce's International Trade Administration, in 2007, 56 million persons traveled to the United States—an increase of 10 percent since 2006.[15]

1.4 Cyber Systems

Members of the Lodging Subcouncil and their hotel and motel properties are not dependent on a subsector-wide base of cyber assets. Each individual hotel company has cyber systems for reservations, property management, human resources, and financial management. Because of the importance of these systems, many hotel companies have backup/offsite facilities. Likewise, individual properties utilize cyber systems and control systems to monitor and operate HVAC systems, elevators and escalators, lighting, and CCTV. The Lodging Subsector would certainly be affected by any mass communications failure. For example, the loss of the ability to make reservations at one hotel chain could result in the public overloading reservations at another hotel chain. However, any event that affects the operations of a hotel company is not likely to affect cyber assets at other hotel companies within the sector.

1.5 Lodging Subsector Key Issues

As a result of discussions held between DHS and members of the Lodging Subsector, the following issues emerged as areas of concern for the subsector:

- **Resistance to a "Fortress Mentality:"** Many hotel companies must balance the need for enhanced security screening with positive customer perception. At the same time, increased security at hotels overseas is accepted and, in some locations, expected as a safety measure. There are many instances where increased security and screening is implemented at hotels, but it is usually at the request of a special guest or client that is either staying at the hotel or participating in some function on hotel grounds.

  Some hotels emphasize the security capabilities offered to former guests and functions in order to attract similar guests and functions in the future. However, hotels have many daily visitors for meetings, luncheons, or similar activities, and increased security could decrease this type of profitable business.

  Until the costs and benefits of security procedures can be marketed in a positive manner (e.g., a reduction in the theft of hotel items), there will be reluctance toward enhancing security.

- **Staff Turnover:** There is a high turnover rate in housekeeping, wait staff, and security personnel at hotels and motels. This necessitates having continuous training underway for staff and, in some cases, hiring employees before a background check can be completed. Security is not just the responsibility of the security staff; it should be emphasized and practiced by all hotel employees. Staff members who are unfamiliar with the hotel facilities and operations are also less likely to be aware of an unusual situation or individual.

- **Industry Vulnerability to Public Fears and Perception:** The Lodging Subsector is supported through business travel and vacation travel funds, which are discretionary in nature. As a result, the subsector is particularly sensitive to any incident that impacts transportation or a gathering in a public place, which, in turn, could result in people choosing not to travel. In major

---

[15] U.S. Department of Commerce, International Trade Administration, Office of Travel and Tourism Industries, Bureau of Economic Analysis.

vacation locations where hotels and motels are clustered together, the economic impact of a downturn in business on both the State and local economies could be significant.

- **Crime and Terrorism:** U.S. hotel companies place an equal emphasis on high-frequency events (e.g., credit card theft, identity theft, etc.) and low-frequency/high-severity events (e.g., terrorist threats).

- **Guest Information:** The release of information on hotel guests without a subpoena is an issue for many hotel companies. Another concern is the management and release of guest information that passes through the hotel's business centers.

- **Access to Threat Information:** The Lodging Subcouncil continues to work with DHS to provide readily available threat information to the owners and operators of subsector facilities regarding potential terrorist threats or other manmade or natural disasters, including cyber threats. The subsector wants the information to be clear, concise, and provided in a timely manner, as well as providing the source of the threat and threat analyses so that the owners and operators can determine an appropriate level of response to individual threat bulletins. DHS is providing the necessary security clearances to key sector members so that the distribution of threat information does not become constrained by the need to classify specific information. The CF SSA is working with US-CERT to share information about cybersecurity threats to all subsectors, including the Lodging Subsector.

- **Information Sharing with the Federal Government:** Members of the Lodging Subcouncil have expressed concern over sharing sensitive or proprietary information on assets or security measures. Facility owners and operators are also concerned with the identification of asset vulnerabilities. DHS is utilizing the PCII program and CIPAC to address these concerns and to facilitate information sharing from the Lodging Subsector.

- **Relationships with Local Law Enforcement:** A sound working relationship with local first responders, particularly law enforcement and fire department officials, is essential for quality security. The nature of these relationships varies from city to city and hotel to hotel and can have a considerable impact on the confidence of hotel companies as they formulate their emergency response plans.

- **Liability:** Hotel companies must reconcile their desire to identify vulnerabilities with the reality of liabilities. Once vulnerabilities are identified, hotel companies have a responsibility to address them in some concrete manner.

1.6 Lodging Goals and Objectives

The Lodging Subcouncil has identified the following goals and objectives:

- Protect employees and guests;
- Protect investors' assets in U.S. hotel properties;
- Share timely and accurate information on terrorist activities and methods of operation; and
- Train property security managers on security matters.

The Lodging Subcouncil may develop additional goals in the future and its goals will continue to be expanded and updated with the addition of members to the subcouncil and the continued development of relationships through the CF-SCC, CF-GCC, and other CIKR partners.

1.7 Authorities

The Lodging Subsector is almost entirely regulated at the State and local levels through building codes geared to life safety requirements and operations. Security concerns have not traditionally played a significant role in these codes. Federal regulation is mostly limited to safety-related OSHA requirements, the Hotel and Motel Fire Safety Act, and National Fire Protection Association (NFPA) standards. Accordingly, the primary regulatory authorities over the Lodging Subsector are State and local governments rather than the Federal Government.

2. Identify Assets and Facilities

AH&LA, through its membership, has both comprehensive and up-to-date information on the hotel industry. This information is collected and utilized by AH&LA to promote the hotel and tourist industry.

The Lodging Subcouncil has identified attributes that can be used to screen hotels for inclusion in the IDW. This screening includes the location of the property (e.g., entertainment/financial districts), clientele (e.g., long-standing arrangements with military organizations, controversial organizations, etc.), proximity to high-risk enterprises (e.g., next to an important Federal or iconic building), and the iconic status of the hotel itself (e.g., historical status, height, etc.). The location of the hotel is its most important attribute. For example, an iconic high-rise building in a major metropolitan city may have a higher threat and vulnerability than a similar hotel located in a small city. Another attribute used to distinguish among hotels involves the types of events held on hotel property or the status of the guests staying at the hotel. A hotel in a small city may not be considered critical until a high-profile target is in the building. Therefore, from time to time, any hotel within the Lodging Subsector may be considered a more critical property. A methodology and system to identify when attribute changes occur is going to be an important piece of information to be conveyed through the IDW.

The Lodging Subcouncil has submitted some information to the IDW. IDW representatives at DHS will work with subcouncil members to further develop that information.

The assets and facilities of the Lodging Subsector are addressed by the NCIPP framework outlined in Section 2.1.2.

3. Assess Risks

Some individual hotel companies have taken various measures to assess risk at their properties, but there is no subsector-wide risk assessment process. Some hotel companies utilize the American Society for Industrial Security (ASIS) risk assessment guide to determine risk at their hotels. Others utilize guides developed by local law enforcement agencies, such as the New York City Police Department (NYPD). These assessments are either performed by in-house staff or by third-party contractors. Many hotel owners have performed risk assessments as one element of the insurance underwriting process where sensitive information is shared with the insurance carrier and participating lenders.

Few hotel companies conduct consequence analyses to measure the impacts of a successful attack on a property, or VAs to determine the degree to which a given property is susceptible to an attack.

Hotel companies must reconcile their desire to utilize risk assessment methodologies with the reality of liabilities. Once risk assessments are performed, hotel companies have a responsibility to address deficiencies.

4. Prioritize the Lodging Infrastructure

Some U.S. hotel companies utilize a methodology for prioritizing properties similar to that used to screen assets for inclusion in the IDW. The criteria for prioritization include facility location, proximity, size, height, function type, and value. DHS will utilize the PCII Program and CIPAC to protect prioritization information, which should address potential concerns related to insurance, business competition, and liability issues.

5. Develop and Implement Protective Programs

There are many protective measures that can be applied to hotel properties. Electronic access control, surveillance cameras, security personnel, proper lighting, emergency response planning, and periodic visitor/bag screening are all protective measures designed to improve the security at hotels and motels.

In general, only those hotel properties that have unique attributes or that showcase high-profile venues have implemented enhanced protective programs. Restricted access and vehicle checkpoints have been employed at hotel properties where significant damage could occur. When employed, perimeter security usually consists of alarms, CCTV, and exterior barriers.

Many hotel companies have developed operational manuals, emergency action plans, and evacuation plans that outline the roles and responsibilities of property staff and others when dealing with a natural disaster or terrorist attack. Many of these documents are written not only to respond to a particular incident but to describe changes in security procedures as the DHS threat level changes.

Protective programs offered by DHS include SAVs and the BZPP. There are also Federal Hazard Mitigation programs offered by FEMA and various DHS training programs, including the Soft Target Awareness course. Recently developed in August 2009, the Hotel and Lodging Advisory Poster is being widely distributed throughout the sector. Also currently under development is a Protective Measures Guide for the U.S. Lodging Industry.

6. Measure Progress

Each individual facility owner or operator determines a need for protective measures through the use of in-house assessments. This need is then considered along with all of the other facility needs and, depending on the overall availability of resources, is fully funded, partially funded, or not funded. The progress made toward completing the project may be tracked by the individual facility owner or operator. It is not currently being tracked by the subsector.

As many members of the subcouncil are competitors in the business world and in-house funding for assessments and protective programs is specific to a facility, there is no universally applicable subsector-wide methodology for assessing the success or effectiveness of protective programs.

Additionally, the lodging subsector has expressed concern over sharing sensitive or proprietary information on assets or security measures with the Federal Government. This concern is specific to the identification of asset vulnerabilities, due to potential legal liabilities. In order to address this concern, the CF SSA is working with the PCII Program Office to widely advertise the PCII among the subsector.

7. Research and Development

Members of the Lodging Subcouncil have expressed interest in the following areas of security R&D:

- Unobtrusive blast protection techniques;
- Cost-effective methods to implement progressive collapse building techniques;
- HVAC and air handlers that are more efficient; detectors for chemical, biological, and radiological agents; and ultraviolet light to destroy agents;
- Wireless Information Technology-driven CCTV cameras; and
- Facial recognition software.

The subcouncil has emphasized that the technology applications must be less obtrusive and less costly in order to be practical. They are interested in any tools that enhance protective security, so long as they are cost-effective and applicable on a broad scale.

Annex 4: Outdoor Events Subsector

The Outdoor Events Subsector represents businesses and associations involved in entertainment, exhibitions, and amusements in outdoor spaces utilized by consumers for entertainment and recreational purposes. These assets operate on the principle of open public access, meaning that the general public can move freely without the deterrent of highly visible security barriers. The assets are generally owned and operated by private sector companies or cooperatives, although local government may own some venues, such as public parks or fair grounds. The assets operate with minimal interaction with the Federal Government or other regulatory agencies. For the most part, the facility owners and operators must be responsible for assessing and mitigating their specific vulnerabilities and practicing prudent risk management and mitigation measures.

This annex was prepared with input from the members of the Outdoor Events Subcouncil.

1. Outdoor Events Subsector Profile and Goals

1.1 Outdoor Events Profile

The Outdoor Events Subsector represents entities that provide the public with a place to meet and gather in outdoor spaces for the purposes of entertainment, education, and recreation. The subsector encompasses a wide array of facilities, events, and activities, ranging significantly in size, scope, and focus, including large and established theme parks and water parks, mobile amusement parks, carnivals and circuses, parks and fairgrounds, community festivals, parades, rallies, air shows, and other celebrations and events.

The size and utilization of outdoor events facilities and activities vary greatly. Theme parks may be seasonal or operated year-round. They may be located in a relatively small area or they may cover many acres. Larger theme parks may include theaters, entertainment centers, and hotels. Attendance at each of the 10 largest theme parks in the United States ranged from approximately 4.5 to 17 million people in 2008. Attendance at agricultural fairs and exhibitions is usually concentrated within a two or three-week period and can range from 5,000 to 200,000 people per day. At major State fairs, two to three million people may be on the fair grounds during a multi-week period. At the other end of the spectrum, mobile carnivals and circuses, in addition to operating at State and county fairs and festivals, may set up for a couple of days in a mall parking lot, church, or community recreational park. Parades or other festivals may last for only a few hours, but still draw thousands of people.

Outdoor events operate under various management formats as well. Theme parks and other outdoor entertainment venues are typically privately owned or corporate-owned and operated. Fairs, exhibitions, and other special event activities may be sponsored by a local governing authority and set up on community land or at community facilities. Carnivals and circuses that are set up for a few days in local parks, churches, and retail mall parking lots are often a major fundraiser for the community or a nonprofit organization.

1.1.2 CIKR Partners

Subcouncil members indicate that there are usually strong relationships and information sharing among local police, fire departments, and emergency services groups for facility operations and activities. Local authorities set the emergency plan requirements for permanent facilities and operations, transient/temporary operations, and special events held in a park or other open area.

The Outdoor Events Subsector shares some characteristics with the Entertainment and Media and Public Assembly subsectors.

1.1.3 Distinguishing Characteristics

The distinguishing characteristics of the Outdoor Events Subsector include the following:

- **Outdoor Events:** The subsector represents those activities and gatherings of people that take place outdoors, although there are usually buildings (e.g., restaurants, snack bars, hotels, shops, barns, and exhibition halls) associated with the activity. The outdoor nature of the event may sometimes result in attendees being spread out over a larger area than they would have been if the event had taken place in an enclosed structure.

- **Diversity:** The Outdoor Events Subsector represents an exceptionally diverse range of facilities and activities, including large, established theme parks with annual attendance in the millions; carnivals or circuses that set up for a week or two, or even a few days, in a temporary location; large State fairs with an attendance of more than a million people in a two or three-week period; and festivals and parades with attendance in the thousands over a period of hours.

- **Perimeter:** Some events (e.g., parades, festivals, and carnivals) take place not only outside, but in an open environment with no established perimeter or access controls.

- **Agricultural Products:** State fairs, local fairs, and exhibitions often involve the temporary showing of livestock and other agricultural products.

- **Seasonality:** Many outdoor events are seasonal or last only a few weeks, days, or hours. Vendors and suppliers, as well as security personnel who service the event, are not permanent employees but are hired for the length of the event. In addition, large numbers of volunteers may be involved in staffing the event.

1.1.4 International Relationships

Some of the companies represented in the subsector own international properties and associations that are members of the subcouncil are either international in nature or have international sister associations. Some fairs and exhibitions travel to and from Canada.

1.1.5 Cyber Systems

Many facilities or events within the Outdoor Events Subsector have cyber systems related to their operations (e.g., ticketing, reservations, lighting, CCTV, property management, human resources, and financial management). The Internet is widely used by the subsector to provide information on facilities, market events, sell tickets, and make reservations. Therefore, subsector facilities would be affected by any sort of mass communications failure.

1.1.6 Key Issues

The Outdoor Events Subsector possesses a number of features that distinguish it from the other CF Subsectors.

- **The Importance of Response:** Outdoor events are considered soft targets. Efforts should be undertaken to minimize the effects of a successful attack or a manmade or natural hazard through the efforts of public-private sector emergency response coordination and more efficient and effective evacuation strategies. Accordingly, should an incident occur, property or event management must have an effective plan for post-incident response to ensure that attendees remain safe and secure. Effective business continuity plans are needed to allow for the resumption of business functions in the event of a large-scale emergency.

- **Access to Threat Information:** The Outdoor Events Subcouncil continues to work with DHS to provide readily available threat information to the owners and operators of subsector facilities regarding potential terrorist threats or other manmade or natural disasters, including cyber threats. The subsector wants the information to be clear, concise, and provided in a timely manner, as well as providing the source of the threat and threat analyses so that the owners and operators can determine an appropriate level of response to individual threat bulletins. DHS is providing the necessary security clearances to key subsector members so that the distribution of threat information does not become constrained by the need to classify specific information. The CF SSA is working with US-CERT to share information about cybersecurity threats to all subsectors, including the Outdoor Events subsector.

- **Information Sharing with the Federal Government and Legal Liability:** Members of the Outdoor Events Subcouncil have expressed concern over sharing sensitive or proprietary information on assets or security measures. Facility owners and operators are also concerned with the identification of asset vulnerabilities. DHS will utilize the PCII Program and CIPAC (see chapter 8) to address these concerns and to facilitate information sharing with the Outdoor Events Subsector.

- **Clearinghouse for Government Resources and Industry Best Practices:** Asset owners and operators would benefit from knowing what resources are available from the Federal Government. Members note that there probably exists information, bulletins, and programs that could be of value to them; however, they have not been made aware of these resources. Likewise, owners, operators, and associations are interested in a clearinghouse for information on the best industry practices and tools to assist them in implementing effective protective security programs. Owners and operators have vastly different information and training needs due to the diversity of the subsector. Access to materials, training, and other resources is important for large-scale events, as well as for smaller, less obvious venues.

1.2 Outdoor Events Subsector Goals

The Outdoor Events Subcouncil's goal is to provide safe and secure environments for guests at those facilities hosting outdoor events and related facilities. The Outdoor Events Subcouncil may develop additional goals in the future and its goals will continue to be expanded and updated with the addition of members to the subcouncil and the continued development of relationships through the CF-SCC, CF-GCC, and other CIKR partners.

1.3 Authorities

Outdoor events are mostly regulated at the State and local levels through building codes geared toward life safety requirements. Security concerns have not traditionally played a significant role in these codes. Federal regulation is mostly limited to safety-related OSHA requirements. Accordingly, the primary regulatory authorities over the subsector and its primary security relationships are with State and local governments rather than with the Federal Government. Federal regulations govern other non-security-related aspects, such as the United States Department of Agriculture's (USDA) oversight of livestock, crops, and exotic animals; the U.S. Consumer Product Safety Commission's oversight of carnival ride safety; and the U.S. Department of Transportation's (DOT) regulations for the mobile amusement industry.

2. Identify Assets

Associations representing different venues within the Outdoor Events Subsector have records of membership information, but not necessarily an inventory of facilities. While many fairs and carnivals utilize land set aside for their use, other small carnivals use properties designated for other uses. Therefore, it is very difficult to identify all of the assets associated with this subsector. Individual owners and operators share specific asset information with their local emergency responders on a case-by-case basis. The assets and facilities of the Outdoor Events Subsector are addressed by the NCIPP framework outlined in Section 2.1.2.

3 and 4. Risk Assessment and Prioritization

Large entities within the Outdoor Events Subsector (e.g., theme parks) conduct VAs internally with their own staff, with staff from another corporate-owned facility, or with private contractors hired for the task. Most fairs, carnivals, and circuses are more concerned with theft, gangs, and petty larceny than with a potential terrorist incident. In some cases, an insurance company may require and perform assessments internally. There is great sensitivity about what vulnerability and risk information is included in a written report. Subsector members do not report utilization of any methodologies that would determine the degree to which a given asset is susceptible to an attack.

Concern over public disclosure plays a significant role in determining what asset information subcouncil members will provide to government agencies. If subcouncil members are confident that the information they provide will not by compromised by public disclosure, they will share what they can with DHS. DHS will utilize the PCII Program and CIPAC to facilitate this information-sharing process in a secure environment.

5. Develop and Implement Protective Programs

Protective measures employed by owners and operators of outdoor events facilities are similar to those employed across the CF Sector. For those assets that are permanently fixed, there may be controlled entrances, access identification, bag checks, vehicle barriers, CCTV and other surveillance systems, metal detectors, personnel and vehicle inspections, and antivirus software or similar cyber defense tools employed. These measures can vary significantly according to the type of event or facility. Established venues that charge admission will have more stringent access controls and surveillance because visitors must have a pass or ticket prior to entry. Coordination among Federal, State, and local law enforcement, development of emergency response plans, and the use of security guards are common measures used at virtually all events, whether large or small, permanent or transient.

Individual asset owners and operators may assess the risk of a security vulnerability and employ protective measures to mitigate risk. The threat of a terrorist attack drives some decisions; however, owners and operators are also influenced by local crime conditions and internal operating conditions. Individuals might consult with other subsector members or with law enforcement agencies based on previously established relationships. Operators of State and community events, fairs, and exhibitions have particularly strong relationships with local law enforcement and the community. In fact, local police, fire, or other emergency personnel may be a part of the event and serve as volunteers.

Budget constraints are the primary impediment to the implementation of protective measures, even for large, established theme parks, but particularly in the case of events that last for only a few weeks or days.

Protective programs available to the Outdoor Events Subsector include such DHS programs as SAVs, the BZPP, and various DHS training programs, such as the Soft Target Awareness course. In addition, FEMA offers Federal Hazard Mitigation Programs. A Protective Measures Guide for the Outdoor Events Subsector is currently being developed by the CF SSA with input from subsector members.

Other Federal, State, and local governments and organizations have developed preparedness and security guides to address protective programs for the Outdoor Events Subsector. The Colorado Office of Preparedness and Security, Homeland Security Section has prepared protective measures guides for a number of the 18 CIKR sectors (e.g., *Terrorism Protective Measures Resource Guide, Recreational Facilities* (October 2005) and *Terrorism Protective Measures Resource Guide, Large Outdoor Public Gatherings* (October 2005)). These guides provide an overview of terrorist objectives and give examples of specific threat categories, available protective measures, implementation of protective measures, and a protective measures matrix. The FEMA online training class, Special Events Contingency Planning for Public Safety Agencies, provides information related to pre-event planning, forming the planning team, event hazard analysis, and responding to incidents during special events.

6. Measure Progress

The Outdoor Events Subsector does not formally measure progress toward facility protection or risk mitigation efforts across the subsector. Each individual facility owner or operator determines a need for protective measures through the use of in-house assessments. This need is then considered along with all of the other facility needs and, depending on the overall availability of resources, is fully funded, partially funded, or not funded. The progress made toward completing the project may be tracked by the individual facility owner or operator; it is not currently being tracked by the subsector.

Because members of the subcouncil are competitors in the business world and in-house funding for assessments and protective programs is specific to a facility or company/organization, there has not been an immediate development of a subsector-wide methodology for assessing the success or effectiveness of protective programs. Over time, as the Outdoor Events Subsector evolves, as specific goals and objectives are created, and as communication mechanisms mature, the methods for monitoring the progress of the implementation of protective programs designed to meet goals and objectives should be put into place.

7. Research and Development

Most owners and operators within the Outdoor Events Subsector rely on trade shows, conferences, word of mouth, associates, and vendors with established products to identify R&D programs that may resolve security vulnerabilities.

Outdoor Events Subcouncil members expressed an interest in several areas of new and improved security-related and detection technologies, but were concerned that new technology may be a lost investment in a couple of years due to rapid changes in the industry. Members emphasized the need to know what developments are on the horizon and whether they are compatible with existing systems. Areas of interest include the following:

- **Explosives Detection:** Current technologies are too labor intensive and time consuming for the inspection of large volumes of vehicles, trucks, and delivery items.

- **Biochemical Detection:** A quick and unobtrusive method to check for biological and chemical substances is needed.

- **Development of strategies** for the quick handling and evacuation of large crowds is recommended.

- **Operational Requirements:** These include standoff detection with high-volume throughput, a low false positive rate, and hazard identification covering a wide spectrum of issues.

Annex 5: Public Assembly Subsector

The Public Assembly Subsector comprises facilities where people tend to meet for the purpose of professional education, meeting/gathering, and entertainment. These facilities operate on the principle of open public access, meaning that the general public may move freely throughout many areas within these facilities without the deterrence of highly visible security barriers. Public Assembly Subsector facilities are owned and operated by local governments, local authorities, or the private sector.

Facility owners and operators are responsible for assessing and mitigating their specific facility vulnerabilities and practicing prudent risk management and mitigation measures. They interact with local regulatory agencies (e.g., fire, police, EMS, and local codes) and Federal safety regulators (e.g., OSHA) to ensure compliance with the necessary standards.

This annex was prepared through the active participation of members of the Public Assembly Subcouncil and IAAM. This annex provides information on the current status of the Public Assembly Subsector's protective programs. This annex will be updated as the protective status of the subsector changes over time. Because many sports leagues facilities are not owned or operated by the Sports Leagues Subsector, but by the Public Assembly Subsector, some information regarding sports leagues facilities is also included in this annex.

1. Public Assembly Subsector Profile and Goals

1.1 Public Assembly Profile

The Public Assembly Subsector represents facilities that provide the general public with a place to meet and gather for entertainment, for the sale of products germane to an event or audience, and for professional education. The types of facilities and associations that are included in the Public Assembly Subsector are arenas, stadiums, motor race tracks, amphitheaters, performing arts centers, convention or conference centers, and exhibition halls. Other facilities include theaters, museums, and zoos.

There are many types of museums in the United States—from the very large collections found in major cities that cover many collection categories, to the very small museums that cover either a particular location in a general way or a particular subject, such as a single, individual notable person. A museum normally houses a core collection of important selected objects in its collection category. Their numbers include both governmental and private museums, aquariums, arboreta, art centers, botanical gardens, children's museums, historic sites, nature centers, planetariums, science and technology centers, and zoos. For the benefit of the animals and the visitors, many zoos in the United States keep animals in enclosures that attempt to replicate their natural habitats. Some zoos keep fewer animals in larger, outdoor enclosures, confining them with moats and fences, rather than in cages. There are also roadside zoos, petting zoos, and animal theme parks, which are a combination of an amusement park and a zoo, mainly for entertainment and commercial purposes.

The size, utilization, and owner–management formats of public assembly facilities vary greatly. Zoos and aquariums can be seasonal or operated year-round. They may be located in a single building or cover many acres. Likewise, a museum may be found in one room of a building or incorporate multiple buildings located throughout a city or State. Other public assembly facilities range from small assembly halls with fewer than 1,000 seats to large stadiums with capacities reaching 100,000 or more. The periods of occupancy and core usages range from several hours to full-day or multiple-day events. Convention centers and exhibition halls range in size from community-based facilities with meeting space only, to those that reach or exceed 1,000,000 square feet of exhibition space. Movie theaters may be located in shopping malls, in stand-alone facilities, or at drive-in facilities. They may contain a single viewing screen or multiple screens. All of the public assembly facilities have various types of management formats under which they are operated. Ownership and operating models include being publicly owned and managed, being publicly owned and privately managed, and being privately owned and managed.

1.1.1 CIKR Partners

The Public Assembly Subcouncil has aggressively worked to develop relationships with Federal, State, and local governments. These include DHS, State and local law enforcement, first responders, and emergency medical personnel. The subcouncil also has a good working relationship with the CF-GCC through its relationships with national homeland security officials, State homeland security offices, and individual communities where public assembly facility operations take place. The Public Assembly Subcouncil also has a good working relationship with the USSS and the FBI as a result of the many events held in public assembly facilities that have national recognition and have been classified as National Special Security Events (NSSEs) (e.g., national political conventions). When an event is designated as an NSSE, the USSS assumes its mandated role as the lead agency for the design and implementation of the event's operational security plan. The USSS works closely with facility owners and operators, as well as with State and local law enforcement and first responders, to provide a safe and secure environment for event participants and the general public.

Members of the subcouncil have participated in exercises conducted jointly by DHS, the FBI, and FEMA. The subcouncil also actively initiates working relationships with the American Red Cross and all local and national stakeholders in public safety.

The Public Assembly Subcouncil has shared information with other CF subcouncils, the CF-GCC, and other CIKR sectors, and it will continue to do so in the future. This subsector works closely with the Sports Leagues Subsector because these two subsectors share many of the same characteristics, facilities, and demographics, and they sometimes have the same type of landlord–tenant relationships that vary from facility to facility. Because of the types of facilities in the Resorts and Lodging subsectors (e.g., conference centers, exhibition halls, etc.), there has been direct contact between the Public Assembly Subcouncil and members of these subsectors. A number of subcouncil members are also involved with the Outdoor Events Subsector through their professional responsibilities with municipal outdoor events.

The Public Assembly Subcouncil meets regularly with other subsectors via conference calls or cross attendance of meetings. Additionally, meetings with representatives of DHS are held on a periodic basis. While each CF subcouncil realizes the importance of the unique attributes of its task, the Sports League and Public Assembly subcouncils are working in unison on numerous issues to further the safety of the attending public. Equally important, the subcouncil has fostered initiatives with agencies and departments at all levels of government and with private institutions.

1.1.2 Distinguishing Characteristics

The Public Assembly Subsector possesses a number of features that distinguish it from the other CF subsectors:

- **Emergency Shelters:** While the Public Assembly Subsector's facilities are geared toward meetings/gatherings, professional education, and entertainment, these facilities have taken on a much different role in the United States during times of national crisis. As recently as fall 2005, due to the weather-related devastation that hit the Gulf Coast, public assembly facilities provided extended shelter and comfort for displaced individuals. Public assembly facilities have demonstrated that they are just as critical during times of need as other critical infrastructure components such as energy or food and agriculture. These facilities may also provide temporary shelter for displaced individuals or serve as emergency services command centers for local and Federal first responders.

- **Sporting Facilities:** The focus of the Public Assembly Subcouncil is on the safe and enjoyable operation of facilities designed to accommodate large and small gatherings of people. These characteristics are shared with the Sports League Subcouncil, which is also geared toward large public gatherings. Both subcouncils are focused on the safety and security of public assembly facilities and those who attend events in these facilities, and on the impact on the communities that have invested in these facilities as community icons.

- **Various Owner and Operator Scenarios:** The Public Assembly Subsector has multiple owner and operator relationships that reflect the security operations and responsibilities at each facility. Some public assembly facilities are publicly owned and operated. In most instances, the security of these facilities is the responsibility of the local law enforcement jurisdiction. For privately owned facilities, security may be the responsibility of local law enforcement, or it may be contracted out to a private company. Public assembly facilities that are privately owned and operated are more likely to utilize a private security company. However, some local jurisdictions require the use of their own law enforcement officers. Other facilities utilize local law enforcement officers because of the potential liability associated with security at events. Therefore, the security planned for a particular event relies on the security arrangements of the owner or operator.

- **Command Center:** Many of the public assembly facilities that play host to a large number of visitors utilize a command center to monitor activities within the facility and to serve as an operations center in the event of a manmade or natural incident. Although each command center varies in sophistication, its primary function is to serve as a central location where facility personnel, emergency responders, and law enforcement personnel can work together to respond to an incident. In many cases, the facility system controls, communications, and monitoring equipment are controlled from the command center.

- **Associations:** The Public Assembly Subcouncil comprises officers and members of national and international associations (e.g., IAAM, SMA, Association of Zoos and Aquariums (AZA), and the American Association (AAM)) that represent the various facility profiles that make up the subsector. The CF SSA works through these associations' officers to reach the individual facility owners and operators. It is through these various associations that subsector infrastructure information is obtained to develop and implement a subsector protective program.

1.1.3 International Relationships

The associations that represent the Public Assembly Subcouncil comprise entities that are either international in nature or have international sister associations. For example, IAAM is an international organization with membership extending around the world. Conversely, AZA, although not international in nature, has strong relationships with its sister organizations throughout the world; these include the European Association of Zoos and Aquaria (EAZA), the Australasian Regional Association of Zoological Parks and Aquaria, the Southeast Asia Zoos Association (SEAZA), and the African Association of Zoos and Aquaria (PAAZAB). Likewise, the International Council of Museums (ICOM) is an international organization of museums.

There is also an international component to the events that take place in public assembly facilities. Museums exhibit international items or items with an international theme, some of which may be controversial for religious or political reasons. Cinemas in the United States show foreign films, theaters perform foreign plays, and foreign theater groups perform in U.S. theaters. Overseas cinemas that are not American-owned often show American movies. Therefore, these theaters are regarded internationally as being predominantly "American" and representative of American culture. Many sporting events include players from foreign countries or have foreign teams participating in the competition. Many international associations, some with controversial missions, hold their meetings in conference centers throughout the United States. A good example of the international component for zoos is the Giant Panda program in place at four zoos throughout the United States, wherein U.S. zoos donate an annual license fee of $1 million to China for panda conservation and nursing sites.

1.1.4 Cyber Systems

The Public Assembly Subsector cyber infrastructure systems include business systems, control systems, access control systems, and warning and alert systems. These cyber systems are utilized for day-to-day operations such as ticketing, reservations, property management, human resources and financial management, controlling HVAC systems, elevator and escalator controls, lighting, and CCTV. The consequences of a cyber-related security event against a public assembly facility asset, system, or network would only affect the operations of a limited number of subsector infrastructure associated with the attack (e.g., ticket sales for a specific event). However, the subsector as a whole would be affected by any sort of mass communications failure, including a mass disruption of the Internet. The Internet is widely used by the subsector to provide information on subsector facilities (e.g., marketing, merchandising, ticket sales, and reservations). Based on what was learned during the response to Hurricane Katrina, the Public Assembly Subcouncil is working to identify communications assets for public assembly facilities that would be viable in the absence of cell phones and local communications resources (e.g., satellite telephone technology).

1.1.5 Key Issues

As a result of discussions held among DHS, members of the Public Assembly Subcouncil, and members of IAAM, the following issues emerged as areas of concern for the subsector:

- **The Importance of Response:** Public assembly facilities are considered soft targets. Efforts should be continued to minimize the effects of a successful attack through endeavors such as public-private sector emergency response coordination, more efficient and effective evacuation strategies, and building and glass structural reinforcement strategies. Accordingly, should an attack occur, property management must have an effective plan for post-incident response to ensure that event attendees remain safe and secure, via either evacuation or sheltering in place. Exercises with State and local authorities reinforce these planned emergency response programs.

- **Access to Threat Information:** The Public Assembly Subcouncil continues to work with DHS to provide readily available threat information to the owners and operators of subsector facilities regarding potential terrorist threats or other manmade or natural disasters, including cyber threats. The subsector wants the information to be clear, concise, and provided in a timely manner, as well as providing the source of the threat and threat analyses so that the owners and operators can determine an appropriate level of response to individual threat bulletins. DHS is providing the necessary security clearances to key subsector members so that the distribution of threat information does not become constrained by the need to classify specific information. The CF SSA is working with US-CERT to share information about cybersecurity threats to all subsectors, including the Public Assembly Subsector.

- **Information Sharing with the Federal Government:** Members of the Public Assembly Subcouncil have expressed concern over sharing sensitive or proprietary information on assets or security measures. Facility owners and operators are also concerned with the identification of asset vulnerabilities. DHS has been successful in utilizing the PCII Program and CIPAC (see chapter 8) to address these concerns and to facilitate information sharing from the Public Assembly Subsector.

- **Relationships with Local Law Enforcement:** A sound working relationship with local first responders, particularly law enforcement and fire department officials, is essential for good security. The quality of these relationships varies from city to city and from facility to facility; however, they have a considerable impact on the confidence of facility owners and operators during emergency response planning.

- **Resistance to a "Fortress Mentality:"** The design and construction of many public assembly facilities is focused on an open-access concept where multiple entrances, glass walls, open atriums, and galleries welcome visitors and attendees. Many owners and operators do not want to limit access or create long lines at security checkpoints, which could imply a potential security threat. Along with this concern over perceived threats, many owners and operators are concerned about the increased costs incurred by the implementation of security measures, the potentially hostile atmosphere it creates for visitors, and the potential liability for owners and operators. At the same time, as the responsible party for the security of the facility, the owner or operator has no choice but to implement protective measures in accordance with the threat. DHS has been working with the subsector to implement security measures that are workable, cost-effective, and as unobtrusive as possible.

1.2 Public Assembly Goals and Objectives

The Public Assembly Subcouncil initiated a process to create its goals and objectives by utilizing IAAM members for a safety and security task force that developed specific best practices recommendations classified by facility type, and by tapping into the resources of IAAM's Life Safety Council, whose specific charge is to address safety and security issues that are related to public assembly facilities. The Life Safety Council and IAAM worked with members of the Public Assembly Subcouncil; other CF subcouncil members; and Federal, State, and local organizations to create the following goals for the Public Assembly Subsector:

- Make public assembly facilities safe and secure for all attendees and employees;

- Communicate information to subsector membership that would allow them to be properly prepared to respond to adversary-specific manmade incidents (e.g., civil disruption, hazardous materials release, terrorist threats, etc.), natural disasters (e.g., earthquakes, tornadoes, hurricanes, etc.), or other types of events that could affect the operation of a public assembly facility;

- Access threat information (manmade or natural) in real time;

- Be aware of and have access to technologies that will allow public assembly facilities to receive operational updates on all areas of safety and security;

- Invest dollars for technology, research, and development;

- Invest dollars for equipment and training of Public Assembly Subcouncil members, employees, and first responders;

- Invest dollars for the appropriate building hardening, vehicle intrusion, and ram protection;

- Facilitate Public Assembly Subcouncil members' coordination with first responders, and Federal, State, and local resources;

- Update all public assembly facilities with the latest advances in safety and security;

- Update and be aware of the latest threats and events that may affect public assembly facilities;

- Communicate with other CF subcouncils and utilize the information and initiatives that they have implemented, as appropriate; and

- Take the best practices and information available today and, through a commitment to communication, continue to identify and upgrade the Public Assembly Subcouncil's procedures and protocols.

The Public Assembly Subcouncil may develop additional goals in the future, and its goals will continue to be expanded and updated with the addition of members to the subcouncil and the continued development of relationships through the CF-SCC, CF-GCC, and other CIKR partners.

1.3 Authorities

The Public Assembly Subsector is almost entirely regulated at the State and local levels through building codes geared toward life safety requirements. Security concerns have not traditionally played a significant role in these codes. Federal regulation is mostly limited to safety-related OSHA requirements, the Americans with Disability Act (ADA), and standards and guides developed by agencies such NFPA. Accordingly, the primary regulatory authorities over the Public Assembly Subsector are State and local governments instead of the Federal Government.

2. Identify Assets, Systems, Networks, and Functions

The Public Assembly Subcouncil, through its member organizations, has both comprehensive and up-to-date information on all assets included in the Public Assembly Subsector. Information is updated on an annual basis by each member organization.

2.1 Defining Information Parameters

The Public Assembly Subsector categorized several attributes to define facilities within the subsector. Primary attributes include the size of the facility in terms of the number of seats, the amount of space, or the number of people that a facility can host. The physical location of the facility is also important. The primary method for contacting a facility, including cell phone and security contact information, is also an important facility attribute. There might be other specific attributes unique to a facility that could make that facility a more attractive target, including the specific event activity taking place in the facility or the audience attending the event.

The Public Assembly Subcouncil has identified attributes that are used to screen or identify facilities for inclusion in the IDW. These include the type of facility, the size of the facility, the number of people that a facility can accommodate, and the types of functions that take place within the facility. The location of the facility is also important. For example, a public assembly facility in Washington, D.C., may have a higher threat and vulnerability than a similar facility located in a small Midwestern city. Other attributes used to distinguish facilities include the facility type and utilization. For example, major professional sports arenas or convention facilities that are located in major metropolitan areas and that broadcast national events would have a higher rating from a critical asset standpoint. Each of these facilities and the other facilities represented within the Public Assembly Subsector may, from time to time, be considered a more critical asset based on the nature of the function(s) taking place within the facility. A methodology and system for identifying when attribute changes occur are critical for updating the IDW.

The assets and facilities of the Public Assembly subsector are addressed by the NCIPP framework outlined in Section 2.1.2.

2.2 Collecting Infrastructure Information

The Public Assembly Subcouncil is providing information to IICD for inclusion in the IDW. There is a specific process in place to collect data and information on subsector assets and facilities. The subcouncil, through IAAM, has submitted a significant amount of information to the IDW and continues to work with IICD representatives to further develop subsector infrastructure information.

2.3 Verifying Infrastructure Information

Subcouncil members update the infrastructure information that pertains to the Public Assembly Subsector on an annual basis. There are methods in place to make the necessary changes as new facilities join or leave the subsector. The CF SSA is working with subcouncil members and IICD to implement the quality control processes, protocols for reviewing infrastructure information, and processes to address incomplete and inaccurate infrastructure data.

2.4 Updating Infrastructure Information

The Public Assembly Subcouncil participates in the population and updating of the IDW. The IICS will display the date when the data from the subsector were last updated. This date is determined by when the original data source was approved and by the predetermined agreements for how often the subcouncil updates the IICS with their data.

The Public Assembly Subcouncil will continue to work directly with IICD representatives by performing an annual review of the public assembly infrastructure data contained in the IDW, and by providing information on new and deleted facilities and assets on an annual basis.

3. Assess Risks

Individual asset owners within the Public Assembly Subsector have taken various measures to assess the risk to their assets, systems, and networks. The subsector has also initiated a subsector-wide risk assessment process through the development and implementation of RSAT. The subsector has become increasingly focused on security and is moving toward the implementation of a subsector-wide robust risk assessment methodology, as called for in the NIPP.

3.1 Use of Risk Assessment in the Public Assembly Subsector

The current risk assessment methodology being used within the Public Assembly Subsector is RSAT, a self-assessment tool for safety and security provided by DHS. A module has been deployed for stadiums and arenas with plans for future modules specific to other subsector facility types. RSATs are self-performed and information can be shared directly with DHS at the user's discretion.

It is a common practice for public assembly facility owners and operators to engage local law enforcement agencies and private consultants in conducting risk assessments. Other risk assessment tools are available to public assembly owners and operators from local law enforcement organizations (e.g., NYPD) and from commercial vendors.

Members of the Public Assembly Subcouncil conduct individualized self-assessments on their own particular assets. Many subcouncil members have done so as one element of the insurance underwriting process where sensitive information is shared with the insurance carrier and participating lenders. Many members of the same corporate organizations perform third-party risk assessments on each others' facilities when they are similar in type and located in the same geographical area. Procedures and protocols for conducting individual risk assessments and third-party organizational risk assessments are evolving throughout the Public Assembly Subsector. The Public Assembly Subcouncil embraces any DHS or other Federal agency efforts to make risk assessments available to subcouncil members.

3.2 Screening Infrastructure

Attributes that may be used to screen public assembly facilities include the following:

- Type of facility;
- Size of facility;
- Number of people attending an event at the facility;
- Types of functions/activities that take place at the facility; and
- Location and surrounding areas of the facility.

3.3 Assessing Consequences

There are many consequence assessments that can assist a Public Assembly Subsector facility owner or operator in assessing the consequences and, ultimately, the risks associated with their facility. These assessments have certain characteristics in order to be useful to support sector risk analyses and DHS resource allocations. These criteria include public health and safety consequences, economic consequences, psychological consequences, and governance/mission impact consequences.

3.4 Assessing Vulnerabilities

A variety of vulnerability assessment methodologies are currently available, either as stand-alone methodologies or as a part of programs being implemented by DHS or other Federal partners. Some of the federally sponsored programs and methodologies employed by DHS include SAVs, BZPs, CSET, and IST.

3.5 Assessing Threats

The Public Assembly Subcouncil has created partnerships with State and local law enforcement and the Joint Terrorism Task Force (JTTF) in order to be advised of potential threats against subsector facilities. DHS HITRAC issues products that include threat information bulletins and security awareness documents.

4. Prioritize the Public Assembly Infrastructure

Individual companies and associations within the Public Assembly Subsector currently perform some type of asset prioritization utilizing their own guidelines and assumptions for prioritizing their specific assets. Examples include the asset's profile (e.g., iconic value), the asset's proximity to high-risk enterprises, the physical location of the asset, the magnitude of the function or activity taking place at the asset, and the clientele or tenants of the asset. However, due to the ever-changing nature of activities within assets (e.g., clientele, tenants, venues, etc.) and activities surrounding the assets (e.g., location, outdoor events, etc.), the critical nature of an asset can go from low risk to a higher priority based on the event activity that is taking place in and around the asset. A sports stadium or convention center may be at more risk of an attack when an event is occurring than when the facility is empty. A methodology that can identify the changes in an asset's priority based on event activity could be an important piece of information to be conveyed through a DHS prioritization system.

5. Develop and Implement Protective Programs

IAAM's Safety and Security Task Force (SSTF) has developed four security planning guides to address the need for selecting security practices based on levels of threat or vulnerability matrixes associated with the DHS HSAS. These guides were developed through a peer review process among IAAM members. The four security guides are:

- Safety and Security Best Practices Security Planning Guide for Arenas, Stadiums, and Amphitheaters;

- Safety and Security Best Practices Security Planning Guide for Convention Centers;

- Safety and Security Best Practices Planning Guide for Emergency Preparedness; and

- Safety and Security Best Practices Planning Guide for Theaters and Performing Arts Centers.

Each of the four planning guides comprises several documents that aid in assessing risk factors and determining terrorist threat levels. A checklist is also provided that can be used in the formulation of safety/security plans at public venues for any given event or related activity.

The IAAM best practices guides recommend that venue management adopt a planning process that includes the following steps:

- Assessing risk factors;

- Determining threat levels; and

- Developing and implementing a safety/security plan.

In response to the weather-related devastation that hit the Gulf Coast in fall 2005, IAAM also prepared a best practices guide for mega-shelter operations entitled, IAAM Mega-Shelter Best Practices Guidelines for Planning, Activation, and Operation. This guide aids facility managers in understanding the activation process, shelter standards, contracting, liability exposure, and how to plan for a predicted storm season. The operations guidelines provide information on command and control systems, security, compassionate care, food service, resident services, medical care, and interaction with mega-shelter partners. This guide is available at **www.iaam.org/members/Sec_pages/Mega-ShelterPlanning&Activation.pdf**.

Other Federal, State, and local governments and organizations have developed preparedness and security guides to address protective programs for the Public Assembly Sector. These guides provide an overview of terrorist objectives and give examples of specific threat categories, available protective measures, implementation of protective measures, and a protective measures matrix.

There are also many international plans that provide protective security advice, that are available to the Public Assembly Subsector, and address terrorist threats from a sector level down to specific types of facilities. Counter Terrorism Protective Security Advice for Stadiums and Arenas, produced by the National Counter Terrorism Security Office within MI5, the United Kingdom's security intelligence agency, provides information to stadium and arena owners and operators who want to reduce the risk of a terrorist attack or limit the damage that terrorism might cause to their facilities.

DHS and the FBI issue Joint Special Assessments and Joint Information Bulletins to members of the Public Assembly Subcouncil that address possible terrorist activities that are related to the subsector. Members of the subcouncil, along with other CIKR partners associated with the Pubic Assembly Subsector, will be able to obtain, analyze, and share information through HSIN. DHS HITRAC issues Private Sector Notes that address topical information and analysis on current security issues of interest to the Public Assembly Subsector. Information derived and shared through both HSIN and HITRAC support protective programs established by the Public Assembly Subsector.

While the preceding paragraphs describe various programmatic protective programs that are in place or available to the Public Assembly Subsector, there are also many protective measures that can be applied at the facility level. Electronic access control, surveillance cameras, security personnel, proper lighting, emergency response planning, and visitor/bag screening are all protective measures designed to improve the security of public assembly facilities.

In general, only those public assembly facilities with unique attributes or high-profile venues have security procedures. When employed, perimeter security usually consists of alarms, CCTV, and exterior barriers. Contractor security guards may be employed. Facility staff and venue/sports personnel may use entrances that are separate from the public entrances. Security screening may occur at public entrances, as well as at entrances to offices, locker rooms, dressing rooms, and storage areas within the facility. Deliveries to the facility may also be screened. Badges may be required to control access to various areas of the facility. Screening of security, maintenance, concession, and custodial staff may also be required.

Many public assembly facilities develop operational manuals, emergency action plans, and evacuation plans that outline the roles and responsibilities of facility staff, law enforcement, emergency responders, and others when dealing with a natural disaster or terrorist attack. Many of these documents are written not only to respond to a particular incident, but to describe changes in security procedures as the DHS threat level changes.

5.1 Determining Protective Program Needs

The development of best practices guides by IAAM has been embraced as a model for preparing safety and security policies and procedures in the Public Assembly Subsector (e.g., Best Practices Planning Guide—Convention Centers/Exhibit Halls, and Best Practices Planning Guide—Arenas, Stadiums, Amphitheaters). Additionally, with DHS collaboration, RSAT has been developed for stadiums and arenas with the goal of creating modules in the future for the other types of public assembly facilities. The Public Assembly Subcouncil and IAAM work with owners and operators of public assembly facilities to communicate the importance and use of RSAT, and how to promote, market, and appropriately train facility personnel in its completion. This has been done through on-site IAAM training, promotion by IAAM at conferences and meetings, and by the National Center for Spectator Sports Safety and Security (NCS4), an organizational member of the Sports League Subsector.

Those owners and operators who apply the principles found in the RSAT threat assessment modules and the various vulnerability matrixes in the IAAM protective guides will be able to identify those protective programs that should be implemented at their individual Public Assembly Subsector facilities.

Individual public assembly facility owners and operators are limited by their operating budgets and the amount of funding available to mitigate risk. This is a constant challenge for security professionals and for the facilities represented within the Public Assembly Subsector. However, by normalizing and prioritizing, facility owners and operators can place themselves in the best possible position to employ what resources they do have in the most efficient and effective manner.

There has been a concerted effort by the CF SSA to make risk assessment tools and protective programs available to the many CIKR partners associated with the Public Assembly Subsector through the various communication and information-sharing mechanisms available to them. Once the subsector has disseminated these tools and the individual facility owners and operators have put them into practice, gaps in security measures and protective programs can be identified and addressed across the subsector in order to prioritize what additional security measure need to be put in place.

5.2 Protective Program Implementation

Protective programs are put into place and implemented on an individual facility basis. Each individual facility or company/organization with multiple facilities is responsible for its own protective program(s). The Public Assembly Subcouncil has worked directly with representatives of other CF subcouncils where interests are parallel (e.g., the Sports Leagues Subcouncil) to further develop these protective programs. The Public Assembly Subsector, via IAAM, has formed the Life Safety Council to focus specifically on protective programs. In addition, IAAM has initiated a professional development training and educational program called the Academy for Venue Safety and Security. IAAM also participates in a variety of professional development and educational programs to bring coordinated policy, procedure, and delivery methods to Public Assembly Subcouncil members. FEMA has provided IAAM with a grant to promote RSAT.

Protective programs offered by DHS and utilized by the Public Assembly Subsector include SAVs, the BZPP, RSAT, the Risk Management Series documents offered by FEMA, and various DHS training programs (e.g., the Soft Target Awareness course).

6. Measure Progress

Each individual owner or operator of a public assembly facility determines the need for protective measures using in-house assessments. This need is then considered along with other facility needs and, depending on the overall availability of resources, is fully funded, partially funded, or not funded. The individual facility owner or operator may track the progress made toward completing the project; the subsector does not currently tracked this information.

Because many members of the subcouncil are competitors in the business world and in-house funding for assessments and protective programs is specific to a facility or company/organization, there has not been an immediate development of a subsector-wide methodology for assessing the success or effectiveness of protective programs. Over time, as the Public Assembly Subsector evolves, as specific goals and objectives are created, and as communication mechanisms mature, the methods for monitoring the progress of implementing protective programs designed to meet goals and objectives should be put into place.

7. Research and Development

Some public assembly facility owners and operators conduct their own R&D based on policies and procedures applicable to their specific operating circumstances. Other facility owners and operators rely on communication within the parent organization or professional organization to find out what type of R&D is underway and how other owners and operators are adapting to meet safety and security needs. Currently, the Public Assembly Subsector is involved in R&D activities sponsored by DHS that are investigating chemical, biological, and explosive detection techniques.

The following are some R&D initiatives that members of the Public Assembly Subcouncil have identified as being valuable to the subsector:

- Training of security personnel and managers via tabletop and full-scale exercises dealing with emergency responses to a weapons of mass destruction incident;

- Rapid and effective van, truck, and vehicle screening equipment that provides acceptable results in a reasonable amount of time, thereby allowing more vehicles to be screened prior to an event;

- Bollard and security camera upgrades to provide better vehicle control and tracking of vehicles in and around a sporting event facility;

- Development of HVAC systems that utilize real-time chemical, biological, and radiological detectors, similar to those employed in laboratories and nuclear power plants;

- Quick and accurate detectors for chemical, biological, and radiological contaminants in order to shorten response time;

- Portable containment devices to isolate contaminants;

- Explosive detection devices (the Public Assembly Subsector views improvised explosive devices (IEDs) as the biggest terrorist threat to facilities); and

- Protection assessments for different types of explosives.

Annex 6: Real Estate Subsector

The Real Estate Subsector comprises commercial office buildings, large residential buildings, multi-family residential units, and self-storage facilities. In short, this subsector contains those commercial facility assets in which Americans live and work every day. Some assets within the Real Estate Subsector are highly recognizable. The World Trade Center was not only a commercial office building, it was a national icon on the New York City skyline.

Traditionally, terrorists have selected buildings (primarily commercial buildings) as the preferred target of attacks. This preference can be easily understood as there is a large inventory of vulnerable buildings throughout the Nation. Buildings are mostly built in accordance with building codes that lack substantial design considerations intended to prevent or minimize the impact caused by terrorist attacks. The collapse or failure of these buildings can have a severe effect on all sectors of the economy and key resources, and can result in significant loss of life.

This annex was prepared with the active participation of members of the Real Estate Subcouncil. Multiple roundtable sessions were held with leading security professionals and industry experts. Numerous individual interviews were conducted with subcouncil members and representatives of real estate owners, real estate investment trusts, brokerage firms, and property management companies throughout the United States. At the request of the subcouncil, these discussions took place on a not-for-attribution basis to encourage candid dialogue.

1. Real Estate Subsector Profile and Goals

1.1 Real Estate Subsector Profile

Approximately 740,000 commercial office buildings exist in the United States, comprising 12 billion square feet and housing approximately 29 million workers. Roughly 2,000 buildings, less than 1 percent of the total number, contain more than 500,000 square feet of floor space, and another 5,000 buildings exceed 200,000 square feet. Together, these buildings account for nearly 30 percent of all commercial office square footage within the United States. Some of the largest commercial office buildings exceed 1 million square feet and are among the Nation's most prominent icons.

Commercial office buildings range from one-story, single-unit office buildings to towering skyscrapers. Many large commercial office buildings contain other businesses, including restaurants, dry cleaners, drug stores, and daycare centers. Underground parking is common.

Large residential or multi-family unit buildings include apartments, condominiums, and cooperatives. Large residential buildings today are typically high-rise structures characterized by controlled-access lobbies, common areas, on-site parking, and a staff to maintain common areas and grounds. These buildings typically contain only residential units; however, some mixed-used developments will have offices, hotel space, or apartments above street-level retail units. According to data in the 2000 Census, there are more than 19 million housing units in residential structures that contain five or more units.

According to the Self Storage Association, there were more than 45,812 primary self-storage facilities in the United States as of December 31, 2005. "Primary" self-storage facilities are those facilities where storage is a primary source of business income. Some 32,000 companies own and operate primary self-storage facilities. Additionally, there are another 9,600 "secondary" mini-storage facilities in the United States wherein storage is a secondary source of revenue.

1.1.1 CIKR Partners

As with any broad sector comprising hundreds of thousands of individual assets, national associations provide an effective mechanism to represent collective interests. The following associations have active representation on the Real Estate Subcouncil:

- The Real Estate Roundtable
- Building Owners and Managers Association (BOMA) International
- National Multi-Housing Council (NMHC)
- National Association of Industrial and Office Properties (NAIOP)
- National Association of Real Estate Investment Trusts (NAREIT)
- National Association of Realtors (NAR)
- National Apartment Association (NAA)
- Self Storage Association
- The Real Estate Board of New York (REBNY)

RE-ISAC, a nonprofit entity, is an outgrowth of a 1998 Presidential Directive and was formally organized in February 2003. Structured as a public-private partnership between the U.S. real estate industry and DHS, RE-ISAC seeks to facilitate information sharing on terrorist threats, warnings, incidents, vulnerabilities, and response planning to counter potential terrorist acts and to protect commercial and residential buildings and their occupants.

RE-ISAC fulfills three key roles:

- Disseminates information from the Federal Government, including terrorist alerts and advisories, to real estate industry participants;
- Facilitates industry reporting to government authorities of credible threats to real estate assets, enables analysis of the information to detect patterns or trends, and develops potentially coordinated actions; and
- Brings public and private sector experts together to share useful information, and discusses and develops best practices on risk assessment, asset protection, and emergency response planning.

1.1.2 Distinguishing Characteristics

The Real Estate Subsector possesses a number of unique features that distinguish it from the other Commercial Facility Subsectors. Whereas most other CF subsectors allow public access into their facilities on a temporary basis (e.g., for a theater performance, a retail outlet shopping trip, or a day at an amusement park), the Real Estate Subsector experiences continuous occupation because the public both lives and works within this subsector's facilities. Accordingly, office building or residential unit tenants maintain extensive control over their immediate suite/residential units, with limited authority and responsibility being exercised by the property owner or manager. For example, a patron at a movie theater is not expected to take measures to ensure his or her own safety while viewing a movie. However, the same cannot be said for an office or residential tenant.

Additionally, many real estate facilities have unique relationships and significant interdependencies with other CIKR, including those represented by the Communications, Banking and Finance, Transportation Systems, and Information Technology Sectors, potentially increasing their overall risk.

This unique relationship between the Real Estate Subsector and its tenants is the basis for a number of distinguishing characteristics, as discussed below:

- **Division of Responsibility Between Owners and Tenants:** Property managers uniformly agree that tenants in both commercial office buildings and residential buildings are responsible for their own safety and that of visitors within their particular suites or apartments in any scenario short of emergency evacuation. In other words, if a situation calls for a shelter-in-place response strategy (see below), it is the tenant who has the duty to ensure that provisions are on hand for the duration. The same approach applies to access to individual office suites or apartments. It is the responsibility of individual tenants to ensure the security of their units inside the facility. On the other hand, the property manager of a facility is always responsible for perimeter access controls and continuity of critical functions (e.g., water pumps, HVAC systems, evacuation planning, etc.).

  Leases are the primary mechanism for defining what duties facility owners and operators are required to execute versus the obligations of the building tenants. Virtually all owners and operators have cited the misconception among individual tenants that the facility owners or operators are responsible for their personal safety. Accordingly, the subcouncil believes that there is a need to raise awareness at the tenant level of individual responsibilities to ensure personal safety.

- **Tenant/Resident Identification:** Owners and operators of residential properties screen all rental applicants using credit reports, criminal background databases, and Federal terrorist watch lists prior to granting residency. This information is used to ensure the suitability of the lessee, financial security for the lessor, and the safety of existing and future building occupants.

- **Control of Parking Areas:** In most commercial office buildings, a separate firm usually operates the parking garage that is attached to or located underneath the property. This arrangement may complicate efforts to coordinate security practices and emergency response. In the aftermath of an incident, for example, the parking garage and the office building may implement contradictory rules on access and inspections. To avoid this and to ensure consistency, carefully crafted leases giving building owners and operators the necessary control is an important factor in emergencies. Additionally, owners and operators expressed the need for active partnership with public transportation officials to enable evacuation from parking garages and to ensure that traffic flows are created to keep vehicles moving once on the street.

1.1.3 International Relationships

The real estate industry is a global business. U.S. real estate corporations, real estate investment trusts (REITs), and self-storage REITs have substantial holdings around the world. Likewise, foreign corporations own real estate in the United States.

Because U.S.-owned real estate holdings abroad are privately controlled, the mission of ensuring the security of these buildings presents a significant challenge. OSAC within the U.S. Department of State has developed a document entitled *Security Guidelines for American Enterprises Abroad* (**www.osac.gov/Reports/report.cfm?contentID=30023**), which provides a set of guidelines for American private sector executives operating outside the United States. The guidelines are developed for areas where serious threats to personnel exist and terrorism is considered a present danger. The recommended security measures can be implemented in a scalable manner in areas where the threat may be reduced or made relatively less significant.

1.1.4 Cyber Issues

Cyber systems are utilized to operate control systems for the facilities within the Real Estate Subsector. Individual properties use Supervisory Control and Data Acquisition (SCADA) systems to monitor and operate HVAC systems, elevators and escalators, lighting, and CCTV. Although the loss of cyber capabilities at one facility may not significantly impact other facilities within the subsector, suspended functionality could present widespread cyber challenges throughout a specific business and even affect that business's client population.

The following issues emerged as areas of concern for the Real Estate Subsector:

- **The Importance of Response:** Mechanisms should be in place to minimize the effects of a successful attack (e.g., public-private sector emergency response coordination, occupant protection within an attacked facility, more efficient and effective evacuation strategies, and building/glass structural reinforcement strategies). Minimal distinction exists between being the target of an attack versus confronting the collateral damage associated with a nearby attack. Both situations require effective emergency response and recovery capabilities.

  Accordingly, if an attack occurs against either a facility or an adjacent site, that property's manager must have an effective response plan for post-incident response to ensure that tenants remain safe and secure. Mutual-aid agreements among neighboring facilities can play a key role. In some cities, security vendors have a Mutual-Aid Plan enabling them to rapidly deploy additional personnel to a crisis site. Some cities require that every commercial facility building devise an Emergency Action Plan. Some building owners have made it mandatory for every individual tenant to initiate and annually repeat an evacuation familiarization exercise using an interactive Web-based model. While these requirements may be too extreme for some cities and regions across the Nation, they can serve as a guidepost.

- **Access to Threat Information:** The Real Estate Subcouncil continues to work with DHS to provide readily available threat information to the owners and operators of subsector facilities regarding potential terrorist threats or other manmade or natural disasters, including cyber threats. The subsector wants the information to be clear, concise, and provided in a timely manner, as well as providing the source of the threat and threat analyses so that the owners and operators can determine an appropriate level of response to individual threat bulletins. DHS is providing the necessary security clearances to key sector members so that the distribution of threat information does not become constrained by the need to classify specific information. The CF SSA is working with US-CERT to share information about cybersecurity threats to all subsectors, including the Real Estate Subsector.

- **Information Sharing with the Federal Government and Legal Liability:** Members of the Real Estate Subcouncil have expressed concern over sharing sensitive or proprietary information on assets or security measures. Facility owners and operators are also concerned with the identification of asset vulnerabilities and potential legal liabilities. DHS will utilize the PCII Program and CIPAC (see chapter 8) to address these concerns and to facilitate information sharing from the Real Estate Subsector.

- **Relationships with Local Law Enforcement:** A sound working relationship with local first responders, particularly law enforcement and fire department officials, is essential. The quality of these relationships (which varies from city to city and from property to property) impacts property owners and operators as they prepare emergency response plans and conduct related exercises. Therefore, developing and maintaining relationships with local police and fire departments is a priority.

- **Resistance to a "Fortress Mentality:"** Some commercial office building owners report resistance on the part of their tenants to increasing security measures. Tenants are concerned over the increased costs incurred by additional security measures and the potentially hostile atmosphere that they may create for guests and visitors. Many security measures can, in fact, be implemented in a non-obtrusive manner.

- **Terrorism Insurance:** While the insurance industry was able to pay out the $40 to $70 billion in damages from the September 11th attacks, most insurance companies either refused to cover damages from terrorist attacks or offered terrorism coverage at very high rates. In 2002, the U.S. Congress passed the Terrorism Risk Insurance Act, which provided a temporary insurance backstop for terrorism-related insurance claims. The program was extended in late 2005 by the Terrorism Risk Insurance Extension Act through 2007, with several changes to the original act. These changes increased the total damages threshold to trigger the program from $5 million in the original law to $50 million in 2006, and again to $100 million in 2007, and they also increased the share of costs incurred by the insurance companies.

The real estate lobby has been a major advocate for creating a permanent public-private solution for commercial insurance coverage in the event of a major terror attack. This insurance coverage would help to mitigate loan default and would allow property owners to obtain financing for future development.

1.2 Goals and Objectives

The Real Estate Subcouncil has identified the following goals for improving the subsector's risk posture:

- Maintain an effective security framework that meets the requirements of the tenants and customers of commercial office and residential buildings while ensuring the continued economic vitality of this subsector;

- Improve information sharing among Federal, State, and local government partners with regard to the threat profile of individual assets or geographic regions in order to make informed security and risk assessment and resource allocation decisions;

- Efficiently provide actionable intelligence to appropriate partners;

- Create standardized training programs with differing levels of sophistication on security awareness and risk assessment methods in order to provide certifications to security personnel;

- Develop training initiatives, materials, and exercises that elevate employee and tenant threat and emergency awareness and preparedness to create a more integrated and effective response to incidents (e.g., shelter-in-place, active shooter, and natural disasters);

- Create more uniform two-way communication mechanisms between local government support and response teams;

- Standardize information on government programs related to homeland security and uniform methods of access; and

- Establish a national/international clearinghouse of at-risk individuals that can be easily searched for pre-qualification of tenants, vendors, and partners.

1.3 Authorities

The Real Estate Subsector is almost entirely regulated at the State and local levels through building codes geared toward safety requirements. Security concerns have not traditionally played a significant role in these codes. Federal regulation is mostly limited to safety-related OSHA requirements. Although not regulatory entities, organizations like NFPA and laws such as ADA, provide additional requirements that focus on improving the safety of commercial facilities.

2. Identify Assets and Facilities

Individual companies and associations within the Real Estate Subsector maintain inventories of their facilities for various reasons, such as marketing and financial purposes, but not for security or protective programs and resilience strategies. Many owners and operators of buildings in the Real Estate Subsector are willing to share facility vulnerability information on an informal basis with trusted local first responders. DHS will utilize the PCII Program and CIPAC to facilitate the formal disclosure of such information to DHS in a building-specific format.

The subsector is reasonably confident that key State and local officials are aware of the "critical" real estate assets within their jurisdictions. This same understanding applies to DHS's knowledge of "nationally critical" real estate facilities. The CF SSA has developed a process for obtaining asset information from those building owners and operators who are willing to submit asset information to DHS.

The assets and facilities of the Real Estate Subsector are addressed by the NCIPP framework outlined in Section 2.1.2.

3. Assess Risk

3.1 Vulnerability Assessment for the Real Estate Subsector

The following factors play a role in the overall vulnerability of a commercial office or residential building to a terrorist attack or other emergency:

- Geographic location;
- Neighborhood or community where a building is located;
- Design and construction of the building; and
- Tenant mix and collective business functions.

Real estate owners and operators may employ a variety of methodologies to develop VAs for their individual properties. Insurance companies also use assessments and methodologies that address vulnerabilities while underwriting risks.

3.2 Risk Assessment

Owners and operators of property in the Real Estate Subsector take the following questions into consideration when evaluating key risk factors:

- Is the property in an urban location in a well-known city?
- Is the property a national or local landmark or icon?
- Is the property a tourist attraction?
- Does the property accommodate a large number of occupants?
- Does the property house sensitive or high-risk tenants?
- Does the property house sensitive or high-risk operations?
- Is the property adjacent to a transportation hub?
- Is the property adjacent to other critical infrastructure?

Owners and operators in the Real Estate Subsector use a variety of risk assessment methodologies, depending on individual circumstances. For example, one large property management firm, in assessing the risks to each of its properties, examines two key elements:

- A normative analysis of the property and its particular location and context from an all-hazards perspective (e.g., the property's location, potential nearby targets that raise the risk for the property, tenant risk, structural issues, and other physical aspects of the property); and
- A threat matrix that identifies the potential specific scenarios that could pose a likely threat to the property. The matrix assigns an assessed probability that a threat could materialize, as well as worst-case consequences.

The results of these assessments are not generally shared with others, although the insurance underwriting process sometimes requires that case-specific information be shared with insurance firms and lenders. Members of the Real Estate Subcouncil have expressed a strong interest in having DHS compile a list of vetted and endorsed risk assessment tools to enhance standardization and uniformity across the CF Sector.

4. Prioritize the Subsector Infrastructure

Members of the Real Estate Subcouncil have expressed considerable concern over making formal decisions on the prioritization of assets (e.g., concluding that one asset is more "at risk" than another). They feel that because the risk environment is so fluid, being based on fluctuating intelligence on current threats, it is neither wise nor fair to permanently brand a particular asset as "high risk."

5. Develop and Implement Protective Programs and Resilience Strategies

Protective measures employed by owners and operators of commercial office and residential buildings are similar to those employed across the CF Sector. Electronic access controls, surveillance cameras, security personnel, and proper lighting are all areas of importance to the Real Estate Subsector. Protective measures are fully voluntary, apart from some building code regulations that focus on structural integrity, safety, and basic emergency response planning (e.g., emergency exits, emergency evacuation plans, and fire prevention mitigation). Protective measures vary widely, depending on the marketplace and State and local requirements.

While a number of commercial office building owners and operators have put rigorous and comprehensive protective measures in place to secure their facilities, many commercial office buildings have limited or no security procedures. In general, only those buildings with high-risk tenants (e.g., foreign government representatives, individual Federal and State government agencies, etc.) or high symbolic recognition (e.g., office towers in high-risk downtown areas of major cities) have extensive security procedures in place. When employed, perimeter security usually consists of alarms, CCTV, exterior barriers, and lighting considerations. Contract and proprietary security personnel may be employed at primary entrances to office buildings, and x-ray and metal detectors may be used for screening visitors and their belongings. Access control measures may differ from floor to floor. Security screening may occur at public entrances, as well as at entrances for high-risk tenants and offices within a building. Deliveries to a building may also be screened. Mail belonging to individual tenants is usually controlled by the U.S. Postal Service and is not generally screened by building security or facility mail handling personnel. Additional deliveries to facilities through the use of courier services (e.g., FedEx, UPS, etc.) is usually unchecked by security personnel and is delivered directly to the addressee inside the tenant space. Maintenance and custodial staff may have to undergo security screening before entering a building.

Common protective measures employed across real estate properties include the following:

- Regular security staff training;
- Loading dock vehicle control;
- Retail arcade access control;
- Lobby access control;
- Elevator access control;
- Stairway access control;
- Building deliveries and contractor access;
- HVAC protection;
- Other critical utility access control;
- Emergency response program; and
- Tenant communications and awareness.

Additional protective measures may be employed during heightened alert levels (e.g., perimeter security control, vehicle inspections, and personnel inspections and bag searches in office lobbies). Some facility owners and operators elect to implement additional security controls in lobby areas utilizing special detection equipment to add additional layers of security to mitigate risk. Such technologies include baggage x-ray; access control and visitor management applications; handheld chemical and radiation detection; biological sampling and comprehensive ultraviolet protection for HVAC filtration; and ion mobility spectrometry for chemicals, explosives, and narcotics detection.

Primary constraints toward instituting or enhancing protective security measures are based on cost and buy-in. Protective measures must meet the needs of the property and should not be viewed as unnecessary or too costly by tenants, operators, and owners.

Real estate owners and operators interact with local police and emergency response officials in the implementation of protective programs and resilience strategies at their facilities. For example, the international Crime Free Multi-Housing Program is an effort that has received increased interest from apartment communities since its inception in 1992. This program is based on a partnership arrangement with local law enforcement that enables a property manager to be certified in crime prevention once specific training has been conducted under the supervision of the local police department. After fulfilling all training components (e.g., management training, law enforcement property assessments, and community awareness training), the property manager can post the International Crime Free Multi-Housing Program sign throughout the apartment community and advertise his or her completion of the program to prospective residents.

The FBI and the USSS may occasionally participate in protective programs based on the level of threat or the type of activities occurring at a particular property. Protective programs offered by DHS and used by the subsector include SAVs, the BZPP, the Federal Hazard Mitigation Programs offered by FEMA, and various DHS training programs (e.g., the Protective Measures Courses, Private Sector Counterterrorism Awareness Workshops, etc.).

Members of the Real Estate Subcouncil have encouraged the Federal Government to act as a clear reference point for private sector owners and operators through the vetting and validation of protective measures, VAs, and risk assessments. Many view the appropriate Federal role as that of a "safe harbor," providing guidance to owners and operators so that they can do the right thing.

5.1 Security Personnel Training

According to the Congressional Research Service (CRS) Report for Congress, *Guarding America: Security Guards and U.S. Critical Infrastructure Protection* (November 2004), there are no Federal requirements for the training of critical infrastructure guards other than airport screeners and nuclear guards. Twenty-two States currently require basic training courses for licensed contract guards. These courses range from 1 hour (Texas) to 24 hours (New York) to 40 hours (California) to 48 hours (Arkansas).

Of those States with training requirements, few specifically require counterterrorism training. Despite the lack of universal, mandatory standards, individual companies have taken it upon themselves to assess their unique risks and to respond accordingly. For example, many companies have instituted robust training procedures, including specific antiterrorism components, which exceed the local jurisdiction's requirements. IP has also invited private security companies to participate in its Protective Measures courses, Private Sector Counterterrorism Awareness workshops, Buffer Zone Protection training programs, and so forth.

State regulations vary regarding criminal background checks for security guards. Sixteen States have no background check regulations. Contract guards' salaries are low and contract guard turnover is high. In the opinion of one large national owner/ operator, increased training and pay alone do not change the fact that a guard's job is frequently not challenging. It is usually not considered a career field and, therefore, attracts low-skilled labor. More advanced and better use of technology could enhance the job, attract better-qualified people, and reduce manpower needs.

Despite the lack of federally mandated training and varying State regulations, the Real Estate Subsector places a heavy emphasis on the proper training of security personnel to secure facilities against a potential attack and handle the aftermath of an attack. Many firms emphasize the use of drills and simulations to help train their personnel on the procedures to be followed in the event of a crisis. For example, NAA sponsored 10 training sessions in the aftermath of the September 11th attacks, with panels involving representatives from industry, DHS, the FBI, and State and local law enforcement agencies. These panels covered topics such as suspicious behaviors and resident screening. In 2005, more than 60 real estate firms participated in the TOPOFF-3 exercise, which involved approximately 10,000 Federal and State officials in a simulated response to a catastrophic incident. The Real Estate Subcouncil was also well-represented during the June 2006 TOPOFF-4 Command Post Exercise.

BOMA of Greater Los Angeles, working with the City of Los Angeles, has established a program called the Accredited Security Organization, which establishes local certifications based on minimum levels of training and the square footage of a building. For example, in those commercial office buildings with more than 1 million rentable square feet, security staff will receive a minimum of 64 hours of training during their first year of service and a minimum of 24 hours of annual training thereafter.

A joint public-private partnership to enhance the security of commercial facilities was developed in the United Kingdom. The City of London Police and the Metropolitan Police joined forces with private security companies across the city to offer counterterrorism awareness training for security officers. The objective was to better protect crowded places, strategic national targets, and commercial/financial facilities. Project Griffin consists of three elements: (1) a counterterrorism awareness day, (2) a weekly conference call between security managers and police updating security guards on crime trends and terrorist threat levels, and (3) the deployment of security officers to work alongside police officers on cordon control in the event of an incident. Four thousand guards in London and 1,500 more across the United Kingdom have been trained, resulting in more than 500 buildings and 500,000 people receiving better protection. Project Griffin has been successfully expanded to other parts of the United Kingdom and was launched internationally in Singapore, South Africa, Hong Kong, and Australia.

In New York City, the police department has developed a public-private partnership called NYPD Shield. This program aims to provide best practices and counterterrorism training opportunities by partnering police officers with private sector security managers.

5.2 Measure Effectiveness

It is difficult for owners and operators of real estate properties to measure the effectiveness of their terrorism prevention measures, although a few companies do audit and/or track some incident trend metrics in an effort to measure the general effectiveness of a protective program (e.g., property thefts, reported breaches of access control protocols, the number of reported access attempts with an invalid ID, and reported suspicious persons and objects).

6. Measure Progress

Each individual facility owner or operator determines the need for protective measures through the use of in-house assessments. This need is then considered along with all of the other facility needs and, depending on the overall availability of resources, is fully funded, partially funded, or not funded. The progress made toward completing the project may be tracked by the individual facility owner or operator; it is not currently being tracked by the subsector.

Because many members of the subcouncil are competitors in the business world and in-house funding for assessments, protective programs, and resilience strategies is specific to a facility or a company/organization, there has not been an immediate development of a subsector-wide methodology for assessing the success or effectiveness of protective programs and resilience strategies. Over time, as the Real Estate Subsector evolves, as specific goals and objectives are created, and as communication mechanisms mature, the methods for monitoring the progress of implementing protective programs and resilience strategies designed to meet goals and objectives should be put into place.

7. Subsector Protection Research and Development

Members of the Real Estate Subcouncil have expressed an interest in R&D with the caveat that technology applications be practical, less obtrusive, and less costly. Property owners and managers are interested in any tools that may enhance protective security as long as they are cost-effective and applicable on a broad scale. Some examples include the following:

- DHS development and/or sponsorship of a blast effects model that would assess the impact of an explosion on a building or facility in order to assist with the implementation of protective measures and provide a common standard for liability;
- Biochemical agent detection;
- Automated CCTV facial recognition of suspected terrorists;
- Real-time and automated identification, verification, and cross-referencing with terrorist watch lists;
- Explosive substances detection for vehicles, persons, packages, and rooms; and
- Minimization of the damaging effects of explosions.

Nevertheless, members have expressed broad skepticism toward the real-world feasibility of these technologies. Subcouncil members have also expressed interest in further analyses of the methodologies employed by suicide bombers and an examination of the use of vehicle-borne improvised explosive devices in other parts of the world.

Annex 7: Retail Subsector

The Retail Subsector comprises a wide range of commercial facilities, ranging from small kiosks to vast shopping centers and malls. In addition to stand-alone locations, retail facilities of varying sizes are located in various commercial facilities (e.g., transportation hubs, hotels, resorts, and office buildings). Given the importance of consumer spending to the U.S. economy, this subsector carries tremendous economic significance, especially in tough economic times.

This annex was prepared with the active participation of members of the Retail Subcouncil. Interviews were conducted with subcouncil members and security professionals representing retail institutions and associations throughout the United States. At the request of the subcouncil, these discussions took place on a not-for-attribution basis in order to encourage candid dialogue.

1. Retail Subsector Profile and Goals

1.1 Retail Profile

Retail facilities are divided into three major categories: enclosed malls, shopping centers/strip malls (e.g., anchor retailers and surrounding shops), and free-standing/high-street establishments. The retail industry is the second largest industry in the United States, with more than 1.6 million establishments conducting $4.6 trillion in annual sales in 2008 and employing about 1 in 5 American workers.[16] The largest retail real estate holders have extensive property holdings, with the top 10 owners controlling more than 1 billion square feet of gross leasable area.

The constant flow of patrons into, around, and out of these establishments frustrates effective and discreet preventive surveillance. It is believed that shoppers in the United States would be reluctant to patronize retail locations that employ highly visible security measures, including numerous armed guards, barbed wire, or concrete barriers. Retailers believe that these security measures would make consumers uneasy, likely cutting into sales and causing economic harm to retailers and the local communities that depend on them. Retail facilities are privately owned; therefore, security measures are the responsibility of the owners and operators, with the government playing only an advisory or limited regulatory role. In large shopping malls with 125 to 300 individual tenants residing in one facility, individual tenants are responsible for their own store's security. As a result, security measures and practices vary widely across the Retail Subsector.

1.1.1 CIKR Partners

As with any broad sector comprised of hundreds of thousands of assets, national associations provide an effective mechanism to represent similar collective interests. The following associations actively participate on the Retail Subcouncil:

---

[16] **www.nrf.com.**

- The National Retail Federation (NRF) represents all aspects of the retail industry. It represents more than 1.6 million retail establishments in the United States. NRF serves as an umbrella organization for more than 100 national, State, and international retail associations;[17]

- The Retail Industry Leaders Association (RILA) member companies include more than 200 retailers,[18] product manufacturers, and service suppliers who operate more than 100,000[19] stores in the United States and account for more than $1.5 trillion in annual sales;[20] and

- The International Council of Shopping Centers (ICSC) is a global trade association for the shopping center industry. Its 70,000 members in the United States, Canada, and other countries include shopping center owners, developers, managers, and retailers, as well as academics and public officials.[21]

Natural and manmade incident information-sharing systems have been created for the Retail Subsector, and mechanisms are being improved on in order to reach a larger share of the subsector. Information is distributed from DHS to subcouncils, retail associations, retailers, and RE-ISAC, which has members in the Retail, Real Estate, and Lodging subsectors. Information is distributed from DHS to the subcouncil. The Retail Subsector has its own subportal on the HSIN portal, which provides members with access to bulletins and alerts from DHS.

1.1.2 Distinguishing Characteristics

The Retail Subsector possesses a number of features that distinguish it from the other CF subsectors.

- **Access and Multiple Access Points:** Retail establishments offer open access to the public without requiring fees, tickets, or reservations. Establishments may have more than one access point for customers, personal vehicles, and delivery trucks.

- **Frequency and Volume of People:** Retail establishments are surrounded daily by a steady flow of traffic because they provide basic necessities to the population. A typical mall, for example, attracts 12 to 25 million visitors per year. In addition to shoppers, retail establishments employ a large number of part-time and full-time employees. In the case of enclosed malls that are landlords to independently owned retail tenants (125 to 300 under one roof), controlling who enters and exits becomes especially difficult. Patrons generally carry bags and packages within shopping facilities, which could easily conceal various types of weapons.

- **Highly Competitive, with Reputations at Stake:** Competition and economic conditions force owners and operators to minimize highly visible or obtrusive protective measures because these can make prospective patrons uneasy. Retailers strive to maintain the highest reputation possible because customers can easily go elsewhere.

- **Dependence on Global Supply Chains:** The retail industry is highly dependent on supply chains that stretch around the globe. Retailers rely on a continuous flow of goods and products, many of which are manufactured overseas and are shipped to the United States, making them vulnerable to supply chain interruption due to port closures, terrorist attacks, or natural disasters. While the U.S. Customs and Border Protection and USCG have taken greater steps since the September 11th attacks to secure ports and inspect overseas shipments, there still remain security gaps and a need for greater coordination among Federal, State, local, and private sector entities. Retail owners and operators emphasize the importance of protecting the security of supply chains, yet they have concerns regarding legislation and regulations that would slow down global trade. The Retail Subsector supports reasonable container inspections (e.g., inspection of cargo that is deemed suspicious versus 100

[17] http://www.nrf.com/modules.php?name=Pages&sp_id=146&pmenu_id=1&mn_type=1.

[18] http://www.rila.org/about/Pages/default.aspx.

[19] http://www.rila.org/about/who/Pages/default.aspx.

[20] http://www.rila.org/about/Pages/default.aspx.

[21] http://www.icsc.org/about/about.php.

percent of the cargo), as well as a Federal Government policy that balances the need for security while allowing the free flow of commerce. The subsector believes that there is currently no single technological solution for supply chain security and that the Federal Government should thoroughly evaluate the use of "smart containers" or "electronic seals," which can be prohibitively expensive and not 100 percent accurate.

- **Retail Stores as Distribution Centers:** The importance of the Retail Subsector extends beyond the potential damage to lives and the economy in the event of a terrorist attack or natural disaster. Retail distribution centers are key resources and many response plans use shopping centers as distribution points, with the assumption that these facilities will still be operational. The retail industry has also proven to be important in the responses to disasters by sharing information and donating supplies, services, and money, as demonstrated during the response to Hurricane Katrina when the retail industry provided essential backup support to FEMA and the Red Cross. Retailers were crucial to logistics before, during, and after Katrina, utilizing their network of stores, trucking fleets, and sophisticated hurricane tracking software in delivering critical supplies.

1.1.3 International Relationships

While the international divisions of the Nation's top retail companies are currently among the fastest-growing components, the economic hardships of 2008 and 2009 have had significant implications for the retail industry in the United States and abroad. As market saturation occurs in overdeveloped areas, emerging markets are of great interest to retailers.

Outside of North America, the areas of greatest new interest are emerging markets such as Brazil, Russia, India, and China. In India, the number of big shopping malls went from zero to more than 100 in the past 5 years.[22]

According to the 2009 A.T. Kearny Global Retail Development Index, which tracks retail investment in 30 emerging countries, Eastern Europe has seen a 5 percent increase since 2008 over Asia and Latin America in the top 20 markets. The Global Retail Development Index ranks India first in retail globalization, followed by Russia and China. The United Arab Emirates has seen the most improvement since 2008, rising from twentieth to fourth.

The Retail Subsector is also concerned with the protection of global supply chains. The subsector relies heavily on imports and foreign manufacturing. For example, retail facilities depend on the continuous flow of goods along lengthy and frequently international supply chains that are highly susceptible to interruption, both from terrorist activity (e.g., a "dirty bomb" attack on a port) and from natural disasters (e.g., hurricanes). A forced closure of the Los Angeles/Long Beach port facilities could result in losses of more than $34 billion.[23] Such an event would result in shortages and attacks on multiple ports could prove crippling to the retail supply lines, and thus to the Nation.

Many U.S. retailers are familiar with the extensive security and protective measures employed by Israeli retail facilities. Israeli shopping malls have been the target of suicide bombers and other terrorist attacks for years and, as a result, security measures at Israeli shopping malls include comprehensive security training, numerous physical security measures, and close cooperation with local law enforcement. In contrast, American shopping malls feature few of these measures. While Israeli mall security is geared toward preventing terrorist attack, American mall security has traditionally focused on theft, vandalism, assault, and other crimes against property and individuals.

Common security measures in Israeli shopping malls include metal detectors, x-ray machines, and armed guards at all entrances; air and water filtration systems to defend against a CBR attack; perimeter fencing and CCTV systems; and armed security, both in uniform and plainclothes. The parking lots and exteriors of the malls are constantly patrolled by armed security guards and patrol cars. Security personnel are evaluated by the police and are subject to a psychiatric examination before

---

[22] Emerging Opportunities in BRIC: Brazil, Russia, India and China. 2009, **http://www.atkearney.com/index.php/Our-expertise/consumer-products-a-retail-research-and-publications.html.**

[23] P. Gordan, J. Moore II, and Q. Pan Richardson, "The Economic Impact of a Terrorist Attack on the Twin Ports of Los Angeles-Long Beach," Center for Risk and Economic Analysis of Terrorism Events (CREATE), **www.usc.edu/dept/create/reports/Report05012.pdf.**

being accepted; they also undergo monthly training. Additionally, Israeli mall security conduct frequent drills for a variety of possible situations, and personnel that consistently fail these drills are laid off. Israeli mall security works closely with the police, conducting joint drills with police and other emergency response teams, and is subject to regular and random police inspections once or twice a month. Additionally, the mall's Chief Security Officer must be approved by the police, attend police seminars, and be in constant contact with local law enforcement officials. These extensive security measures are regulated, but they also stem from the attitude of Israeli customers toward security measures. Because of the very real risk of terrorist attacks in that nation, Israeli shoppers will not go to malls if they believe that security is inadequate. American retailers and shoppers are currently not prepared to adopt Israeli measures; however, some techniques (e.g., recognizing suspicious behavior) are making their way into security guard training in the United States.

1.1.4 Cyber Systems

Cyber systems are a major concern for the retail industry. A significant amount of shopping now occurs over the Internet and cyber attacks on retail Web sites are an important consideration for retailers. The Census Bureau estimates that U.S. retail e-commerce sales for the first quarter of 2009 were $31.7 billion.[24] In addition, ordering processes, supply chain management, electronic transactions and credit card activities, telecommunications, and electronic systems (e.g., store security systems) that utilize the Internet are all vulnerable to a cyber attack. Retail facilities use control systems to monitor and operate HVAC systems, elevators and escalators, lighting, and CCTV. In some cases, manipulation of the systems that control access to entrances and exits at retail facilities may be used to restrict egress after an attack.

1.1.5 Key Issues

Because of the meetings and discussions held with members of the Retail Subsector and associations representing the Retail Subsector, the following issues emerged as areas of concern for the subsector:

- **Response and Business Continuity:** Because retail assets fall within the category of "soft targets," retailers feel that their focus should be on efforts to minimize the effects of a successful attack (e.g., public-private sector emergency response coordination, occupant protection within an attacked facility, more efficient and effective evacuation strategies, and building/glass structural reinforcement strategies). It is crucial for retailers to respond immediately and effectively, to have business continuity/restoration plans in place in order to get their establishments up and running, and to provide some sense of normalcy.

- **Cost:** Fierce competition among retail companies means that any expense, including security, must be economically justifiable. While visible security measures, such as armed guards and bomb-sniffing dogs, may improve security at shopping facilities, studies have shown that such measures increase anxiety among shoppers, driving away business and causing losses to the retailers. Passive security measures, although less effective, are more economically viable. However, many retailers, particularly smaller ones, have not implemented these measures. According to an online poll conducted by *Retail Traffic*, 40 percent of responders stated that the most common reason for not increasing security is the cost, followed by not wanting to scare off customers.

- **Terrorism Insurance:** While the insurance industry was able to pay out the $40 to $70 billion in damages from the September 11th attacks, most insurance companies either refuse to cover damages from terrorist attacks or offer terrorism coverage at very high rates. In 2002, Congress passed the Terrorism Risk Insurance Act, which provided a temporary insurance backstop for terrorism-related insurance claims. The program was extended in late 2005 by the Terrorism Risk Insurance Extension Act through 2007, with several changes to the original act. These changes increased the total damages threshold to trigger the program from $5 million in the original law to $50 million in 2006, and again to $100 million in 2007, and it also increased the share of the costs borne by the insurance companies. The retail industry supports having the Federal Government permanently shoulder at least part of the terrorism insurance burden.

---

[24] http://www.census.gov/retail/#arts.

- **Information Sharing with the Federal Government and Legal Liability:** Members of the Retail Subcouncil have expressed concern over sharing sensitive or proprietary information on assets or security measures. Facility owners and operators are also concerned with the identification of asset vulnerabilities and potential legal liabilities. DHS will utilize the PCII Program and CIPAC to address these concerns and to facilitate information sharing from the Retail Subsector.

  The Support Antiterrorism by Fostering Effective Technologies Act of 2002 (the SAFETY Act) provides liability protection to businesses that provide security products, as well as to their customers and contractors, if these products are found to be effective by the Secretary of Homeland Security.

- **Access to Threat Information:** The Retail Subcouncil continues to work with DHS to provide readily available threat information to the owners and operators of subsector facilities regarding potential terrorist threats or other manmade or natural disasters, including cyber threats. The subsector wants the information to be clear, concise, and provided in a timely manner, as well as providing the source of the threat and threat analyses so that the owners and operators can determine an appropriate level of response to individual threat bulletins. DHS is providing the necessary security clearances to key sector members so that the distribution of threat information does not become constrained by the need to classify specific information. The CF SSA is working with US-CERT to share information about cybersecurity threats to all subsectors, including the Retail Subsector.

1.2 Goals and Objectives

The Retail Subcouncil identified the following goals and objectives:

- Deter and prevent threats of terrorism against retail facilities;

- Protect all assets, employees, and shoppers;

- Enhance training for retail security personnel;

- Prepare for emergencies and engage in all forms of contingency planning;

- Respond to crisis situations while protecting customers, employees, and businesses; and

- Recover from attacks by ensuring business continuity; and

- Focus on responding quickly and effectively, restoring operations, and establishing deterrence.

1.3 Authorities

The Retail Subsector is almost entirely regulated at the State and local levels through building codes geared toward safety requirements. Security concerns have traditionally not played a significant role in these codes. Federal regulation is mostly limited to safety-related OSHA requirements.

2. Identify Assets and Facilities

Individual companies and associations within the Retail Subsector maintain inventories of their facilities for various reasons (e.g., marketing and financial purposes), but not for security or protective programs. Many owners and operators of buildings in the Retail Subsector are willing to share facility vulnerability information on an informal basis with trusted local first responders. DHS will utilize the PCII Program and CIPAC to facilitate the formal disclosure of such information to DHS in a building-specific format.

The subsector is reasonably confident that key State and local officials are aware of the "critical" retail assets within their jurisdictions. This same understanding applies to DHS's knowledge of "nationally critical" real estate facilities. The SSA will develop a process for obtaining asset information from those building owners and operators who are willing to submit asset information to DHS.

Many of the larger corporate members of the Retail Subsector have advanced logistical systems that can highlight specific items and the quantities purchased. These purchases can then be compared against a Hazardous Materials List created by the FBI and the Bureau of Alcohol, Tobacco, Firearms, and Explosives (ATF) to determine whether a purchase exceeds what is normally bought or includes large quantities of more than one of the listed items. Such purchases can then be flagged and shared with law enforcement, the JTTF, and the NICC. Additionally, members of the Retail Subsector utilize the Bomb-Making Materials Awareness Program cards.

The assets and facilities of the Retail Subsector are addressed by the NCIPP framework outlined in Section 2.1.2.

3. Assess Risks

While there is no established general vulnerability and risk assessment methodology for the Retail Subsector, there are several factors that play a role in affecting the vulnerability of any retail facility to terrorist attack or other emergencies:

- Geographic location;
- Neighborhood or community where the establishment is located;
- Design and construction of a building; and
- Numbers and flow of people.

According to the Retail Subcouncil, all retailers perform some kind of in-house risk assessment based on their individual needs. Owners and operators in the Retail Subsector do not use standardized risk assessment methodologies for their facilities; instead, they use different frameworks for each of their properties, depending on their individual situations and characteristics.

Members of the Retail Subcouncil take the following questions into consideration when evaluating key risk factors:

- Is the retail facility in an urban location in a well-known city?
- Is the retail facility a national or local landmark or icon?
- Is the retail facility a tourist attraction?
- Does the retail facility accommodate a large number of patrons?
- Does the retail facility sell high-risk or hazardous materials?
- Is the retail facility adjacent to a transportation hub?
- Is the retail facility adjacent to other critical infrastructure?
- Does the retail facility accommodate a large number of employees?
- Does the retail facility carry a large amount of inventory or high-value inventory?

4. Prioritize the Subsector Infrastructure

The Retail Subsector does not currently have a methodology or process for prioritizing its assets because individual stores and shopping centers are privately owned. Members of the Retail Subcouncil have expressed considerable concern over making formal decisions on the prioritization of assets (e.g., concluding that one asset is more "at risk" than another). They feel that because the risk environment is so fluid based on fluctuating intelligence on current threats, it is neither wise nor fair to permanently brand a particular asset as "high risk."

However, the CF Sector has determined that rapid restoration of retail centers following a disaster is vital to community revitalization and resilience. Prioritization during an incident can help to focus planning, foster coordination, and support effective resource allocation and incident management decisions. Resource identification and prioritization supports the sector's goal of having systems in place to ensure a timely response to and recovery from natural or manmade incidents.

5. Develop and Implement Protective Programs and Resilience Strategies

The protective measures used by the retail industry are similar to those used across the CF Sector. The most common security measures implemented at retail establishments are as follows:

- Installation of surveillance equipment and cameras;
- Training for security personnel and the hiring of new security personnel;
- Preparation of evacuation and security plans;
- Good lighting;
- Well-placed phones that allow instant contact with mall security;
- Installation of shatterproof glass;
- Placement of concrete planters around entrances and plazas to deter car and truck bombs;
- Improved coordination with local law enforcement and emergency services;
- Patrol vehicles; and
- Preparation of business continuity and operational contingency plans.

5.1 Security Guard Training

According to the CRS Report for Congress, *Guarding America: Security Guards and U.S. Critical Infrastructure Protection* (November 2004), there are no Federal requirements for the training of critical infrastructure guards other than airport screeners and nuclear facility guards. Twenty-two States require basic training for licensed contract guards (e.g., 1 hour in Texas, 24 hours in New York, 40 hours in California, and 48 hours in Arkansas).

Of the States with training requirements, few specifically require counterterrorism training. Despite the lack of universal, mandatory standards, individual companies have taken it upon themselves to assess their unique risks and to respond accordingly. For example, many companies have instituted robust training procedures, including specific antiterrorism components, which exceed the local jurisdiction's requirements. IP has also invited private security companies to participate in its Soft Target Awareness course.

State regulations vary regarding criminal background checks for security guards. Sixteen States have no background check regulations.

Contract guard turnover is high. Two-thirds of retailers have no security guards at all, particularly those located outside of shopping malls and centers.

The International Council of Shopping Centers, in cooperation with The George Washington University, recently launched a 16-hour interactive computer training program to train mall security personnel with recognition, avoidance, isolation, and notification techniques when confronted with potential weapons of mass destruction. Presently, 53 companies nationwide participate and almost 9,000 personnel have received the training.

6. Measure Progress

Each individual facility owner or operator determines a need for protective measures through the use of in-house assessments. This need is then considered along with other facility needs and, depending on the overall availability of resources, is fully funded, partially funded, or not funded. The progress made toward completing the project may be tracked by the individual facility owner or operator; it is not currently being tracked by the subsector.

Because many members of the subcouncil are competitors in the business world and in-house funding for assessments, protective programs, and resilience strategies is specific to a facility or a company/organization, there has not been an immediate development of a subsector-wide methodology for assessing the success or effectiveness of protective programs and resilience strategies. Over time, as the Retail Subsector evolves, as specific goals and objectives are created, and as communication mechanisms mature, the methods for monitoring the progress of implementing protective programs and resilience strategies designed to meet goals and objectives should be put into place.

7. Research and Development

Individual retailers have identified several technologies that effectively enhance security at retail facilities. These include facial recognition software, license plate screening, an up-to-date terrorist watch list, and weapon detection. Other promising technologies, some originally developed for airport and government facility security, include video surveillance networks run on Internet protocols, which would allow offsite security officers and managers (e.g., at the corporate headquarters) to use the system; high-quality video cameras capable of resolving images as small as a fingernail; handheld cameras that scan using radio waves, allowing differentiation among objects with a high liquid content (e.g., human beings) and other objects (e.g., guns, knives, explosive belts); biometric and facial recognition devices for securing restricted areas (e.g., utility rooms or the roof); and wireless technology, allowing cameras and call boxes to be placed easily in various locations.

Retail Subcouncil members have noted that the range of technologies for security enhancements in the marketplace is quite broad and sometimes overwhelming. The subcouncil has suggested that it would be helpful for the Federal Government to provide assistance in identifying sensible technologies for the subsector to invest in while steering clear of those products that do not work. The industry welcomes partnerships with the Federal Government and would like the Government to facilitate the sharing of technology information between Government entities (e.g., military technology, if applicable) and the private sector.

Annex 8: Sports Leagues Subsector

The Sports Leagues Subsector represents those sports leagues and teams that utilize stadiums, arenas, and motor racetracks where people meet for the purpose of viewing sports events. The facilities utilized by this subsector operate on the principle of open public access, meaning that the general public can move freely throughout these facilities without the deterrent of highly visible security barriers. The majority of the facilities utilized by the sports leagues and teams are owned and operated by local governments, local authorities, or the private sector. (Some facilities are owned by individual sports teams.) There is minimal interaction with the Federal Government and other regulatory entities over the operations of these facilities. The sports leagues work to provide a safe environment for fans and teams in those facilities owned by the teams, as well as in those facilities utilized by the leagues and teams. For the most part, facility owners and operators (whether local government, local authority, or private sector) are responsible for assessing and mitigating their specific facility vulnerabilities and practicing prudent risk management and mitigation measures.

This annex was prepared with the active participation of members of the Sports Leagues Subcouncil, as well as individual sports leagues. The information contained in this annex reflects the current activities employed by the sports leagues to provide a safe environment where the public can enjoy sporting events. This annex will be updated as the protective status of facilities within the Sports Leagues Subsector changes over time.

1. Sports Leagues Subsector Profile and Goals

1.1 Sports Leagues Profile

The Sports Leagues Subsector represents those sports leagues and teams that utilize or own facilities that are also part of the Public Assembly Subsector. These facilities share many of the same characteristics; demographics; and, in many cases, owner–management relationships (i.e., league owned and operated, privately owned and operated, publicly owned and operated, or publicly owned and privately operated) as Public Assembly Subsector facilities. The types of associations/leagues that are active members of the Sports Leagues Subcouncil include the Indy Racing League (IRL), Major League Baseball (MLB), Major League Soccer (MLS), NASCAR, the National Basketball Association (NBA), the National Football League (NFL), the National Hockey League (NHL), the United States Tennis Association (USTA), the National Tennis Center, the National Collegiate Athletic Association (NCAA), and ESPN.

- **Indy Racing League:** IRL is the sanctioning body of the predominately oval-based, open-wheel racing series in the United States. The centerpiece race is the Indianapolis 500. The league consists of two series—the IndyCar Series (synonymous with the Indy Racing League) and the Firestone Indy Lights Series (a developmental series for the IndyCar). IRL conducts events in the United States, Canada, Japan, and, in 2010, Brazil. The Indianapolis Motor Speedway covers more than 559 acres, with a combined seating capacity of more than 400,000 people.

- **Major League Baseball:** MLB is composed of 30 teams, 14 in the American League and 16 in the National League. Spring training begins in February, and the season ends with the World Series in late October. During spring training, teams train at ball parks located in either Florida or Arizona, and play exhibition games through the Grapefruit and Cactus leagues. Major league teams play or practice in ball parks or stadiums that are operated under various owner–management relationships.

  Minor League Baseball (MiLB) teams are either independently owned or owned by a major league team. All players are assigned by their major league affiliates. Ownership and management models of the ball parks and stadiums utilized by MiLB teams are as varied as the MLB teams' owner–management relationships.

- **Major League Soccer:** MLS will have 16 teams in 2010, with 8 teams each in the Eastern and Western Conferences. MLS will expand by two more teams in 2011—Portland and Vancouver. Each team plays a 30-game schedule, with the regular season opening in March and ending in October. The MLS Cup playoffs run from late October to November. MLS is structured as a single, limited liability company (single entity). In the single-entity business structure, club operators own a financial stake in the league, not just their individual team.

- **Soccer United Marketing (SUM):** SUM, a soccer business company in North America, holds the exclusive rights to the most important soccer properties in the region, including all commercial rights to MLS; the United States Soccer Federation; promotional and marketing rights to Mexican National Team games played in the United States; the marketing and promotion of the CONCACAF Gold Cup™; and marketing, promotional, and broadcast rights to the eight-team Mexican club tournament InterLiga™. SUM also manages promotional and marketing rights in the United States for Mexico's sports team, Club Deportivo Guadalajara (Chivas).

- **National Association for Stock Car Auto Racing (NASCAR):** The NASCAR National Touring Series schedules comprise events across the United States and Canada. Beginning in February at the Daytona International Speedway and concluding in November at the Homestead–Miami Speedway, the Sprint Cup Series, Nationwide Series, and Camping World Truck Series visit a combined total of 30 tracks, including Circuit Gilles Villeneuve in Montreal. Races are held at a variety of track types, including short tracks, intermediate tracks, superspeedways, and road courses. The majority of the events are held at facilities operated by International Speedway Corporation or Speedway Motorsports, Inc.

  The NASCAR International Series includes the Canadian Tire Series, which runs from May through October. The NASCAR Canadian Tire Series is the premier racing series in Canada and home to the nation's top driving talent. NASCAR's Mexico Series brings the thrills and excitement of NASCAR racing on oval tracks and road courses to fans throughout Mexico.

  NASCAR's Regional and Local Series provides family-friendly entertainment featuring grassroots racing in a setting that is close to home. Consisting of dozens of tracks on the regional and local levels throughout North America, NASCAR Home Tracks are the foundation of NASCAR and an important part of the NASCAR experience. These include the following:

  - Camping World Series: Racing in two regions of the country—east and west—the Camping World Series is the premier regional racing series in American motorsports.

  - Whelen Modified Tour: The Whelen Modified Tour holds races throughout New Hampshire, Pennsylvania, Massachusetts, Connecticut, and New York on tracks ranging in size from a quarter mile to the 1.058-mile New Hampshire Motor Speedway.

  - Whelen Southern Modified Tour: The Whelen Southern Modified Tour was established in 2005 and is a close cousin to the northern-based Whelen Modified Tour. Races take place in the Southeastern United States, including stops in North Carolina and Virginia.

  - Whelen All-American Series: With racing at more than 50 tracks throughout North America, this series' drivers compete for local track championships, State titles, and positions in the prestigious national standings.

- **National Basketball Association (NBA):** NBA membership is divided into two conferences, each with three divisions. The Eastern Conference consists of the Atlantic Division, the Central Division, and the Southwestern Division. The Western

Conference consists of the Northwestern Division, the Pacific Division, and the Southwestern Division. Each division has 5 teams for a total of 30 teams. Training camp begins in October with the regular season beginning the first week in November and ending in April, followed by the play-offs, which end in June. Games are played in arenas, sports centers, and other venues where the arrangement of the owner or operator for the NBA games varies from venue to venue.

- **National Football League (NFL):** NFL teams are divided into two conferences: the American Football Conference and the National Football Conference (NFC). Each conference is then further divided into four divisions consisting of four teams each: East, West, North, and South. During the NFL's regular season, each team plays 16 games over a 17-week period, generally from September to January. At the end of each regular season, the six best teams from each conference play in the NFL playoffs, which is a 12-team single-elimination tournament. This culminates with the Super Bowl, which is held at a pre-selected site (typically in a city that hosts an NFL team or a popular college stadium). NFL teams play or practice in stadiums that are operated under various types of owner–management relationships.

- **National Hockey League (NHL):** The NHL consists of 30 teams in 2 conferences and 6 divisions. The Eastern Conference includes the Atlantic Division, the Northeast Division, and the Southeast Division. The Western Conference includes the Central Division, the Northwest Division, and the Pacific Division (five teams each). At the end of the regular winter season, the top teams in each division engage in a play-off (best-of-seven-games series) for the Stanley Cup. The playing season runs from October to the beginning of April. Hockey games are played at arenas, civic centers, and other venues where the arrangement of the owner or operator for the hockey games varies from venue to venue.

- **U.S. Tennis Association (USTA):** USTA is the national governing body for the sport of tennis and the leader in promoting and developing the sport's growth on every level in the United States, from local communities to the international professional contest, the U.S. Open. It oversees three professional tour events, 94 Pro Circuit events nationwide, and all operations of the USTA Billie Jean King National Tennis Center (NTC), and manages and selects the U.S. teams for the Davis Cup, the Fed Cup, the Olympics, and the Paralympic Games.

  USTA is the largest tennis organization in the world, with 17 geographical sections, more than 700,000 individual members and 7,000 organizational members, thousands of volunteers, and a professional staff dedicated to growing the game. The Professional Tennis Division manages all aspects of USTA's involvement in the professional sport, including the U.S. Open—the world's most attended annual sporting event—and the Olympus U.S. Open Series, which links 10 summer tournaments to the U.S. Open.

  The USTA Billie Jean King NTC is the largest public tennis facility in the world, and covering 46.5 acres. It has a total of 46 courts for play—34 outdoor courts (not including the Arthur Ashe Stadium, the Louis Armstrong Stadium, and the Grandstand Stadium) and an additional 12 indoor courts that are available year-round to the public. In addition to the U.S. Open, the NTC hosts many tournaments throughout the year and conducts tennis camps throughout the summer. Located in Flushing Meadows Corona Park, it is operated by USTA year-round, pursuant to a long-term lease between USTA and the City of New York. Other venues where recreational and professional tennis are played have various owner/operator arrangements.

- **National Collegiate Athletic Association (NCAA):** NCAA is a voluntary association of about 1,281 institutions, conferences, organizations, and individuals that organizes the athletic programs of many colleges and universities in the United States and Canada.

  In August 1973, the current three-division setup of Division I, Division II, and Division III was adopted by the NCAA membership in a special convention. Under NCAA rules, Division I and Division II schools can offer scholarships to athletes for playing a sport. Division III schools may not offer any athletic scholarships. Generally, larger schools compete in Division I and smaller schools in Divisions II and III. Division I football was further divided into I-A and I-AA in 1978. Subsequently, the term "Division I-AAA" was added to delineate Division I schools that do not field a football program at all. In 2006, Divisions I-A and I-AA were renamed the Football Bowl Subdivision (FBS) and the Football Championship Subdivision (FCS), respectively.

Sports sanctioned by the NCAA include basketball, baseball (men), softball (women), football (men), cross country, field hockey (women), bowling (women), golf, fencing (coeducational), lacrosse, soccer, gymnastics, rowing (women only), volleyball, ice hockey, water polo, rifle (coeducational), tennis, skiing (coeducational), track and field, swimming and diving, and wrestling (men).

1.1.1 Best Practices

A majority of the sports leagues have developed best practices security guides that are used by the teams and shared with the facilities where they play. These guides utilize information contained in IAAM's Best Practices Guide, as well as in guides developed by local first responders and law enforcement. The CF SSA has partnered with the Sports Leagues Subcouncil to develop a Protective Measures Guide for use by Sports Leagues Subsector members. In most instances, the sports leagues are merely tenants in a facility, so their best practices are simply guidelines that the facility may choose to follow. In order to encourage the use of their best practices security guides, some sports leagues and teams include a clause in their contracts that a facility must utilize their best practices security guides. Verification is accomplished through assessments conducted by the sports leagues. RSAT, which has a module for stadiums and arenas, is available to facility owners and the sports leagues. The facility owner is responsible for implementation of protective programs, resilience strategies, and installation of security systems.

Many sports league teams work with facility owners to develop guides specific to each facility's needs and to provide information and direction to facility staff on operations during sporting events, as well as procedures to follow when responding to safety and emergency situations. Visiting teams usually follow the security best practices of the home team. Some leagues employ their own security representatives in the city of each respective team to conduct a walk-through with the facility security director before each game; this walk-through includes an inspection of security and infrastructure systems, and verification that the sports league's best practices security guide is being utilized. Many sports leagues have security staff that meet on a regular basis to review facility assessments and best practices across facilities and teams to regularly update best practices security guides.

The security best practices employed by most of the minor league teams are the result of the influence of the major league teams, which either own or have some affiliation with the minor league teams. Best practices security guides are shared between major and minor league teams and the facility owner responsible for the implementation of protective programs, resilience strategies, and the installation of security systems.

While traveling, most sports league teams utilize security agents who act as liaisons with hotels and bus companies to ensure that security is in place for the teams. Likewise, sports league teams contract with major airline carriers and work with TSA to screen luggage, equipment, and the players.

Security staffing is usually the responsibility of the facility owner or operator, but this depends on the relationship between the owner or operator of the facility and the local government. Security may be provided by the sports league, by the facility, or by local law enforcement. If a sporting event has been classified as NSSE, then the Federal Government also provides security. During high-profile major sporting events, security may include bomb sweeps and air monitoring.

On December 19, 2008, the NFL's *Best Practices for Stadium Security* was granted Safety Act approval. These guidelines for stadium security management are designed to deter and defend against terrorist attacks at sports stadiums. They include standards for non-game-day operations, game-day operations, and threat assessments and emergency plans. These guidelines also include the hiring, vetting, and training of personnel used to provide the services.

1.1.2 Critical Infrastructure and Key Resources Partners

The Sports Leagues Subcouncil has aggressively worked toward developing relationships with all Federal, State, and local governments. This includes DHS, State and local law enforcement, first responders, and emergency medical personnel. The Sports

Leagues Subcouncil also has an excellent relationship with the USSS, ATF, ICE, the Civil Support Teams in the National Guard, and the U.S. Marshals as a result of the many sporting events that have national recognition.

The Sports Leagues Subcouncil has shared information with other CF subcouncils and it will continue to do so in the future. This subsector works closely with the Public Assembly Subsector because these two subsectors share many of the same facilities.

1.1.3 Common Distinguishing Characteristics

The Sports Leagues Subsector possesses a number of features that distinguish it from the other CF subsectors.

- **Owner–Lessee Agreements:** In most situations, another entity (e.g., a local government or authority) owns the facility where sports teams hold their events. Although there are some sports teams that own their facility, this is not the norm. Likewise, the operation of these facilities may be handled either by the owner or by an organization or company other than the owner. In many cases, these facilities are also considered multipurpose in that different sporting events (e.g., basketball and ice hockey, baseball and football), as well as other activities (e.g., trade shows, conventions, conferences, and concerts), are held in the same facility. The facility owner is responsible for implementation of protective programs, resilience strategies, and the installation of security systems.

- **Emergency Shelters:** The Sports Leagues Subsector utilizes facilities that may be designated as a mega-shelter and used to house evacuees from a major disaster area. These facilities may also act as temporary shelter for displaced individuals or as an emergency services command center for local and Federal first responders. This may impact the sports leagues' utilization of the facility.

- **Security:** As stated above, the Sports Leagues Subsector has multiple owner/operator relationships that reflect the security operations and responsibilities at each facility utilized by sports leagues and teams. Some sports league facilities are publicly owned and operated. In most instances, the security of these facilities is the responsibility of the local law enforcement jurisdiction. For publicly owned and privately operated facilities, security may be contracted out to a private company. Sports league facilities that are privately owned and operated are more likely to utilize a private security company. Some local jurisdictions require the use of their own law enforcement officers, even though the facility is not publicly owned. Other facilities utilize local law enforcement officers because of the potential liability associated with security at events. Therefore, the security planned for a particular event relies on the security arrangement of the owner or operator.

- **Command Centers:** Many of the sports league facilities that play host to a large number of visitors utilize a command center to monitor activities within the facility and to serve as an operations center in the event of a manmade or natural incident. Although each command center varies in sophistication, its primary function is to serve as a central location where facility personnel, emergency responders, and law enforcement can work together to respond to an incident. In many instances, facility system controls, communications, and monitoring equipment are controlled by the command center.

1.1.4 International Relationships

There are many international facets to the Sports Leagues Subsector. Both MLB and the NHL have teams in Canada. Every MLB team has an academy in the Dominican Republic and in Venezuela. Formed in 1989, Major League Baseball International (MLBI) is focused on the worldwide growth of baseball through game development, broadcasting, special events, sponsorship, and licensing. MLBI currently has offices in New York, London, Sydney, and Tokyo. As baseball's popularity continues to grow around the world, so will the role of MLBI.

NASCAR has held exhibition races in Japan and Australia and sanctions races in Canada and Mexico. The IRL has also sanctioned races in Japan.

SUM created SuperLiga, the innovative professional tournament between MLS and Mexico's First Division clubs that debuted in 2007, as well as the Pan-Pacific Championship, an international soccer tournament that crowns the top club from the

Pan-Pacific region. In 2008, SUM entered into a long-term partnership with FC Barcelona, which includes tours with the Spanish club.

The NBA sponsors Basketball without Borders, a global basketball development and community outreach program. Each Basketball without Borders camp features current and former NBA players and team personnel acting as coaches to promote education, leadership, character, healthy living, and HIV/AIDS awareness and prevention.

The NFL has taken teams overseas for exhibition games in the spring and during the pre-season. The NFL plays at least one regular season game abroad. In recent years, the game has been played in London, England. The NFL is also a member of OSAC, a Federal Advisory Committee with a U.S. Government Charter to promote security cooperation between the American government and private sector interests worldwide.

When traveling overseas, sports leagues usually employ their own security programs and staff, supplementing their programs with the security program of their host country, their host team, or their host city.

1.1.5 Cyber Systems

The Sports Leagues Subsector cyber infrastructure systems include business systems, control systems, access control systems, and warning and alert systems. These cyber systems are utilized for day-to-day operations such as ticketing, reservations, property management, human resources and financial management, controlling HVAC systems, elevator and escalator controls, lighting, and CCTV.

Conversations with members of the Sports Leagues Subcouncil did not result in the identification of any operations that are dependent on cyber assets on a league-wide basis. Each individual sports league and stadium, arena, or motor racetrack utilized by sports leagues employs cyber systems; however, any incident affecting the operation of one sports league's facilities is not likely to affect a broader group or a broader element within the subsector. As with the Public Assembly Subsector, the facilities utilized by the Sports Leagues Subsector would be affected by any sort of mass Internet failure.

While sporting events are held as live spectator sports, they also have come to rely on radio and television as a primary source of revenue. The disruption of telecommunications before or during a televised sporting event would have an impact on the television viewing audience and would be costly to advertisers.

The Internet is widely used by sports leagues for marketing merchandise, selling tickets, and offering live and archived video Webcasts of games. The loss of Internet services would have a financial impact on sports leagues.

1.1.6 Key Issues

As a result of the meetings and discussions held with members of the Sports Leagues Subcouncil and individual sports leagues, the following issues emerged as areas of concern for the subsector:

- **Temporary Flight Restrictions:** The Federal Aviation Administration (FAA) can issue a Temporary Flight Restriction (TFR) in the proximity of stadiums and other sporting events from 1 hour before the scheduled time of the event until 1 hour after the event has ended, thus prohibiting all aircraft and parachute operations below 3,000 feet within a 3-nautical-mile radius of any stadium having a seating capacity of at least 30,000 people in which an MLB, NFL, NCAA Division I football, or major motor speedway event (Sprint Cup Series) is occurring. The FAA can also issue a more restrictive TFR during the Super Bowl. A TFR has also been granted by the FAA for the USTA U.S. Open tournament.

  The Sports Leagues Subcouncil would like to see TFRs be made more restrictive in order to provide stadiums and arenas with increased protection from a potential aircraft attack. In many instances, variances are given to advertisers and news media. The Sports Leagues Subcouncil believes that the TFR should be expanded to include both pre- and post-season games and should extend restrictive operations to include a period greater than 1 hour before and after the event. During major sporting events, venues fill up many hours ahead of time, and it takes several hours to empty a venue after an event. The Sports Leagues Subcouncil also believes that a 3,000-foot elevation and a 3-nautical-mile radius should be extended to provide additional response time for preempting an aircraft attack.

- **Staff Turnover:** There is a high turnover rate among the event staff hired for the majority of sporting events. This creates a situation where newly hired individuals may not have adequate training to be knowledgeable about the facility's layout and its emergency response procedures. It also creates a situation where background checks may not always be conducted prior to hiring. There is a need to motivate event staff to remain throughout the season and to provide them with adequate equipment and training.

- **End-of-Event Security:** There is a significant amount of effort placed on security procedures and practices prior to a sporting event. However, once an event has ended, the same level of vigilance may not be applied to attendees exiting the facility or to those individuals who may want to enter the facility at that time. In some instances, security and event staff have been assigned other duties or have left the facility. With the mass exodus of so many people at one time, there is an equal need both before and after the event for crowd and vehicle traffic control.

- **Funding for Assessment Findings:** The majority of sports leagues and teams have lease agreements with the stadiums, arenas, and motor racetracks that they utilize. Therefore, they have no control over the funding for protective programs and resilience strategies at these facilities. Funding to address assessment deficiencies must come from the facility's owner or the local municipality.

- **The Importance of Response Authority:** Each sporting event should have an emergency response document that clearly identifies who has the authority to make decisions with regard to a manmade or natural incident. This authority includes such actions as halting the event, dealing with the containment of the facility, evacuating the facility, or coordinating shelter-in-place. The information needed to make relevant decisions, the authority needed to implement them, and the resources needed to carry them out must be clearly stated and agreed to by all parties involved (e.g., the sports club, the facility owner, and State and local governments).

- **Access to Threat Information:** The Sports Leagues Subcouncil continues to work with DHS to provide readily available threat information to the owners and operators of subsector facilities regarding potential terrorist threats or other manmade or natural disasters, including cyber threats. The subsector wants the information to be clear, concise, and provided in a timely manner, as well as providing the source of the threat and threat analyses so that the owners and operators can determine an appropriate level of response to individual threat bulletins. DHS is providing the necessary security clearances to key subsector members so that the distribution of threat information does not become constrained by the need to classify specific information. The CF SSA is working with US-CERT to share information about cybersecurity threats to all subsectors, including the Sports League Subsector.

- **Information Sharing with the Federal Government and Legal Liability:** Members of the Sports Leagues Subcouncil have expressed concern over sharing sensitive or proprietary information on assets or security measures. Facility owners and operators are also concerned with the identification of asset vulnerabilities and potential legal liabilities. DHS has been successful in utilizing the PCII Program and CIPAC (see chapter 8) to address these concerns and to facilitate information sharing from the Sports Leagues Subsector.

- **Relationships with Local Law Enforcement:** A sound, ongoing working relationship with local first responders (particularly with law enforcement, emergency services, and fire department officials) is essential for effective security. The quality of these relationships varies from city to city and from facility to facility; however, they have a considerable impact on the confidence of facility owners and operators during their emergency response planning. Understanding the roles and responsibilities of local law enforcement at each sporting facility is essential for a timely response to a manmade or natural incident.

1.2 Sports Leagues Goals and Objectives

Discussions with individual members of the various sports leagues have revealed that all of the sports leagues want the facilities they utilize to be made safe and secure for all attendees, employees, and teams. This can be accomplished through the implementation of protective programs and resilience strategies across the subsector and at each sports facility. As stated previously, the sports leagues utilize facilities that are also part of the Public Assembly Subsector. Therefore, the goals and objectives outlined in Annex 5: Public Assembly, are also embraced by the Sports Leagues Subsector. Some of those goals include the following:

- Make sports league facilities safe and secure for all attendees and employees;
- Access threat information (manmade or natural) in real time;
- Be aware of and have access to technologies that will allow sports league facilities to receive operational updates on all areas of safety and security;
- Invest funds in technology and R&D;
- Invest funds in the appropriate building hardening, vehicle intrusion, and ram protection;
- Update and be aware of the latest threats and events that may affect sports league facilities; and
- Communicate with other CF subcouncils and utilize the information and initiatives that they have implemented, as appropriate.

1.3 Authorities

The Sports Leagues Subsector is almost entirely regulated at the State and local levels through building codes geared toward life safety requirements. Security concerns have not traditionally played a significant role in these codes. Federal regulation is mostly limited to safety-related OSHA requirements or to NFPA codes. Accordingly, the primary regulatory authorities over the facilities utilized by the Sports Leagues Subsector are State and local governments rather than the Federal Government.

There are several key authorities that govern the Sports Leagues Subsector's approach to infrastructure protection. They include NFPA 1600, Standard on Disaster/Emergency Management and Business Continuity Programs, and FEMA's Reference Manual to Mitigate Potential Terrorist Attacks Against Buildings.

2. Identify Assets and Facilities

The sports leagues do not own the majority of the facilities that they utilize for their sporting events. In many instances, they are owned by local governments or authorities. Therefore, the sports leagues have no authority or control over these leased facilities. There are also many training facilities associated with each of these sports leagues, as well as facilities utilized by other Sports Leagues Subcouncil members. Information associated with these facilities is provided to DHS through the Public Assembly Subsector.

The assets and facilities of the Sports Leagues Subsector are addressed by the NCIPP framework outlined in Section 2.1.2.

3. Assess Risks

Individual facility owners within the Public Assembly Facilities Subsector may have taken various measures to assess risk; however, there is no Sports Leagues Subsector-wide risk assessment process. Individual sports leagues may utilize their security best practices guides (or those of local law enforcement) to conduct risk self-assessments of the facilities owned by and leased to the sports teams.

The Sports Leagues Subsector is aware of RSAT, which contains a stadium and arena module. However, it is up to a facility owner to utilize the RSAT process and to choose to share the information with DHS.

Some of the sports leagues do classify or rank the facilities that they utilize based on criteria to determine which facilities are the most visible or distinctive. Criteria examples include the following:

- Type of facility;
- Size of the facility;
- Number of people attending a sporting event at the facility;
- Type of sporting event; and
- Location and surrounding areas of the facility.

4. Prioritize the Sports Leagues Infrastructure

Facilities utilized by the Sports Leagues Subsector are prioritized according to the methodology used by the Public Assembly Subsector.

5. Develop and Implement Protective Programs and Resilience Strategies

The Sports Leagues Subcouncil has a vested interest in the operations and security of the sports facility during a sporting event. Many sports leagues have developed security best practices guides that they implement or the facility implements before, during, and after a sporting event. These guides may provide security best practices that are unique to the sporting event or that supplement existing security best practices at the facility. The Sports Leagues Subcouncil works closely with the Public Assembly Subcouncil with regard to facility operations and security because many of the assets utilized by the Sports Leagues Subsector are similar to or, in many instances, actually are Public Assembly Subsector facilities.

The CF SSA has partnered with the Sports Leagues Subcouncil to develop a Protective Measures Guide for use by Sports Leagues Subsector members. The guide incorporates participating sports leagues' best practices, which have been shared with DHS by subsector members. The guide addresses perimeter control and stadium security, gate access and management, credentialing, setting up a command post, protocols for threat assessments, emergency plans, event day security, and post-event evaluations.

IAAM's Safety and Security Task Force has developed four security planning guides to address the need for selecting security practices based on the levels of threat or the vulnerability matrixes associated with the DHS HSAS. The Safety and Security Best Practices Security Planning Guide for Arenas, Stadiums, and Amphitheaters is particularly relevant to facilities utilized by sports leagues.

DHS and the FBI issue Joint Special Assessments and Joint Information Bulletins to members of the Sports Leagues Subcouncil that address possible terrorist activities as they relate to the Sports Leagues Subsector. Members of the subcouncil, along with other CIKR partners associated with the Sports Leagues Subsector, are also able to obtain, analyze, and share information through HSIN. Information derived and shared through HSIN supports protective programs and resilience strategies established by the Sports Leagues Subsector.

While the paragraphs above describe various programmatic protective programs and resilience strategies that are in place or are available to the Sports Leagues Subsector, there are also many protective measures that can be applied at the facilities that are utilized by sports leagues. Electronic access controls, surveillance cameras, security personnel, proper lighting, emergency response planning, and visitor/bag screening are all protective measures designed to improve the security of these facilities. Perimeter security may consist of alarms, CCTV, and exterior barriers. Facility staff and venue/sports league personnel may utilize separate entrances from the public entrances. Security screening may occur at public entrances, as well as at the entrances to offices, locker rooms, dressing rooms, and storage areas within the facility. Deliveries to the facility may also be screened. Badges may be required to control access into various areas of the facility. Also, security screening of security, maintenance, concession, and custodial staff may be required.

Many sports leagues and their teams encourage the facilities that they utilize to develop operational manuals, emergency action plans, and evacuation plans that outline the roles and responsibilities of the sports teams, facility staff, law enforcement, emergency response personnel, and others when dealing with a natural disaster or a terrorist attack. The CF SSA has prepared an evacuation planning guide for stadiums for use by both the Public Assembly and the Sports Leagues subsectors. Many of these documents are written not only to respond to a particular incident, but also to describe changes in security procedures as the DHS threat level changes.

Protective programs and resilience strategies offered by DHS and utilized by the Sports Leagues Subsector include SAVs, the BZPP, RSAT, the Federal Hazard Mitigation Programs offered by FEMA, and various DHS training programs (e.g., the Soft Target Awareness course).

6. Measure Progress

Each individual facility owner or operator determines the need for protective measures through the use of in-house assessments. This need is then considered along with other facility needs and, depending on the overall availability of resources, is fully funded, partially funded, or not funded. The progress made toward completing the project may be tracked by the individual facility's owner or operator; it is not currently being tracked by the subsector.

Because many members of the subcouncil are competitors in the business world and in-house funding for assessments, protective programs, and resilience strategies is specific to a facility or a company/organization, there has not been an immediate development of a subsector-wide methodology for assessing the success or effectiveness of protective programs and resilience strategies. Over time, as the Sports Leagues Subsector continues to evolve, as specific goals and objectives are created, and as communication mechanisms mature, the methods for monitoring the progress of implementing protective programs and resilience strategies designed to meet goals and objectives should be put into place.

7. Research and Development

The following are R&D initiatives that members of the Sports Leagues Subcouncil have identified as being valuable to the Sports Leagues Subsector:

- Rapid and effective van, truck, and vehicle screening equipment that provides acceptable results in a reasonable amount of time, thereby allowing more vehicles to be screened prior to an event;

- Bollard and security camera upgrades to provide better vehicle control and tracking of vehicles in and around the sporting event facility;

- Development of HVAC systems that utilize real-time chemical, biological, and radiological detectors, similar to those employed in laboratories and nuclear power plants;

- Quick and accurate detectors for chemical, biological, and radiological contaminants in order to shorten response time;

- Portable containment devices to isolate contaminants; and

- Explosive detection devices (IEDs are seen by the sports leagues as being the biggest terrorist threat to sporting events).

Appendix 1: List of Acronyms and Abbreviations

ACAMS	Automated Critical Asset Management System
ADA	Americans with Disabilities Act
AGA	American Gaming Association
AH&LA	American Hotel and Lodging Association
ASCE	American Society of Civil Engineers
ASHRAE	American Society of Heating, Refrigeration, and Air Conditioning Engineers
ASIS	American Society for Industrial Security
ATF	Bureau of Alcohol, Tobacco, Firearms, and Explosives
AZA	Association of Zoos and Aquariums
BOCA	Building Officials and Code Administrators
BOMA	Building Owners and Managers Association
BSTP	Building Security Technology Program
BZP	Buffer Zone Plan
BZPP	Buffer Zone Protection Program
C3	Comprehensive Consensus Codes
CANJ	Casino Association of New Jersey
CARRI	Community and Regional Resilience Initiative
CARVER	Criticality, Accessibility, Recuperability, Vulnerability, Effect, Recognizability
CBR	Chemical/Biological/Radiological
CCTV	Closed-Circuit Television
CCV	Characteristics and Common Vulnerabilities
CDC	Centers for Disease Control and Prevention
CDI	Cyberterrorism Defense Initiative
CF	Commercial Facilities
CF-GCC	Commercial Facilities Government Coordinating Council
CF-SCC	Commercial Facilities Sector Coordinating Council

CF-SSP	Commercial Facilities Sector-Specific Plan
CII	Critical Infrastructure Information
CIIA	Critical Infrastructure Information Act
CIKR	Critical Infrastructure and Key Resources
CIP	Critical Infrastructure Protection
CIP CS	Critical Infrastructure Program CyberSecurity Program
CIPAC	Critical Infrastructure Partnership Advisory Council
CITA	Critical Infrastructure Threat Analysis Division
COTS	Commercial Off-the-Shelf
CRS	Congressional Research Service
CS&C	Office of Cybersecurity and Communications
CSCSWG	Cross-Sector Cybersecurity Working Group
CSET	Cyber Security Evaluation Tool
CSSP	Control Systems Security Program
CWIN	Critical Infrastructure Warning Information Network
DHS	U.S. Department of Homeland Security
DoD	U.S. Department of Defense
DOE	U.S. Department of Energy
DOI	U.S. Department of the Interior
DOJ	U.S. Department of Justice
DOL	U.S. Department of Labor
ECIP	Enhanced Critical Infrastructure Program
EMO	Executive Management Office
ENS	Emergency Notification Services
EPA	U.S. Environmental Protection Agency
ESS	Emergency Services Sector
FAA	Federal Aviation Administration
FBI	Federal Bureau of Investigation
FEMA	Federal Emergency Management Agency
FOIA	Freedom of Information Act
FOUO	For Official Use Only
FPS	Federal Protective Service
FSLC	Federal Senior Leadership Council
FSP	Facility Security Plan
GCC	Government Coordinating Council

GSA	General Services Administration
HHS	U.S. Department of Health and Human Services
HITRAC	Homeland Infrastructure Threat and Risk Analysis Center
HSA	Homeland Security Advisor
HSAS	Homeland Security Advisory System
HSIN	Homeland Security Information Network
HSIP	Homeland Security Infrastructure Program
HSPD	Homeland Security Presidential Directive
HUD	U.S. Department of Housing and Urban Development
HVAC	Heating, Ventilating, and Air Conditioning
I&A	Office of Intelligence and Analysis
IAAM	International Association of Assembly Managers
IAPMO	International Association of Plumbing and Mechanical Officials
ICAV	Integrated Common Analytical Viewer
ICBO	International Conference of Building Officials
ICE	U.S. Immigration and Customs Enforcement
ICSC	International Council of Shopping Centers
IDM	Infrastructure Data Management
IDW	Infrastructure Data Warehouse
IED	Improvised Explosive Device
IICD	Infrastructure Information Collection Division
IICS	Infrastructure Information Collection System
IP	Office of Infrastructure Protection
IPT	Integrated Product Team
IRAPP	Infrastructure Risk Analysis Partnership Program
IRL	Indy Racing League
ISAC	Information Sharing and Analysis Center
ISE	Information-Sharing Environment
ISMA	International Security Managers Association
IST	Infrastructure Security Tool
IT	Information Technology
JTTF	Joint Terrorism Task Force
MiLB	Minor League Baseball
MLB	Major League Baseball
MLBI	Major League Baseball International

MLS	Major League Soccer
MTSA	Maritime Transportation Security Act
NAA	National Apartment Association
NASCAR	National Association for Stock Car Auto Racing
NBA	National Basketball Association
NCAA	National Collegiate Athletic Association
NCIPP	National Critical Infrastructure Prioritization Program
NCIP R&D	National Critical Infrastructure Protection Research and Development
NCP	National Contingency Plan
NCSD	National Cybersecurity Division
NEA	National Endowment for the Arts
NFC	National Football Conference
NFL	National Football League
NFPA	National Fire Protection Association
NHL	National Hockey League
NICC	National Infrastructure Coordination Center
NIGA	National Indian Gaming Association
NIOSH	National Institute for Occupational Safety and Health
NIPP	National Infrastructure Protection Plan
NIST	National Institute of Standards and Technology
NOC	National Operations Center
NRF	National Retail Federation
NSSE	National Security Special Event
NTC	National Tennis Center
NYPD	New York Police Department
OSAC	Overseas Security Advisory Council
OSHA	Occupational Safety and Health Administration
PCII	Protected Critical Infrastructure Information
PCIS	Partnership for Critical Infrastructure Security
PI	Potential Indicators of Terrorist Activity
PM	Protective Measure
PMP	Project Management Plan
PNWER	Pacific Northwest Economic Region
PSA	Protective Security Advisor
PSCD	Protective Security Coordination Division

PSO	Private Sector Office
QA	Quality Assurance
R&D	Research and Development
RCCC	Regional Consortium Coordinating Council
RE-ISAC	Real Estate Information Sharing and Analysis Center
REIT	Real Estate Investment Trust
RFI	Request for Information
RILA	Retail Industry Leaders Association
RSAT	Risk Self Assessment Tool
S&T	Science and Technology
SAP	Software Assurance Program
SAR	Sector Annual Report
SAV	Site Assistance Visit
SAVER	System Assessment and Validation for Emergency Responders
SBCCI	Southern Building Code Congress International
SCADA	Supervisory Control and Data Acquisition
SCC	Sector Coordinating Council
SERRI	Southeast Region Research Initiative
SHIRA	Strategic Homeland Infrastructure Risk Analysis
SLTTGCC	State, Local, Tribal, and Territorial Government Coordinating Council
SMA	Stadium Managers Association
SSA	Sector-Specific Agency
SSP	Sector-Specific Plan
SSTF	Safety and Security Task Force
SUM	Soccer United Marketing
TFR	Temporary Flight Restriction
TOPOFF	Top Officials Exercise Series
TSA	Transportation Security Administration
US-CERT	United States Computer Emergency Readiness Team
USCG	United States Coast Guard
USDA	United States Department of Agriculture
USSS	United States Secret Service
USTA	United States Tennis Association
VA	Vulnerability Assessment
WFCA	Western Fire Chiefs Association

Appendix 2: Glossary of Key Terms

Asset. Contracts, facilities, property, electronic and non-electronic records and documents, unobligated or unexpended balances of appropriations, and other funds or resources (other than personnel).

Business Continuity. The ability of an organization to continue to function before, during, and after a disaster.

CIKR Partner. Those Federal, State, regional, local, tribal, and territorial government entities, private sector owners and operators and representative organizations, academic and professional entities, and certain not-for-profit and private volunteer organizations that share in the responsibility for protecting the Nation's CIKR.

Consequence. The result of a terrorist attack or other hazard that reflects the level, duration, and nature of the loss resulting from the incident. For the purposes of the NIPP, consequences are divided into four main categories: public health and safety, economic, psychological, and governance impacts.

Critical Infrastructure. Assets, systems, and networks, whether physical or virtual, that are so vital to the United States that the incapacity or destruction of such assets, systems, or networks would have a debilitating impact on security, national economic security, public health or safety, or any combination thereof.

Critical Infrastructure Information (CII). Information not customarily in the public domain related to the security of critical infrastructure or protected systems, and voluntarily provided to the government. CII includes any planned or past assessment, projection, estimate, operational problem, or solution regarding critical infrastructure or the ability of protected systems to resist any actual, potential, or threatened unlawful interference with, attack on, compromise of, or incapacitation of these infrastructure or systems by either physical or computer-based attack.

Cybersecurity. The prevention of damage to, unauthorized use of, or exploitation of, and, if needed, the restoration of electronic information and communications systems and the information contained therein to ensure confidentiality, integrity, and availability. Includes protection and restoration, when needed, of information networks and wireline, wireless, satellite, public safety answering points, and 911 communications systems and control systems.

Government Coordinating Council (GCC). The government counterpart to the Sector Coordinating Council (SCC) for each sector, established to enable interagency coordination. The GCC comprises representatives from across various levels of government (Federal, State, local, tribal, and territorial) as appropriate to the security and operational landscape of each individual sector.

Incident. An occurrence or event, natural or human-engineered, that requires an emergency response to protect life or property. Incidents may include major disasters, emergencies, terrorist attacks, terrorist threats, wildfires and urban fires, floods, hazardous materials spills, nuclear accidents, aircraft accidents, earthquakes, hurricanes, tornadoes, tropical storms, war-related disasters, public health and medical emergencies, and other occurrences requiring an emergency response.

Infrastructure. The framework of interdependent networks and systems comprise identifiable industries, institutions (including people and procedures), and distribution capabilities that provide a reliable flow of products and services that are essential to the defense and economic security of the United States, the smooth functioning of government at all levels, and society as a whole. Consistent with the definition in the Homeland Security Act, infrastructure includes physical, cyber, and human elements.

Interdependency. The multi- or bidirectional reliance of an asset, system, network, or collection thereof, within or across sectors, on input, interaction, or other requirement from other sources in order to function properly.

Key Resources. As defined by the Homeland Security Act of 2002, key resources are publicly or privately controlled resources essential to the minimal operations of the economy and government.

Mitigation. Activities designed to reduce or eliminate risks to persons or property or to lessen the actual or potential effects or consequences of an incident. Mitigation measures may be implemented prior to, during, or after an incident.

Normalize. In the context of the NIPP, the process of transforming risk-related data into comparable units.

Owners and Operators. Those entities responsible for day-to-day operations and investment in a particular asset or system.

Preparedness. The range of deliberate critical tasks and activities necessary to build, sustain, and improve the operational capability to prevent, protect against, respond to, and recover from domestic incidents.

Prioritization. In the context of the NIPP, prioritization is the process of using risk assessment results to identify where risk reduction or mitigation efforts are most needed and subsequently determine which protective actions should be instituted in order to have the greatest effect.

Protection. Actions to mitigate the overall risk to CIKR assets, systems, networks, or their interconnecting links resulting from exposure, injury, destruction, incapacitation, or exploitation. In the context of the NIPP, protection includes actions to deter the threat, mitigate vulnerabilities, or minimize the consequences associated with a terrorist attack or other incident. Protection can include a wide range of activities, such as hardening facilities, incorporating hazard resistance into initial facility design, initiating active or passive countermeasures, installing security systems, promoting workforce surety, and implementing cyber-security measures, among various others.

Recovery. The development, coordination, and execution of service- and site-restoration plans for impacted communities and the reconstitution of government operations and services through individual, private sector, nongovernmental, and public assistance programs that identify needs and define resources; provide housing and promote restoration; address long-term care and treatment of affected persons; implement additional measures for community restoration; incorporate mitigation measures and techniques, as feasible; evaluate the incident to identify lessons learned; and develop initiatives to mitigate the effects of future incidents.

Response. Activities that address the short-term, direct effects of an incident, including immediate actions to save lives, protect property, and meet basic human needs. Response also includes the execution of emergency operations plans and incident mitigation activities designed to limit the loss of life, personal injury, property damage, and other unfavorable outcomes. As indicated by the situation, response activities include application of intelligence and other information to lessen the effects or consequences of an incident; increased security operations; continuing investigations into the nature and source of the threat; ongoing surveillance and testing processes; immunizations, isolation, or quarantine; and specific law enforcement operations aimed at preempting, interdicting, or disrupting illegal activity, and apprehending actual perpetrators and bringing them to justice.

Risk. A measure of potential harm that encompasses threat, vulnerability, and consequence. In the context of the NIPP, risk is the expected magnitude of loss due to a terrorist attack, natural disaster, or other incident, along with the likelihood of such an event occurring and causing that loss.

Risk Management Framework. A planning methodology that outlines the process for setting security goals; identifying assets, systems, networks, and functions; assessing risks; prioritizing and implementing protective programs; measuring performance; and taking corrective action. Public and private sector entities often include risk management frameworks in their business continuity plans.

Sector. A logical collection of assets, systems, or networks that provide a common function to the economy, government, or society. The NIPP addresses 18 CIKR sectors as defined in Homeland Security Presidential Directive 7 (HSPD-7).

Sector Coordinating Council (SCC). The private-sector counterpart to the GCC, this council is a self-organized, self-run, and self-governed organization that is representative of a spectrum of key stakeholders within a sector. SCCs serve as the government's principal point of entry into each sector for developing and coordinating a wide range of CIKR protection activities and issues.

Sector Partnership Model. The framework used to promote and facilitate sector and cross-sector planning and coordination, collaboration, and information sharing for CIKR protection involving all levels of government and private sector entities.

Sector-Specific Agency (SSA). Federal departments and agencies identified in HSPD-7 as being responsible for CIKR protection activities in specified CIKR sectors.

Sector-Specific Plan (SSP). Augmenting plans that complement and extend the NIPP Base Plan and detail the application of the NIPP framework specific to each CIKR sector. SSPs are developed by the SSAs in close collaboration with other partners.

System. In the context of the NIPP, a system is a collection of assets, resources, or elements that performs a process that provides infrastructure services to the Nation.

Terrorism. Any activity that (1) involves an act that is (a) dangerous to human life or potentially destructive of critical infrastructure or key resources, and (b) a violation of the criminal laws of the United States or of any State or other subdivision of the United States; and (2) appears to be intended to (a) intimidate or coerce a civilian population, (b) influence the policy of a government by intimidation or coercion, or (c) affect the conduct of a government by mass destruction, assassination, or kidnapping.

Threat. The intention and capability of an adversary to undertake actions that would be detrimental to CIKR.

Value Proposition. A statement that outlines the national and homeland security interest in protecting the Nation's CIKR and articulates the benefits gained by all partners through the risk management framework and public-private partnerships described in the NIPP.

Vulnerability. A weakness in the design, implementation, or operation of an asset, system, or network that can be exploited by an adversary or disrupted by a natural hazard or technological failure.

Appendix 3: Review of Authorities

While most authorities reside at the State and local levels, a wide range of existing governing authorities pertain to the CF Sector. These authorities impact the actions that DHS will facilitate, and they provide opportunities to expand on existing strategies and increase protective measures.

1.1 Commercial Facilities Sector Federal Authorities

Authorities at the Federal level are applicable to the protection of assets, systems, and networks within the CF Sector, as well as other CIKR sectors. The authorities identified below provide the opportunity to enhance protective programs and resilience strategies.

1.1.1 U.S. Department of Homeland Security

DHS's authority is derived from the Homeland Security Act, Public Law 107-296, 116 Stat. 2135 (2002). On December 17, 2003, President George W. Bush issued HSPD-7, which "establishes a national policy for Federal departments and agencies to identify and prioritize United States CIKR and to protect them from terrorist attack." Pursuant to HSPD-7, DHS "shall coordinate with appropriate departments and agencies to ensure the protection of other key resources, including ... commercial facilities."

Also in response to the Homeland Security Act of 2002, Congress enacted the Support Anti-Terrorism by Fostering Effective Technologies Act of 2002 (the SAFETY Act) to encourage the development and deployment of antiterrorism technologies by creating a system of risk and liability management. The purpose of the act is to ensure that the threat of liability does not deter manufacturers of antiterrorism technologies from developing and commercializing technologies that could significantly reduce the risks or effects of terrorist events. Specifically, the act creates liability limitations for claims arising out of, relating to, or resulting from an act of terrorism.

HSPD-8 establishes policies "to strengthen the preparedness of the United States to prevent and respond to threatened or actual domestic terrorist attacks, major disasters, and other emergencies."

The Critical Infrastructure Information Act (CIIA) of 2002 (also known as Title II of the Homeland Security Act of 2002) established the PCII program to manage private sector infrastructure protection information that is exempt from the Freedom of Information Act (FOIA). The PCII Program Office, which is part of the DHS National Protection and Programs Directorate (NPPD), manages and controls PCII. At its core, PCII is information that owners and operators submit voluntarily to protect critical infrastructure or protected systems. PCII is used by DHS for analysis, warning, interdependency study, recovery, reconstitution, or other informational purposes. The PCII program provides the private sector with the needed assurances that they will guard sensitive infrastructure protection information from disclosure to the public.

The National Strategy for the Physical Protection of Critical Infrastructures and Key Assets, developed in February 2003, identifies a clear set of national goals and objectives and outlines the guiding principles that will underpin the Nation's efforts to secure the infrastructure and assets that are vital to national security, governance, public health and safety, the economy, and public confidence. This National Strategy also provides a unifying organization and identifies specific initiatives to drive near-term national protection priorities and inform the resource allocation process. Most importantly, it establishes a foundation for building and fostering the cooperative environment in which government, industry, and private citizens can carry out their respective protection responsibilities more effectively and efficiently.

1.1.2 U.S. Department of Commerce, National Institute of Standards and Technology

The National Institute of Standards and Technology (NIST) is a non-regulatory Federal agency within the U.S. Department of Commerce's Technology Administration. NIST's mission is to develop and promote measurement, standards, and technologies to enhance productivity, facilitate trade, and improve the quality of life. It carries out its mission through four cooperative programs:

- The NIST Laboratories conduct research that advances the Nation's technology infrastructure and is needed by U.S. industry to continually improve products and services.

- The Malcolm Baldrige National Quality Program promotes performance excellence among U.S. manufacturers, service companies, educational institutions, and health care providers.

- The Manufacturing Extension Partnership is a nationwide network of local centers that offer technical and business assistance to smaller manufacturers.

- The Advanced Technology Program accelerates the development of innovative technologies for broad national benefit by co-funding R&D partnerships with the private sector.

In addition, NIST's Buildings and Fire Research Laboratory studies building materials; computer-integrated construction practices; fire science and fire safety engineering; and structural, mechanical, and environmental engineering. Products of the laboratory's research include measurements and test methods, performance criteria, and technical data that support innovations by industry and are incorporated into building and fire standards and codes.

1.1.3 U.S. Environmental Protection Agency

Historically, EPA has maintained oversight over indoor environmental issues, although not with formal regulatory authority. EPA remains the preeminent source of information on bioterrorism and chemical weapons issues as they relate to potential entry via building HVAC systems. In addition, HSPDs 5, 7, 9, and 10 assign general responsibility for decontamination to EPA. EPA may utilize the following laws and regulations to respond to terrorist activities:

- The Comprehensive Environmental Response, Compensation, and Liability Act (CERCLA, 42 U.S.C. 9601 et seq.), as amended by the Superfund Amendments and Reauthorization Act of 1986, authorizes EPA to respond to releases, or substantial threats of releases, of hazardous substances to the environment, and to respond to releases, or substantial threats of releases, of pollutants or contaminants that may present an imminent and substantial danger to the public health or welfare. This act might be used by EPA to accomplish the following:

  - Develop and provide scientific and technical information on sampling and analysis methods, protocols, and procedures for use by emergency and remedial responders in the event of a terrorist threat or actual attack;

  - Advance, through testing and evaluation, decontamination techniques and technologies for indoor and outdoor attacks for use by emergency and remedial responders; and

- Develop and refine scientific methods and tools for risk assessors and others who must make decisions based on risk information associated with acute, mid-term, and longer-term exposures to chemical and biological agents and other materials employed in intentional attacks.

- The National Oil and Hazardous Substances Pollution Contingency Plan (NCP, 40 CFR Part 300) implements the authorities provided to EPA and other agencies under CERCLA, the Clean Water Act, and Executive Order 12580. It sets forth the process for activating the national response system; specifies responsibilities among Federal, State, and local governments; and describes resources that are available for response.

1.1.4 Federal Emergency Management Agency

FEMA has published a series of risk management manuals and primers directed at providing design guidance for mitigating multi-hazard events. The objective of the series is to reduce the physical damage to structural and nonstructural components of buildings and related infrastructure, and to reduce the resultant casualties during natural and manmade disasters. The intended audience includes architects and engineers working for private institutions; building owners, operators, and managers; and State and local government officials working in the building sciences community. Examples of manuals with applicability to the CF Sector include the following:

- The *Reference Manual to Mitigate Potential Terrorist Attacks Against Buildings*, FEMA 426, Washington, D.C., December 2003, presents incremental approaches that can be implemented over time to decrease the vulnerability of buildings to terrorist threats. The appendices describe design considerations for electronic security systems and provide a listing of associations and organizations currently working in the building sciences security area.

- The *Primer for Design of Commercial Buildings to Mitigate Terrorist Attacks*, FEMA 427, Washington, D.C., December 2003, introduces a series of concepts to mitigate the threat of hazards resulting from terrorist attacks on new buildings. FEMA 427 specifically addresses four high-population, private sector building types, one of which is the commercial office building. The manual focuses primarily on explosions, but also addresses CBR attacks.

- The *Risk Management Series, Insurance, Finance, and Regulation Primer for Terrorism Risk Management in Buildings*, FEMA 429, Washington, D.C., December 2003, provides information related to insurance and the Terrorism Risk Insurance Act of 2002. It highlights current building regulations related to terrorism risk, due diligence, and vulnerability. The manual also includes a Building Security Checklist categorized by data collection, attack delivery methods, and attack mechanism parameters.

- The *Risk Management Series, Site and Urban Design for Security: Guidance Against Potential Terrorist Attacks*, FEMA 430, Washington, D.C., December 2007, addresses security issues in high-population private sector buildings. It is a companion to the *Reference Manual to Mitigate Potential Terrorist Attacks Against Buildings* (FEMA 426).

- The *Risk Management Series, Risk Assessment, A How-To Guide to Mitigate Potential Terrorist Attacks Against Buildings*, FEMA 452, Washington, D.C., January 2005, outlines methods for identifying the critical assets and functions within buildings, determining the threats to those assets, and assessing the vulnerabilities associated with those threats.

- The *Risk Management Series, Design Guidance for Shelters and Safe Rooms*, FEMA 453, Washington, D.C., May 2006, provides information pertaining to the design and construction of shelters in the work place, in the home, or in community buildings that will provide protection in response to manmade hazards.

- The *Risk Management Series, Incremental Protection for Existing Commercial Buildings from Terrorist Attack: Providing Protection to People and Buildings*, FEMA 459, Washington, D.C., April 2009, provides guidance on security and operational enhancements to address vulnerabilities to explosive blasts and chemical, biological, and radiological hazards.

- The *Risk Management Series, Design Guide for Improving Critical Facility Safety from Flooding and High Winds: Providing Protection to People and Buildings*, FEMA 543, Washington, D.C.

FEMA also prepared a report entitled *The Oklahoma City Bombing: Improving Building Performance Through Multi-Hazard Mitigation*, FEMA 277, Washington, D.C., August 1996, which focuses on the nine-story portion of the Alfred P. Murrah Building that incurred significant damage and partial collapse as a result of the bombing on April 19, 1995. The purpose of the mitigation assessment team's investigation was to review damage caused by the blast, determine the failure mechanism for the building, and review engineering strategies for reducing such damage to new and existing buildings in the future. Specifically, mechanisms for multi-hazard mitigation, including mitigation of wind and earthquake effects, were considered.

Future FEMA Risk Management Series publications include FEMA 455, *Rapid Visual Screening for Building Security*; FEMA 452, *A How-To Guide to Mitigate Multi-hazard Events (CBR, Explosives, Earthquakes, Floods, and High Winds) Against Buildings*; and FEMA 582, *Design Guide for Improving Commercial Building Safety in Earthquakes, Floods, and High Winds*.

1.1.5 National Institute for Occupational Safety and Health

The National Institute for Occupational Safety and Health (NIOSH), within the U.S. Department of Health and Human Services, Centers for Disease Control and Prevention, issued *Guidance for Protecting Building Environments from Airborne Chemical, Biological, or Radiological Attacks* in May 2002. The document identifies actions that owners and managers of offices and other public and private sector buildings can implement to enhance occupant protection from an airborne chemical, biological, or radiological attack. Recommendations are made in four categories (what not to do; physical security; ventilation and filtration; and maintenance, administration, and training) and include such actions as preventing access to outdoor air intakes, mechanical areas, and building roofs; securing return air grilles; and several specific actions that can be implemented reasonably quickly and cost-effectively to both existing and new buildings (NIOSH, 2002).

1.1.6 U.S. Centers for Disease Control and Prevention

The U.S. Centers for Disease Control and Prevention (CDC), in conjunction with NIOSH, issued a comprehensive report entitled *CDC–NIOSH Guidance for Protecting Building Environments from Airborne Chemical, Biological, or Radiological Attacks*, Publication No. 2002-139, May 2002. The guidance details preventive steps that owners and operators can take to reduce the likelihood and mitigate the impact of threats and potential hazards associated with CBR terrorism. Although this document discusses buildings in general rather than malls in particular, many of the vulnerabilities and recommendations are applicable.

The CDC has also issued a document entitled *Guidance for Filtration and Air Cleaning Systems to Protect Building Environments from Airborne Chemical, Biological, or Radiological Attacks*, Publication No. 2003-136, April 2003, that provides preventive measures that building owners and managers can implement to protect building air environments from a terrorist release of chemical, biological, or radiological contaminants.

1.1.7 U.S. Department of Labor

All facilities employing staff under the CF Sector must comply with Federal laws that the U.S. Department of Labor (DOL) enforces. DOL fosters and promotes the welfare of job seekers, wage earners, and retirees. Among other items, DOL administers a variety of Federal labor laws, including those that guarantee a worker's right to safe and healthful working conditions.

1.1.8 General Services Administration

The GSA Building Security Technology Program (BSTP) team is responsible for developing the policy and requirements for building security used in the design and construction of GSA buildings. The BSTP team performs explosive testing, develops design tools, and provides technical assistance to project managers. This program supports the mission of GSA, as well as other Federal agencies and departments.

1.1.9 U.S. Department of Justice

The mission of the U.S. Department of Justice is to enforce the law and defend the interests of the United States according to the law; ensure public safety against threats foreign and domestic; provide Federal leadership in preventing and controlling crime; seek just punishment for those who are guilty of unlawful behavior; and ensure fair and impartial administration of justice for all Americans.

1.1.9.1 National Institute of Justice

The National Institute of Justice (NIJ) is the research, development, and evaluation agency of DOJ and is dedicated to researching crime control and justice issues. NIJ provides objective, independent, evidence-based knowledge and tools to meet the challenges of crime and justice, particularly at the State and local levels. NIJ's principal authorities are derived from the Omnibus Crime Control and Safe Streets Act of 1968, as amended (see 42 U.S.C. 3721–3723) and Title II of the Homeland Security Act of 2002.

NIJ prepared *Crime Prevention Through Environmental Design and Community Policing* in August 1996.

1.1.9.2 Federal Bureau of Investigation

The FBI InfraGard program is an association of businesses, academic institutions, State and local law enforcement agencies, and other participants dedicated to sharing information and intelligence to prevent hostile acts against the United States. The relationship supports information sharing at the national and local levels; its objectives are as follows:

* Increase the level of information and reporting between InfraGard members and the FBI on matters related to counterterrorism, cyber crime, and other major crime programs;

* Increase the interaction and information sharing between InfraGard members and the FBI regarding threats to critical infrastructure, vulnerabilities, and interdependencies;

* Provide members with value-added threat advisories, alerts, and warnings;

* Promote effective liaison with Federal, State, and local agencies, to include DHS; and

* Provide members with a forum for education and training on counterterrorism, counterintelligence cyber crime, and other matters related to informed reporting of potential crimes and attacks on the Nation and U.S. interests.

1.1.10 Federal Aviation Administration

FAA has the authority to issue TFRs for commercial facilities. An example of a TFR involves sporting events and is pursuant to 14 CFR 99.7, Special Security Instructions, which stipulates that from 1 hour before an event until 1 hour after an event, all aircraft and parachute operations are prohibited at and below 3,000 feet above ground level (AGL) within a 3-nautical-mile radius of any stadium having a seating capacity of 30,000 or more people in which an MLB, NFL, NCAA Division I football, or major motor speedway event is occurring.

1.2 State and Local Governments

State and local governments enact and enforce the vast preponderance of government authorities and regulations vis-à-vis the CF Sector through zoning standards, fire and safety regulations, and other measures. Accordingly, there is some diversity in how particular States and counties regulate commercial facilities. In developing an SSP for the CF Sector, it will be important to consider the impact of these varied authorities.

1.2.1 State Police Fusion Programs

Important intelligence that may forewarn of a future terrorist attack may be derived from information collected by State, local, tribal, and territorial government personnel through crime control and other routine activities and by people living and working in our local communities. Successful counterterrorism efforts require that Federal, State, local, tribal, territorial, and private sector entities have an effective information-sharing and collaboration capability to ensure that they can seamlessly collect, blend, analyze, disseminate, and use information regarding threats, vulnerabilities, and consequences in support of prevention, response, and consequence management efforts.

The President and Congress have directed that an information-sharing environment (ISE) be created to facilitate information-sharing and collaboration activities within the Federal Government (horizontally) and among Federal, State, local, tribal, and territorial governments, as well as private sector entities (vertically). The concept of intelligence/information fusion has emerged as the fundamental process (or processes) for facilitating the sharing of homeland security-related information and intelligence at a national level and, therefore, has become a guiding principle in defining the ISE.

1.3 Private Sector Authorities

Although not formally vested with the power of law, many private associations have acquired internal authorities to set standards for their member companies in various areas, including national and international building codes and best practices standards. Groups including ASIS International, the American Society of Mechanical Engineers (ASME), NFPA, the International Code Council (ICC), the American Society of Heating, Refrigeration, and Air Conditioning Experts (ASHRAE), and the American Society of Civil Engineers (ASCE) have standard-setting authority to implement vigorous vulnerability assessments and protective measures at commercial facility assets.

1.3.1 American Society for Industrial Security International

Although there is limited Federal regulation of commercial facilities with regard to security, the policies and requirements of at least three private sector industries—the lending community, insurance underwriters, and investors/rating agencies—may influence facility managers' decisions. In addition, emerging tort law in the area of building security will also be a powerful motivation for managers to ensure that facility security meets the current legal standard of care.

ASIS International has published several guidelines to help the private sector secure its business and critical infrastructure, whether from natural disasters, accidents, or planned actions (e.g., terrorist attacks or vandalism). The Business Continuity Guidelines outline a series of interrelated processes and activities, including readiness, prevention, response, recovery and resumption, testing and training, and evaluation and maintenance, that will assist in creating, assessing, and sustaining a comprehensive plan for use in the event of a crisis that threatens the viability and continuity of an organization. The ASIS International General Security Risk Assessment Guidelines are a seven-step process that creates a methodology by which security risks at a specific location can be identified and communicated, along with the appropriate solutions. The Threat Advisory Response Guideline provides private business and industry with possible actions that could be implemented based on DHS Alert Levels.

1.3.2 National Fire Protection Association

In NFPA 1600, Standard on Disaster/Emergency Management and Business Continuity Programs (2007), the association has established a common set of criteria for disaster management, emergency management, and business continuity programs. This standard provides those who have responsibility for disaster and emergency management and business continuity programs with criteria to assess current programs or to develop, implement, and maintain a program to prevent, mitigate, prepare for, respond to, and recover from disasters and emergencies.

Many vulnerability studies have suggested remedies for dealing with potential incidents that are not terrorism-related but have similar scenarios and consequences. Vulnerability to a fire and mitigating the effects is one example. There are obvious differences in preventive measures; however, once a fire occurs (regardless of the cause), facility vulnerabilities are the same. The same is true of safety measures such as sprinkler systems and fire doors. NFPA has produced many publications and reports related to fire prevention, including codes and standards, preventive measures, and alarm and signaling systems.

1.3.3 International Code Council

Building codes establish the minimum acceptable standards necessary for protecting people and property. Although enforced at the State and local levels, they are generally based on or are identical to national model building codes. These national codes include requirements to design for loads that might be imposed by natural disasters, but not by acts of war or terrorism. Currently, two associations develop model-building codes in the United States—the International Code Council (ICC) and NFPA. ICC is made up of many of the experts from three former model code associations: the Building Officials and Code Administrators (BOCA) International, the International Conference of Building Officials (ICBO), and the Southern Building Code Congress International (SBCCI). It publishes the International Building Code, which is based on a combination of the previous National, Uniform, and Standard Building Codes, along with several others.

NFPA's Comprehensive Consensus Codes (C3), which include NFPA 5000, Building Construction and Safety Code; the NFPA Uniform Fire Code; and others, have been developed through American National Standards Institute-approved processes. Developers of the C3 codes include NFPA, the International Association of Plumbing and Mechanical Officials (IAPMO), the Western Fire Chiefs Association (WFCA), and the ASHRAE engineers.

ICC and NFPA codes are similar in their disaster-resistant requirements because they reference the same standard for determining design loads. Periodically, ASCE updates this standard (Minimum Design Loads for Buildings and Other Structures). Other standards referenced in the model building codes are used for assessing the performance of construction materials under design conditions.

1.3.4 American Society for Testing and Materials

The American Society for Testing and Materials (ASTM) E119 Standard Fire Test is the standard method of testing to evaluate fire resistance. It is a comparison of relative specimen behavior under controlled conditions and does not intend to predict actual behavior. A popular misconception concerning fire-resistance ratings for walls, columns, floors, and other building components is that the ratings imply the length of time that a building component will remain in place when exposed to an actual fire. For example, a 2-hour fire-resistant wall is expected to remain standing for 2 hours when exposed to an actual fire. However, the time to collapse for such a wall in an actual fire may be greater or less than two hours.

ASTM Committee 54 addresses issues related to standards and guidance materials for homeland security applications with a specific focus on infrastructure protection; decontamination; security controls; and chemical, biological, radiological, nuclear, and high-yield explosives (CBRNE) sensors and detectors. Additionally, the committee coordinates existing standardization (ASTM generated, as well as external) related to homeland security needs.

1.3.5 National Research Council

The National Research Council (NRC) is part of the National Academies, which comprises the National Academy of Sciences (NAS), the National Academy of Engineering (NAE), and the Institute of Medicine. They are private, nonprofit institutions that provide science, technology, and health policy advice under a congressional charter. NRC was organized by NAS in 1916 to associate the broad community of science and technology with the academy's purposes of furthering knowledge and advising the Federal Government. Functioning in accordance with general policies determined by the Academy, NRC has become the principal operating agency of both NAS and NAE in providing services to the government, the public, and the scientific and engineering communities. The Research Council is administered jointly by both academies and the Institute of Medicine through the NRC Governing Board. Guides prepared by NRC include the following:

- Protecting Buildings and People from Terrorism: Technology Transfer for Blast-Effects Mitigation, National Academy Press, Washington, D.C., 2001.

- Protecting Buildings from Bomb Blast: The Transfer of Blast-Effects Mitigation Technologies from Military to Civilian Applications, National Academy Press, Washington, D.C., 1995.

1.4 Other Guides

Many private sector associations have published guides or studies that provide information and guidance on safety and security issues, strategies, and lessons learned.

American Institute of Architects

- *Building Security Through Design* offers architects up-to-date, indepth material on building security issues (**www.aia.org**).

American Society of Civil Engineers

- *Blast Effects on Buildings: Design of Buildings to Optimize Resistance to Blast Loading*, G.C. Mays and P.D. Smith, Thomas Telford, Ltd, London, 1995, **www.pubs.asce.org/BOOKdisplay.cgi?9990338**.

- "Blast-Resistant Design of Commercial Buildings," M. Ettouney, R. Smilowitz, and T. Rittenhouse, *Practice Periodical on Structural Design and Construction*, Vol. 1, February 1996, **www.wai.com/Applied Science/Blast/blast-struct-design.html**.

- *Lessons from the Oklahoma City Bombing: Defensive Design Techniques*, Eve E. Hinman and David J. Hammond, American Society of Civil Engineers Press, Reston, VA, January 1997, **www.asce.org/publications/booksdisplay.cfm?tyoe=9702295**.

- *Structural Design for Physical Security: State of the Practice*, Edward Conrath, et al., Structural Engineering Institute of the American Society of Civil Engineers, Reston, VA, 1999, **www.pubs/asce/org/BOOKdisplay.cgi?9990571**.

- *Vulnerability and Protection of Infrastructure Systems: The State of the Art*, An ASCE Journals Special Publication compiling articles from 2002 and earlier, **https://ascestore.aip.org/OA_HTML/aipCCtpItmDspRte.jsp?a=b&item=39885**.

American Society of Heating, Refrigerating, and Air Conditioning Engineers

- "Defensive Filtration," James D. Miller, ASHRAE Journal, December 2002, **http://resourcecenter.ashrae.org/store/ashrae/newstore.cgi?itemid=9346&view+item&categoryid=409&page=1&1oginid=29483**.

- *Risk Management Guidance for Health and Safety Under Extraordinary Incidents*, ASHRAE 2002 Winter Meeting Report, January 12, 2002, **http://atfp.nfesc.navy.mil/pdf/ASHRAE%20CBR%20Guidance.pdf**.

Council on Tall Buildings and Urban Habitat

- Building Safety Enhancement Guidebook, 2002, **www.ctbuh.org**.

- *Task Force on Tall Buildings: "The Future,"* October 15, 2001, **www.ctbuh.org/htmlfiles/hot_links/report.pdf**.

Lawrence Berkeley National Laboratory

- *Combating Terrorism: Prioritizing Vulnerabilities and Developing Mitigation Strategies*, Publication No. LBNL/PUB-51959, January 10, 2003, **http://securebuildings.lbl.gov/images/bldgadvice.pdf**.

- *Protecting Buildings from a Biological or Chemical Attack: Actions to Take Before or During a Release*, Publication No. LBNL/PUB-51959, January 10, 2003, **http://securebuildings.lbl.gov/images/bldgadvice.pdf**.

The Institute of Structural Engineers

- *The Structural Engineer's Response to Explosives Damage*. SETO, Ltd., London.

National Institute of Building Sciences

- "Provide Security for Building Occupants and Assets," Whole Building Design Guide (online security-related design information), **www.wbdg.org/design/provide_security.php**.

1.5 Commercial Facilities Subsector Authorities

1.5.1 Entertainment and Media Subsector Authorities

There are various national, Federal, and international standard-setting organizations, and State and local government-issued rules, regulations, standards, and policies (see above) that may be applicable to the protection of assets associated with the Entertainment and Media Subsector.

1.5.2 Gaming Facilities Subsector Authorities

Typically, State gaming control boards or commissions, which manage the enforcement and compliance divisions that oversee daily activities for gaming operations, regulate commercial casinos. This involves criminal activity, game regulation, game integrity (fairness), compliance of the gaming operator to established rules, regulations and laws, and customer dispute resolution. They also conduct due diligence of persons or companies licensed to operate gaming businesses. There is Federal oversight related to the USA PATRIOT Act, the Sarbanes–Oxley Act, and Title 31. Physical security, as it relates to terrorist threats and attacks, has not traditionally been an issue addressed by these entities.

The Indian Gaming Regulatory Act established the jurisdictional framework that presently governs tribal casinos. In general, tribal casinos were established and operate in conformance with a compact entered into by the Tribal Nation and the State. The regulatory concerns and authorities addressed by such compacts are similar to those described above for commercial casinos.

Riverboat and dockside casinos fall under the USCG regulations that implement the MTSA. The regulations specify the requirements for security assessments; development of security plans; implementation of measures to address access control and security monitoring; and physical, passenger, personnel, baggage, and cargo security.

ASIS International has established councils that are subsector-specific, such as the Gaming and Wagering Protection Council, founded in 1996.

The International Master of Gaming Law deals with legal issues related to operating a gaming business. These matters span any aspect of the legal system, be it regulatory, risk management, compliance, defense, or lobbyist related.

There are various other national, Federal, and international standard-setting organizations, and State and local government-issued rules, regulations, standards, and policies (see above) that may be applicable to the protection of assets associated with the Gaming Facilities Subsector.

1.5.3 Lodging Subsector Authorities

There are various national, Federal, and international standard-setting organizations, and State and local government-issued rules, regulations, standards, and policies (see above) that may be applicable to the protection of assets associated with the Lodging Subsector. Specifically, local building codes that apply to hotels generally address the following:

- Fire resistance of the structure;

- Compartmentalization of use areas;

- Flame spread;

- Fire resistance of furnishings;

- Fire detection alarms and fire suppression systems;

- Occupant load; and

- Exit requirements.

1.5.4 Outdoor Events Subsector Authorities

Most of the published standards for the regulation of theme parks have focused on the area of ride safety. Since 1978, ASTM International has worked with members of the U.S. amusement industry in the development of ride safety standards. ASTM Committee F24 on Amusement Rides and Devices has established standards for design and manufacturing, testing, operation, maintenance, inspection, and quality assurance. Albeit voluntary, these standards have been widely adopted by the industry. Some States have given these standards the force of law, such as in Massachusetts, where the General Law states, "Owners of permanent or traveling amusement parks shall comply with the standards of the American Society for Testing and Materials on amusement rides and devices ..." (Chapter 140, Section 205A).

There are no national or even statewide standards, rules, or regulations pertaining to the various types of large, outdoor public gatherings on non-Federal or State property. Normally, local rules, codes, ordinances, standards, and regulations govern events involving an assembly of people on public property (e.g., streets and parks) or even on private property (e.g., traffic control and health and safety standards). Permits are required for parades, the sale and consumption of alcohol, and the sale of food items. Fire safety inspections are also required. Permission may also be required if it will be necessary to close certain adjacent or peripheral roads or streets. A permit may be required for the mass gathering itself. The FEMA manual entitled IS-15, Special Events Contingency Planning for Public Safety Agencies (March 2004), addresses an event's operational considerations, giving a basic overview of the incident command system and instructions on how to implement it both in the planning stage and at the time of an incident. In addition, it includes planning checklists for certain affected parties, including promoters, local law enforcement, fire/emergency and public health services, and utilities and public works departments. The types of incidents discussed include bomb threats, assaults on government or important officials, civil disturbances, hostage-taking (without terrorism), sustained power interruptions, and weather hazards. The manual also stresses, however, that every event is different and the guidance is not intended to override any existing legislation or local emergency management procedures.

There are various national, Federal, and international standard-setting organizations, and State and local government-issued rules, regulations, standards, and policies (see above) that may be applicable to the protection of assets associated with the Outdoor Events Subsector.

1.5.5 Public Assembly Subsector Authorities

Security planning guides from IAAM's Safety and Security Task Force address the need for selecting security practices based on levels of threat or vulnerability matrixes associated with the DHS HSAS. These guides were developed through a peer review process among IAAM members. Titles in this series include Safety and Security Best Practices Security Planning Guide for Arenas, Stadiums, and Amphitheaters; Safety and Security Best Practices Security Planning Guide for Convention Centers; Safety and Security Best Practices Planning Guide for Emergency Preparedness; and Safety and Security Best Practices Planning Guide for Theaters and Performing Arts Centers. Other guides by IAAM include Special Event Security Management, Loss Prevention, and Emergency Services; Public Assembly Facility Law; Life Safety Code and Handbook (NFPA 101); and the No Excuses Risk Management Guide. IAAM's Mega-Shelter Best Practices for Planning and Activation provides facility managers with important information that can be helpful in deliberations with government authorities regarding the use of their facility in response to major disasters, as well as operating a mega-shelter.

The Evacuation Planning Guide for Stadiums, produced in conjunction with DHS and members of the Public Assembly and Sports Leagues subsectors, includes a template that can be used to create an Evacuation Plan that will represent the unique policies and procedures of State and local governments, surrounding communities, and specific stadium characteristics. The guide contains three sections consisting of subsection topics that include questions for consideration and statements for supporting actions. Answering the questions for consideration and implementing the supporting action statements should provide the information and knowledge necessary for preparing the corresponding section of the Evacuation Plan template.

Resource guides from the Colorado Office of Preparedness and Security assist in determining areas within facilities that are vulnerable to a terrorist attack and ways to protect them. Titles in this series are *Resource Guide Large Outdoor Public Gatherings, Resource Guide Recreation,* and *Resource Guide Restaurants and Night Clubs.*

There are various other national, Federal, and international standard-setting organizations, and State and local government-issued rules, regulations, standards, and policies (see above) that may be applicable to the protection of assets associated with the Public Assembly Subsector.

1.5.6 Real Estate Subsector Authorities

Progressive collapse occurs when the local failure of a primary structural component leads to the collapse of adjoining members, which, in turn, leads to additional collapse. Thus, the extent of total damage is disproportionate to the original cause. Progressive collapse can also be described as a chain reaction or the propagation of failures following damage to a relatively small portion of a structure where the removal of one primary supporting element results in the collapse of a large portion or possibly the entire structure. For example, the destruction and the majority of deaths at the Alfred P. Murrah Federal Building in Oklahoma City resulted from the progressive collapse of that structure. Several building codes worldwide address the topic of progressive collapse (e.g., ASCE 7-02, The American Society of Civil Engineers Minimum Design Loads for Buildings and Other Structures (ASCE, 2002); ACI 318-02, The American Concrete Institute Building Code Requirements for Structural Concrete (ACI, 2002); GSA PBS Facilities Standards 2003 (GSA, 2005)); however, there is no explicit engineering design method available that pertains to progressive collapse (GSA, 2004).

1.5.6.1 Residential Units

This section lists and briefly summarizes standards that apply to large residential buildings, with a focus on those that have security implications.

- Building codes establish the minimum acceptable standards necessary for protecting people and property. Although State and local governments enforce these codes, they are generally based on or are identical to national model building codes. These national codes include requirements to design for loads that might be imposed by natural disasters, but not by acts of war or terrorism. Currently, two associations develop model-building codes in the United States—ICC and NFPA.

- ICC is composed of experts from three former model code associations: BOCA, ICBO, and SBCCI. ICC publishes the International Building Code, which is based on a combination of the previous National Uniform and Standard Building Codes, along with several others.

- NFPA's C3, which includes NFPA 5000, Building Construction and Safety Code, and the NFPA Uniform Fire Code, has been developed through American National Standards Institute-approved processes. Developers of the C3 codes include NFPA, IAPMO, WFCA, and the ASHRAE Engineers.

There are various national, Federal, and international standard-setting organizations, and State and local government-issued rules, regulations, standards, and policies (see above) that may be applicable to the protection of assets associated with Real Estate Subsector.

1.5.7 Retail Subsector Authorities

Shopping malls are vulnerable to a number of natural events, such as tornados, hurricanes, and earthquakes. Building codes and construction standards have been designed and adopted to address these threats. There are also ongoing studies investigating how buildings can be improved to withstand the impact of tornados, microbursts, and other wind-driven events. In many ways, these events are applicable to the potential structural impact of explosions caused by bombs.

There are various national, Federal, and international standard-setting organizations, and State and local government-issued rules, regulations, standards, and policies (see above) that may be applicable to the protection of assets associated with the Retail Subsector.

In addition to physical security, recent developments in data storage have impacted the retail subsector. The Payment Card Industry Data Security Standard (PCI-DSS) established worldwide information security standards that were created to help organizations that process card payments prevent credit card fraud through increased controls around data and its exposure to compromise. The standard not only applies to retail operations, but to all organizations that hold, process, or pass cardholder information from any card branded with the logo of one of the card brands. The Payment Card Industry Security Standards Council (PCI SSC) assembled the standard. American Express, Discover Financial Services, JCB International, MasterCard Worldwide, and Visa, Inc. founded the organization.

1.5.8 Sports Leagues Subsector Authorities

Many sports leagues have developed security best practices guides that they implement or the facility implements before, during, and after a sporting event. These guides may provide security best practices that are unique to the sporting event, or that supplement security best practices already in place at the sports facility. The Sports Leagues Subcouncil works closely with the Public Assembly Subcouncil with regard to facility operations and security because many of the assets utilized by the Sports League Subsector are similar to or, in many instances, actually are Public Assembly Subsector facilities.

IAAM's SSTF has developed four security planning guides to address the need for selecting security practices based on levels of threat or vulnerability matrixes associated with the DHS HSAS. The Safety and Security Best Practices Security Planning Guide for Arenas, Stadiums, and Amphitheaters is particularly relevant to facilities utilized by sports leagues.

The *Protective Measures Guide for U.S. Sports Leagues*, developed as a collaborative effort between DHS and U.S. sports leagues, provides an overview of protective measures that can be implemented to assist sports teams and owners and operators of sporting event facilities in planning and managing security at their facilities. The guide addresses perimeter control and stadium security, gate access and management, credentialing, setting up a command post, protocols for threat assessments, emergency plans, pre-event activities, event day security, and post-event evaluations.

The NFL's SAFETY Act-approved NFL Best Practices for Stadium Security is a set of guidelines for stadium security management designed to deter and defend against terrorist attacks at sports stadiums. It includes standards for non-game-day operations, game-day operations, and threat assessments and emergency plans. The guidelines also include the hiring, vetting, and training of personnel used to provide the services.

There are various national, Federal, and international standard-setting organizations, and State and local government-issued rules, regulations, standards, and policies (see above) that may be applicable to the protection of assets associated with the Sports Leagues Subsector.

www.ingramcontent.com/pod-product-compliance
Lightning Source LLC
Chambersburg PA
CBHW080250290526
45790CB00005B/1756